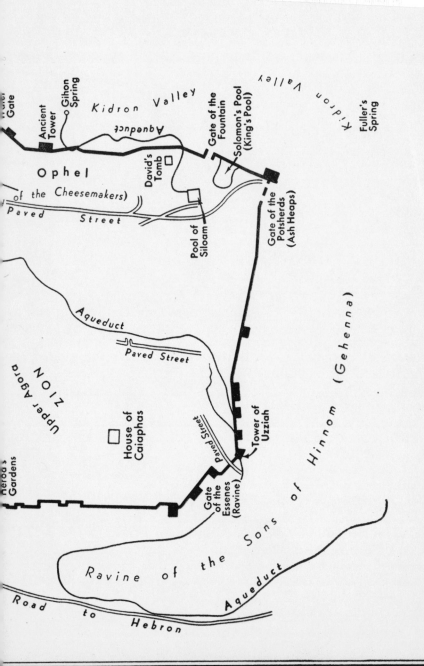

Water Gate

Ancient Tower

Gihon Spring

Kidron Valley

Aqueduct

Gate of the Fountain

Solomon's Pool (King's Pool)

Kidron Valley

Fuller's Spring

Ophel

David's Tomb

of the Cheesemakers)

Paved Street

Pool of Siloam

Gate of the Potsherds (Ash Heaps)

Aqueduct

Paved Street

Upper Agora

ZION

House of Caiaphas

Paved Street

Tower of Uzziah

Ravine of the Sons of Hinnom (Gehenna)

Herod's Gardens

Gate of the Essenes (Ravine)

Aqueduct

Road to Hebron

JESUS
In The Light of History

By A. T. Olmstead

HISTORY OF ASSYRIA

HISTORY OF PALESTINE AND SYRIA

Jesus

In The Light of History

By

A. T. Olmstead

Professor of Oriental History
Oriental Institute, University of Chicago

NEW YORK

Charles Scribner's Sons

1942

BT 301
.04

0243123

To

CLETA PAYNE OLMSTEAD
Companion in Bible Lands

PREFACE

WHO was Jesus of Nazareth? When did he live? Where was his home? What was his environment? How did he act? What did he teach? Why did he die?

The historian is able to answer similar questions in the case of every other outstanding man in world history; is Jesus the lone exception? Must the historian abandon all attempt to picture the historical Jesus? Must he remain content to write a book which simply repeats what the disciples thought about their Master? Must Jesus always be to us a dimly recognizable figure, seen vaguely through wavering clouds of doubt? Or can the historian report in all honesty that he has met the great Prophet face to face under the blazing light of history?

When did Jesus live and preach and die? No longer dare the chronologer attempt an answer based on data from Greek and Roman authors alone. He studies Babylonian astronomy and the calendar evolved therefrom. He discovers how that calendar was adapted to Jewish practice, on what day the various feasts were celebrated, on what sabbath the proper extracts from Law and Prophet were read in the synagogue. Then, by aid of tables recently calculated, he turns these Babylonian-Jewish dates into those of our own era. The reward for these labors is unexpected, even startling; in terms of our own calendar, exact to the day, he knows when Jesus began his public ministry in the Nazareth synagogue, how long was that ministry, on what day he visited Jerusalem for each of the feasts, the Sunday of his last entrance into the Holy City, the Thursday of the Last Supper, the Friday of

his crucifixion, the date of the first Easter. With the chronological framework thus firmly established, authentic history
becomes at last possible.

Where was Jesus' home? We visit the Holy Land. Far
and wide we tramp the country until no spot Jesus once trod
has escaped our notice. We journey to Nazareth and climb
the hill behind the village to feast our eyes on the same wide
vista of historic sites which once inspired the Master. Like
him, we spend long weeks in the Holy City. Every street and
alley and courtyard becomes familiar as those of our own
home town. We secure permission to examine the Temple
Area. Bible and Josephus in hand, we repeatedly make the
circuit of the walls. We crawl through dirty passages, peer
into cellars and cisterns, and descend into every excavated
hole. By the aid of underground Jerusalem, the Holy City is
being recreated before our eyes as it was in Jesus' day.

What was Jesus' social environment? We strike up acquaintance with the people, for the inhabitants of Palestine
have changed little in the last nineteen centuries. We talk to
them on the way, and, however haltingly, in their own
tongue. To be sure, this is now Arabic, but Arabic could
never so easily have supplanted Hebrew and Aramaic had it
not been so akin in vocabulary and structure. Sometimes, if
only we have ears to hear, we may listen to the very words
and phrases once spoken by Jesus, scarcely concealed by a
peasant brogue. By night, we sleep in the villages to remark
customs once observed by the Master. As we come to respect
and even admire these men of so alien a race and religion,
we increase our understanding of Jesus.

What was Jesus' religious environment? We reread our
Bible, no longer as preparation for a History of Palestine,
but to learn this time what Law and Prophet and Psalm

meant to Jesus himself. We study the Targums, those paraphrases of the Sacred Books prepared for recitation on the
sabbath that all might hear the Word of God in their own
Aramaic language; Jesus each sabbath heard the Targum
recited after the reading of Law and Prophet, to him it became as much the Sacred Book as the Hebrew original, which
he interpreted by its assistance. Did Jesus read other books?
We turn to the literature produced in the centuries immediately preceding his birth and discover that Jesus did read
certain of these books and thought them worthy of citation
in his own preaching. We come to realize how close was
Jesus to the Pharisees; not too many of their own sayings
have been preserved, but with due caution much of value may
be obtained from the works of their successors, the rabbis
who composed the Mishna, the Jerusalem and Babylonian
Talmuds, and the Midrash.

How did Jesus act? His life is described in our four
canonical Gospels. At times they are in flat disagreement,
again they agree so well we are convinced the information
goes back to a single common source. Always the accounts
are colored by the faith of the infant church. But to guarantee authentic history, we must pass far beyond mere source
criticism. Each asserted fact must be examined by itself and
in context; then by the painstaking jig-saw puzzle method
we fit each fact we have accepted into every other accepted
fact until gradually there emerges the completed picture.
Finally, this picture must be filled out from the contemporary
background and the whole must be locked into the chronological framework.

Already we have learned much of interest about Jesus but
Jesus himself we still do not know. To secure this insight,
we now ask: What did he teach? Even our best sources quote

sayings in answer to questions not raised until the days of
the early church; these we shall carefully remove for inclusion in a history of the Apostolic Age. The remainder we
accept as authentic and fit into the chronological framework.
Every word of Jesus is precious and should be presented
exactly.

How may we secure the desired precision? We cannot do
better than follow the example set by the men of King James.
Those great scholars had no intention of producing an
example of Elizabethan English. Their ears were never offended by the Semitic cast of their translations of Old Testament and Gospels; their predecessors, Greek, Latin, and English, had already standardized a sacred language, and their
only task was to conform their own revision still more closely
to the sacred text. They did better than they knew. Were not
our ears so attuned to the familiar phrases of the Authorized Version, the outlandish phraseology and syntax, the
monotonous repetition of "and" and "for," the constant appearance of apparently superfluous "therefores," the highly
irregular sequence of tenses, the large number of strangely
placed participles, all would have warned us that we were
reading an Aramaic-English jargon.

Our task, then, is to translate the Greek back into the
Aramaic which Jesus spoke, for the Greek alone is preserved.
This must be done literally and to the best of our ability.
Like the scholars of King James, we shall not be troubled if
our own literal translation of this reconstructed Aramaic
now and then shocks the sensibilities of the English purists;
our reply to their objections is that so Jesus actually did
speak. Much of what Jesus taught was expressed in poetic
form. This form also must be reproduced; the result will not
be English poetry but through it we better understand the

mind of Jesus. In the same fashion we shall repeat the conversations, often as vivid as life itself. So far as possible, we shall present the narratives of the Evangelists in their own words. We shall call the actors in the drama by their own Jewish names, which we shall spell as we find them in the ancient Jewish writings.

Why did Jesus die? The blame for the crucifixion must be placed, not on the innocent Jewish people, but squarely on the shoulders of the high priests and of their attendant scribes. We ask, therefore, how they came to win their power and this involves a study of the later Jewish history. Jesus was condemned by a Roman procurator; we investigate the reasons for the gradual absorption of the entire Mediterranean world by the great republic of the west and we are startled and alarmed by the close parallels in the development of our own United States. To understand the trial before Pilate, we even make a flying visit to the imperial palace of Tiberius.

Who, then, was Jesus of Nazareth? The answer is presented in the following pages. At long last, Jesus makes his own appearance in the full light of history.

A. T. OLMSTEAD

Oriental Institute,
    University of Chicago.
        March 23, 1942.

Contents

MAPS

JESUS

In The Light of History

CHAPTER I

NAZARETH

JESUS of Nazareth is the central figure of world history. He stands at the landmark which separates the old from the new. This epochal division is to our own day witnessed appropriately by the custom which reckons all dates after his birth according to the "Year of our Lord." Yet, in actual fact, we do not know even the approximate year of that birth.

The lack is not so strange as might seem at first glance. Ancient biographers were not interested in the birthdays of their heroes. What counted was the period of their activity, and this fortunately we can state precisely in the case of Jesus. When interest in the question developed, conflicting answers were set forth; our authorities agree on one point alone, that Jesus was born while Herod, misnamed the Great, was ruling as vassal King of the Jews.[1] Herod reigned from 37 B.C. to 4 B.C., a sufficiently wide margin for disagreement, but exact enough to prove that the traditional beginning of our era is much too late.

There was no need for his Jewish followers to ask his exact age. It would be taken for granted that he was of a sufficient maturity to justify the assumption of a prophet's authority, and that would mean that he was at a minimum about fifty.[2] Such was the fact, as is proved by the objection raised against him by his opponents: Jesus was "not yet fifty,"[3] therefore in their view too young to pose as a rival to the

---

[1]Mt. 2:1, 19; Lk. 1:5, 26.
[2]This necessity was not understood by the Greek Luke, who therefore conjectures "about thirty," 3:23.
[3]Jn. 8:57.

hierarchical scribes. Since Jesus was executed in 30 A.D., his birth must be placed about 20 B.C.[4]

Jesus' father was Joseph,[5] Eli's son,[6] a joiner by trade[7] and so of the artizan class. His mother was Mariam, Mary as we say, so called from Moses' sister.[8]

Joseph and Mary named their first-born son,[9] Yeshua, which in Greek would be Jesus. To them it was identical with Yehoshua or Yoshua, our Joshua, and this meant "The Lord saves"; the interpretation was seized upon by the primitive church as prediction of their Master's mission.[10] But it does not explain the actual form. This we first read on a cuneiform tablet sent to an Egyptian king from a chieftain across Jordan; in the Iashuia there mentioned we have the historical Joshua. A little later we find a Yeshua as the owner of a Phœnician seal. It was the name of the high priest contemporary with Zerubbabel. Yeshua ben Sira wrote in Hebrew a book of wise sayings with which Jesus was acquainted. As for the Greek form Jesus, Josephus mentions more than twenty different Jews under that heading. The name was therefore common.[11]

Family surnames were unknown in the ancient world. Jesus would accordingly be distinguished from others of that name in his own village by his patronymic, Joseph's son, or as the joiner's son,[12] for the little settlement would need but one. After his father's death, he might be called Mary's son.[13] When his reputation became national, he was "Jesus,

---

[4]For fuller discussion, cf. A. T. Olmstead, "The Chronology of Jesus' Life," *Anglican Theological Review*, XXIV, 1942, 23 ff.

[5]Jn. 1:45; 6:42; Mt. 1:16, 18–20, 24; 2:13, 19; Lk. 1:27; 2:4, 16, 43; 4:22.

[6]Lk. 3:23; the last section of the genealogy in Luke is obviously authentic.

[7]Mk. 6:3; Mt. 13:55.

[8]Mt. 1:16, 18, 20; 2:11; 13:55; Mk. 6:3; Lk. 1:27, 30, 41; 2:5, 16, 19; Acts 1:14.

[9]Lk. 2:7.

[10]Mt. 1:21.

[11]Cf. A. T. Olmstead, *History of Palestine and Syria*, 1931, 201.

[12]Jn. 1:45; 6:42; Mt. 13:55.

[13]Mk. 6:3.

who is from Nazareth of Galilee,"[14] "Jesus the Nazarene,"[15] or "Jesus the Nazoræan,"[16] while his sect was that of the Nazoræans.[17]

Quite literally, Jesus might have been called "the first born among many brethren."[18] Joseph and Mary should have been happy; their prayers were blessed with a goodly number of children. After Jesus came Jacob or James, to die as head of the infant church; Joseph or Joses, so named from his father; Judah or Jude, who was to write the church a letter; and lastly Simon. Jesus had also at least two sisters; in accordance with custom, their names were not thought worthy of mention.[19]

For almost half a century Jesus lived an obscure life in Nazareth.[20] It must have been a tiny hamlet. The Hebrew Bible does not mention it; after the references in the Lives of Jesus, our canonical Gospels, and in the literature dependent on them, Nazareth does not again make a casual appearance on the historical scene until almost two centuries had elapsed.

Amid the numerous ancient and modern churches and sacred sites of present-day Nasira, it is difficult to recover in our imagination the Nazareth of Jesus' day. We do better to visit a near-by "Arab" village. On the plains he so often crossed, the building material might be clay, dug from a pit close by, and moulded into large bricks dried in the sun. Not only was clay very cheap, it was a good non-conductor, keep-

---

[14]Mt. 21:11; from Nazareth, Jn. 1:45; Acts 10:38.

[15]Mk. 1:24; 10:47; 14:67; 16:6; Lk. 4:34.

[16]Jn. 18:5, 7; 19:19; Mt. 2:23; Lk. 18:37; 24:19; Acts 2:22; 3:6; 4:10; 6:14; 22:8; 26:9.

[17]Acts 24:5.

[18]Rom. 8:29.

[19]Mk. 6:3; Mt. 13:55, where the order of Judah and Simon is reversed. James: Acts 12:17; 15:13; 21:18; I Cor. 15:7; Gal. 1:19; 2:9, 12; Jas. 1:1; Jud. 1:1. Unnamed brothers: Acts 1:14; I Cor. 9:5.

[20]Jn. 1:46; Mt. 2:23; 4:13; Lk. 1:26; 2:51.

ing the house cool in summer and warm in winter. Only when the rains descended would the mud roof leak and the house become clammy and damp; as soon as the downpour ceased, the occupants could sun themselves outside.

In contrast to the swampy and malarial though fertile plains, Nazareth was fortunate. Just north of the Great Plain but shut off by a hill, it snuggled high up in a pleasant nook, its winding lanes climbing still upward to the orchards and vineyards which fringed the rocky surrounding hills. Here the cheapest building material was stone, picked up to clear the fields, and laid in roughly horizontal courses on a foundation of blocks slightly squared. The roofs were constructed of poles stripped of the bark but otherwise untrimmed; they could be seen from the interior, since there was no proper ceiling and the houses were one-storied. Above the poles were laid branches through whose dead leaves the mice, snakes, and scorpions would rustle by night; too often they might drop to the floor, and in the morning painful would be the experience of the child who mistook the scorpion for an egg![21] Over the branches in turn was a thick layer of mud, kept flat by a stone roller.

The entrance was a single low door of wood, which in some parts of the orient the tenant himself must supply if the house was rented. Windows were scarcely necessary when the house served as little more than a refuge from the rain and the sun. Outside would be no break in the stone walls, inside there were niches in which the scant supply of extra clothing would be kept or the bedding bundled up for the day. There was no need of bedsteads; at night the bedding was spread on rugs of local manufacture, woven on primitive looms, and bright with vivid colors, which covered the beaten clay floors.

---

[21] Cf., Lk. 11:12.

There was no need of chairs, visitors could squat or recline on the rugs and the piled-up cushions.

In the dry half of the year or during the intervals between the showers of the wet season, food would be cooked outside the house over a small charcoal brazier. When it rained a chimney permitted cooking within; in winter the occupants huddled around the brazier. Food was brought on a wooden platter or a metal tray and set down on the floor or on a low table, around which the men would recline on cushions. Before the meal, the hands and feet were washed by water poured from a metal ewer; after the meal, the hands required another cleansing, since fingers were substituted for cutlery. Grace would be said before meat.

Foundation of the meal was bread—barley for the poor, wheat for their betters. The grain would come from their own fields close by, since the harvests of the broader fields in the plains were exported to feed Tyre[22] and the adjacent mercantile cities. Meal was ground by the women of the house with the same primitive mills whose clatter each morning still awakens the overnight visitor in the modern village. Baked into round flat loaves which served also as plates, the bread still preserved traces of the grit rubbed off from the millstones.

The remainder of the meal was equally simple. A vegetable or two came from the village gardens, a little fruit or a few ripe olives from the orchards, a bunch of grapes from the vineyards, clabbered milk of course from the flocks, perhaps a bit of white goat's cheese, even a relish of fish from the Lake of Galilee. Meat would be tasted only on feast days or at weddings, when poultry, mutton, or goat would be served; killing the fatted calf would be a rare event indeed. Eating

---

[22]*Cf.* Acts 12:20.

of the unclean pork was banned; only the heathen along the coast and in the semi-independent cities of the Decapolis across Jordan thus defiled themselves.

The town spring under the hill furnished an abundance of sweet cold water; contrasted with the scant brackish supply offered in many villages, it would give cause for local boasting. Each feast was cheered with bowls of wine pressed at little cost by the feet of the youths and maidens in the neighboring winepresses from the grapes raised on the slopes. While the women and children ate the remnants, the men gossiped or danced to melancholy music. If the night was clear and warm, the family then climbed the outer stair and spread their bedding on the flat roof.

With the rising sun, the village was wide awake. The women went off to the spring and returned bearing on their heads the enormous water jars which compelled magnificent carriage and prematurely aged them. The men walked to the olive orchards and vineyards or to the grain fields, for Nazareth was first of all an agricultural hamlet. The soil was the strong red earth of a limestone country, but so thin that oxen could stir it with the primitive wooden plow shod with an iron plow tip. There were flocks of sheep and goats to be herded by the boys and girls. A shopkeeper or two, a few artizans completed the population. Joseph would be the lone joiner in the hamlet; his most important task would be keeping the farm implements in repair. Jesus would succeed to his father's trade without competition. It was a simple but pleasant life; every one was busy, there were no rich and no poor, there should have been no beggars.

Social life in the hamlet would be outdoors. The women would chat at the spring or over the cooking. After the day's work, the men would assemble in the square to talk over the events of the day and no doubt their talk ranged far. Here the village chief would give his judgement on disputed matters. If the year was good, there would be great rejoicing as each crop came in, the dancing in the vineyards when the maidens looked for mates, the pressing of the wine and of the olive, the gathering of the first sheaf of harvest. Each sabbath they rested from their labors. In the synagogue, a tiny replica of the gorgeous ruins we may yet view at Capernaum, they worshipped Israel's God and listened to His word as announced by the Law and the Prophets. If their scanty means permitted, they pilgrimaged on foot to Jerusalem for each feast.

The peasants, artizans, and shopkeepers of Nazareth spoke Aramaic at home. They could boast that it was in every sense a world language. Over a millennium before, their ancestors had introduced the language into Canaan when they invaded the Promised Land as part of the widespread Aramæan invasion. In their Law they could still read how "Your father was a wandering Aramæan." But while elsewhere along the whole margin of the Fertile Crescent the invaders retained their native tongue and in the eighth century before our era began to write it down in the consonantal alphabet borrowed from the Phœnicians, their own ancestors had also borrowed the "lip of Canaan," so close to the Phœnician language, and made it their sacred language, Hebrew.

Aramaic had its revenge. As the official language of the Achæmenid chancellery, it was known throughout the Persian Empire. At the height of its expansion, it could be read by scribes from Greece and Lydia to Egypt, Iran, and even India. It had begun to drive out the clay tablet and the cuneiform writing from Babylonia and Assyria and the sacred language of the Jews from Palestine. The returned Zionists found Aramaic spoken around them, the very rescripts from the Persian monarch which guaranteed their rights were in that tongue, and they succumbed to the influence. When Ezra the scribe introduced to Jerusalem the new Book of the Law of Moses written in the old sacred language, not all could understand and it was necessary to have interpreters.[23] Thus began the custom of Targum, the oral translation of the Bible into Aramaic. Hebrew continued to be written, especially for religious literature, but no longer was it pure, more and more it was infected with Aramaisms. Aramaic was now the language of everyday life, the sacred tongue was dying out.

This tendency was powerfully influenced by the developments beyond Palestine's borders. After the conquests of Alexander the Great, Greek had expelled Aramaic from Egypt and Asia Minor; it was the court language at the great Hellenistic capitals, but it did not penetrate the back country. The quick decline of the Seleucid and Ptolemaic empires and the rise of native states in their place were to the disadvantage of Greek, and Aramaic became all the more firmly entrenched in Mesopotamia, Syria, and Palestine. While Greek was disappearing from the eastern half of Alexander's former empire and Rome had barely commenced to support Greek in the western half to which their rule was to be henceforth confined, Aramaic dominated all the lands in which Semitic languages had once been spoken. Thus by its geographical extent Aramaic was international in a degree to which Greek could never pretend. It was spoken and written with equal facility on either side the frontier of the two great empires, the Roman and the Parthian, which between them divided the civilized world. It was natural there-

---

[23]Neh. 8:7.

fore that it should be the language of that people which already was proving itself international to the highest degree, for at least half the Jews lived east of the international boundary. It was no accident that the words of the founder of an international religion were all spoken in the international language, Aramaic.

Jews of Egypt made wealthy by the opportunities of Alexandria's trade might forget their native Aramaic. It might be necessary to import from Jerusalem scholars to translate the Law into Greek. Historians like Demetrius and Eupolemos might utilize the new translation to inform pagans of past Jewish glories. Ezekielus could imitate Sophocles in preparing a drama on the Exodus. The author of Fourth Maccabees could preach a sermon modelled on the principles of Stoic philosophy. Philo could adjust the Platonic Logos to the Law of Moses. Their writings were to be read by Gentile Christians and so came to exercise an important influence on Gentile Christianity, but they meant little to the great mass of Jews, and none of them would be found at Nazareth.

In Palestine the natural prejudice against the encroaching Greek was reinforced by definite prohibition. When the pro-Roman historian Josephus two full generations later wrote his *Jewish Wars* as warning to his co-religionists, the book was written in Aramaic and sent to the subjects of the Parthian empire; only later was a Greek edition prepared for Roman subjects and in Greek. When, still later, he issued his *Jewish Archæology* as propaganda for sophisticated Greeks and Romans, he must hire the services of professional literary assistants. In the preface, he confesses the difficulty of writing according to "a usage of language to us foreign and strange"; despite his eager study of Greek "grammar," he could never pronounce the Greek correctly. His excuse is that his people does not encourage the study of foreign languages.[24] Another generation and we learn that during the war of Quietus (117 A.D.), it was forbidden a man to teach his son Greek.[25]

No doubt Jesus had picked up some Greek, about as much as the Palestinian knows of English today. He might even have written out in Greek characters the bill for the pagan traveller who visited his shop. It is highly improbable that he ever read a line of Greek "literature," even of the character which was just beginning to straggle into the newly Hellenized cities which ringed Nazareth about. Aramaic was spoken at home, in the shop, and in the market place. If he travelled abroad, Aramaic would take him anywhere in Palestine and Syria, in many of whose corners Greek would be quite unknown. Had his mission taken him beyond their bounds, he would have found Aramaic-speaking Jews in both the empires. For instance, Rabbi Gamaliel I, contemporary of Jesus and teacher of Paul, wrote Aramaic pastoral letters to the brethren of Daroma to the south of Palestine, of Galilee, of Babylonia, of Media, as well as to the brethren among the Javan, the Greeks. Before the eruption of Vesuvius in 79 A.D., the first sneer against the Christians had been scrawled on the walls of a house church at Pompeii by a Jew writing Aramaic in Latin characters.[26]

When Jesus at last began his ministry he must preach in Aramaic, the only language he spoke fluently and the only one of which the peasants and villagers who formed his audience had more than a smattering. To understand the

---

[24]Joseph. *Wars* i, 3; *contra Apion,* i, 50; *Ant.* i, 7; xx, 263.
[25]Mishna, Sotah 9:14.
[26]G. Dalman, *Aramäische Dialektproben,* 2 ed., 1927, 3; W. R. Newbold, "Five transliterated Aramaic Inscriptions," *American Journal of Archæology,* XXX, 1926, 288 ff.

inner meaning of his sayings, it is imperative that we attempt
to retranslate back into his own speech as nearly as possible
the Greek in which alone they have been preserved. Fortunately, our extant Gospels preserve all the phenomena of
"translation Greek."[27]

Although Jesus did not read Greek literature, this does
not imply that he was illiterate or that there was no Aramaic
literature to read. The fortunate discovery of archives from
a fifth-century Jewish mercenary colony settled at Elephantine
in Egypt proves the wide use of Aramaic writing; it also
proves a collection of books, which included the autobiogra-
phy of King Darius and the history and proverbs of the wise
Ahiqar. Toward the end of the third pre-Christian century,
there were widely circulated and variant stories of how the
Watchers descended from their heavenly abodes to wed the
daughters of men and thus introduced evil into the world.
Another Aramaic tale, that of Daniel, despite the handicap
of language, actually was accepted into the biblical canon, as
had been earlier certain portions of Ezra. Through the centuries, Aramaic inscriptions by the hundreds, their number
constantly increasing, bear testimony to a considerable literature in that language now lost. From the lifetime of Jesus
alone, we have twenty-four dated to the year and all from
the neighboring Nabatæans and Palmyrenes.

For a time the old sacred Hebrew appeared dead, preserved
only by the Law and the Prophets; it was brought back by
Jeshua, son of Sira, whose wise sayings have been recovered
in our own day in the original Hebrew, after two thousand
years during which our predecessors were dependent solely
on a Greek translation. A whole library of other contemporary

[27]A. T. Olmstead, "Could an   nal of Near Eastern Studies, I, 1942,
Aramaic Gospel be Written?" Jour-   41 ff.

religious treatises has been preserved, though as yet only in "translation Greek."

Jesus could have had no formal education. Public schools for the study of the Bible had, to be sure, been established some decades before his birth, but they were confined to Jerusalem; it was decades after his death before they were extended to the countryside. For our picture of Jesus' boyhood we cannot therefore invoke the familiar modern sight of the children seated on the floor around the teacher and chanting the sacred words in unison. There was no famous scholar to whose sect Jesus might attach himself in little Nazareth. Joseph must teach his son the reading and writing needed for the joiner's simple bookkeeping. As a pious Jew, Joseph recognized a higher duty: the Law itself commanded: "These words . . . you shall teach diligently to your children, and shall talk of them when you sit in your house and when you walk by the way, when you lie down and when you rise up."[28] From his father, then, Jesus learned to read the sacred rolls in their original Hebrew, not too difficult a task since grammar, syntax, vocabulary, and style were so close to his native Aramaic.

But Joseph was no recognized scholar, only a pious artizan. His pupil Jesus ranked no higher in the sight of the learned. Sneeringly they demanded: "How does this fellow know letters, never having been a student?" He was one of the "people of the soil," no better than a peasant. When he set up as a teacher, he only showed himself an "ignoramus," which *they*, thanks be to God, were not. His fellow townsmen were outraged by his daring to preach in their synagogue; did they not know his artizan career, his lowly parents and relatives? His auditors sensed that he was teach-

---

[28]Deut. 6:7; 11:19.

ing by his own authority, not like the scribes who could cite a precedent for every statement.[29]

In public, Jesus could read his Bible in Hebrew. There was much he could understand without difficulty by its closeness to the speech of every day. There were other sections where the Hebrew itself was antique and tested the ingenuity of the professional scribes. Every single individual word was the voice of God and so must have meaning. How could an uneducated joiner understand what he read?

Like his fellow Galilæans, Jesus depended for his knowledge of the Bible largely on the Targums, the translations or rather paraphrases into Aramaic. Sabbath after sabbath in the synagogue, he listened to the reading of the Law in Hebrew, and after each verse an oral translation into the familiar Aramaic; the Prophets were then read with the same solemnity, except that the translation came only after three verses. Like all orientals, Jesus' memory was retentive, unspoiled by too much reading, and a long lifetime of synagogue attendance must have made the whole Law and much of the Prophets his own, while the Targum taught him its meaning.

Synagogue procedure demanded that the Targum should be recited so that it could never be confused with the true Hebrew scripture which was read. But the translation obviously could not be left to the individual skill or lack of skill of the individual reciter. Long before the birth of Jesus, official translations had been prepared and were available in written form to those who needed or desired them.

Already by 200 B.C. we have evidence for a written Targum of Job. Like all these early Targums, the translation was loose and there was much expansion by what was called Midrash,

---

[29]Jn. 7:15; Lk. 4:22; Mt. 13:54; Mk. 6:2; Mt. 7:29; Mk. 1:22.

edifying exposition often illustrated by stories. Such an expansion was the additional information on the hero's genealogy which the earliest Greek translators "translated from the Syriac book" and added as an appendix to their own version. This Aramaic translation, with most though not all of its Midrashic improvements now cut out may yet be read in print.

An Aramaic version of the Writings, the third and last division of the scriptures and the last to be canonized, implies an earlier version of the Prophets. Such a version we have; it is assigned to Jonathan, son of Uzziel, a student of the great Rabbi Hillel, and so earlier than the ministry of Jesus. Obviously, Jonathan was only one of the editors; the original translator must have been considerably earlier.

A Targum on the prophets implies in turn a still earlier Targum on the Five Books of Moses, which might well trace back to the draft prepared for the reading before Ezra. Another Targum has been wrongly ascribed to this same Jonathan. It was last revised in the days of Muhammad, for the prophet's wife is referred to by name. For the most part, however, it bears the marks of an earlier revision, whose traces extend from near the close of the third pre-Christian century to about our era. We find contemporary references to the decisive battle of Raphia in 217 B.C. and to the "circle of Popilius Laenas," the Roman commander whose cane traced the limits within which Antiochus Epiphanes must decide to abandon Egypt or wage war with Rome, a diplomatic defeat which sent the Seleucid ruler back humiliated to salve his spirit by persecuting the pious Jews. John Hyrcanus is glorified by name about 107 B.C. for his successes against Shechem and the Samaritans. His descendants are blamed for assuming rights of kingship which belonged to Judah.

There is further blame for Herod and his Edomites, who represent the fourth world kingdom. Cæsarea, the city founded by Herod's son Philip at the Jordan sources, is known.

There are fragments of a yet earlier version in which these contemporary references are missing. In them we may find traces of the earliest extant Targum, that of the Law. Whatever their exact date, never again can we assert that written Targums were not available to Jesus.

That Jesus did use the Targums is strikingly proved. Centuries later, the Talmud of Palestine reproved "those who targumized: 'My people, sons of Israel, as I am merciful in heaven, so shall you be merciful on earth,'" inserting this saying as introduction to the genuine passage from the Law: "Whether cow or ewe, you shall not kill both it and its young on the same day." Despite the reproof, the interpolation remained and may be read today in the printed Targum. It is fortunate that it has remained, since it gives the proof that Jesus took one of his own sayings from the Targumizer, whose expansion he has treated as scripture.[30]

Jesus was essentially a man of one book and that book the Bible. This was not entirely for lack of other literature to read. In picturing the first century of our era, we must be as careful not to underestimate as not to overestimate the reading of the educated general public. That century reached the highest literacy ever attained in the ancient world, a literacy, in fact, never again paralleled until within a few centuries of our own day. Already the Jews had made clear one of their most enduring characteristics, their intense love of reading and of writing, as a surprising quantity of literature has survived to prove. At Rome, Greek and Latin books were

---

[30]Lk. 6:36; Mt. 5:48; Lev. 22:28; Palestinian Talmud, Berakot, 5:1.

published on a mass production basis, large numbers of slaves copying papyri at the dictation of one reader. Such was not the way of the orient, particularly of the Jews. Copying the scripture was the work of the scribe, not an educated slave but a gentleman and a man of God, held in high honor as an interpreter of the oracles of the Lord. Men with the same standards would be demanded to copy the other religious works. The cost in time and labor was high, but the books were precious.

Jerusalem no doubt was filled with books, but they would not be available to the general public, least of all to the "people of the soil." Serious students would find all they needed available in the little collections, perhaps a hundred or two parchments or papyri at most, stored in their teacher's home. But Nazareth was not Jerusalem. Aside from the synagogue, there would be few rolls; peasants and artizans did not have enough wealth to buy them for themselves. At that, few of the books in the synagogue would have been purchased; the rolls of the Law and of the Prophets, the Targums, the rare works of a more generally religious nature, would be there because some inhabitant had copied as a pious duty what was to be found in synagogue storerooms of a more favored village.

Yet that Jesus, despite these disadvantages, did read certain books, either in his own possession, in neighboring houses, or in the synagogue, can be proved definitely. For instance, he knew the wisdom of Ahiqar, a wise and learned scribe, who held the office of "Great Seal" under Sennacherib, king of Assyria. Having no son of his own, Ahiqar adopted his sister's son Nadin and gave him every instruction in virtue. Sennacherib died and was succeeded by Esarhaddon, to whom Ahiqar presented Nadin as a worthy successor. Once in power, Nadin showed the basest ingratitude by persuading the king that his adoptive father was disloyal.

The cavalry leader Nabu-sum-iskun was sent to kill Ahiqar. Once, the Great Seal had hidden Nabu-sum-iskun from the wrath of Sennacherib and had brought him forth again from concealment when the king repented and regretted his execution. Now Ahiqar asked repayment and in his turn was hidden. Sure enough, the new king did regret the loss of his father's aged counsellor. Ahiqar came out of hiding and was restored to his former exalted office, while the ungrateful Nadin was handed over for a punishment which consisted in listening to a great number of proverbs and parables intended to restore him to his senses.[31]

All three protagonists appear as high officials in Assyrian business documents and letters dating from the reigns of Sennacherib (705–681 B.C.) and Esarhaddon (681–669 B.C.), and the story doubtless has some historical basis.[32] It was written in Aramaic not long after the events in question, for the Jewish mercenary colony at Elephantine possessed a copy before the end of the fifth century. The story, however, served only as a peg on which to hang proverbs and parables collected from every quarter, including the wise sayings of Assyrian and Babylonian sages. Ahiqar's popularity was wide. He was known to Democritus the Greek philosopher and to Æsop the Phrygian slave and collector of fables, to the Jewish author of Daniel and the reviser of Tobit. One parable, that of the barren palm tree, so clung to

---

[31]F. C. Conybeare, J. R. Harris, and Agnes S. Lewis, *The Story of Ahikar*, 2 ed., 1913.
[32]A. T. Olmstead, "Intertesta-mental Studies," *Journal of American Oriental Society*, LVI, 1936, 242 f.

Jesus' memory that three times he quoted it, once as the
basis for a parable of his own.[33]

Another story read by Jesus was that of Tobit, a pious
Jew from Naphtali, who on the fall of Samaria was deported
to Nineveh. At home he alone of all his tribesmen had gone
on regular pilgrimage to Jerusalem, he alone had followed
all the prescriptions of Moses; as reward, he was granted
favor in the sight of King Shalmaneser, who made him his
regular purchasing agent and inevitably Tobit became very
rich. On his purchasing trips to Media, he left certain purses
with a fellow Jew for safety.

Shalmaneser died and was followed by his son Sennacherib.
On his return from his unsuccessful siege of Jerusalem, the
angered monarch killed many Jews and exposed their corpses.
Tobit obeyed the call of duty and buried them; Sennacherib
was informed and confiscated all Tobit's wealth and drove
him into hiding. On the accession of Esarhaddon, Tobit
could again appear openly, but he was now desperately poor
and so discouraged that when the burial of another exposed
Jew brought only blindness, he begged God to take away his
useless life.

Now that he was about to die, Tobit began to think of his
unfortunate family. He recalled the purses he had deposited
in Media. His son Tobias did not know the way and a guide
must be found. A young man turned up—as you must know
he was the angel Raphael, "God heals" by name, in disguise
—and they went on to Media where the money was recovered.
By the angel's medical art the demon, whose unclean love for
the maiden Sarah had slain her seven bridegrooms on their
wedding nights, was driven off. Sarah was discovered to be
next of kin to Tobias and promptly married to a naturally

---

[33] Ahiqar, Syriac recension, 8 :34 f.; *cf.* Lk. 13 :6–9; 15 :15; 16 :11.

somewhat hesitant husband. The party returned to cure
Tobit's blindness and to reveal that the guide was an angel.

As with Ahiqar, the story was only a coating for the
moral sayings. In this booklet, Jesus found the earliest expression of the negative Golden Rule, later assigned to the
famous teacher Hillel.[34] Phrases of the story were remembered for later parables.[35] But the strongest impression made
on Jesus was by Tobit's outstanding interest, the overwhelming importance of almsgiving.[36]

These two were in Aramaic, others were in Hebrew. By
his reading of the scripture in its original tongue, Jesus had
gained some knowledge of that language; it was easily applied, for the revived neo-Hebraic was either in close imitation of the Biblical phraseology or had been strongly influenced by the current Aramaic. One such was the wisdom of
his namesake Jeshua, the son of Sira. Long since it had
been forgotten that Jeshua's tractate originally was propaganda urging the ruling high priest Simeon II as independent
king,[37] but the appeal of its teaching remained. Not for Jesus
the pompous invitation of Jeshua to students; he had never
known such a teacher and he had no intention of becoming
one himself.[38] But much of the advice was sound. The Son
of Sira urged forgiveness of neighbors that one's own sins
be forgiven.[39] Like Tobit, he looked upon alms as stored-up
treasures.[40] From him Jesus remembered some of the most
effective phrases to be used in the parable of the Rich Fool.[41]

The last of the four books Jesus certainly read was also

[34]Tobit 4:15.
[35]Tobit 5:15; 8:19, 21; 10:10;
11:9; cf. Mt. 20:2; Lk. 15:24;
12:20.
[36]Tobit 4:7–10; 12:8–10; cf. Lk.
12:33 f.; 11:41; Mt. 6:19–21; 6:1–4.
[37]A. T. Olmstead, "Intertestamental Studies," ibid., 246.

[38]Ecclesiasticus 51:23–30; contrast Mt. 11:28–30.
[39]Ecclus. 28:2; cf. Mt. 6:14 f.;
18:35; Mk. 11:25.
[40]Ecclus. 29:12.
[41]Ecclus. 11:18 f.; 31:2; cf. Lk.
12:16–21.

written originally for an ephemeral purpose. As propaganda for John Hyrcanus, son of Simon the Maccabee, about 107 B.C. a Pharisee composed the *Testaments of the Twelve Patriarchs,* in imitation of the biblical "Blessing of Jacob" spoken to these same ancestors of the twelve tribes. Scattered among these propaganda passages were sayings which deserved to rank among the noblest products of Jewish thought.[42] Here for the first time the Golden Rule was made positive: "You shall love the Lord with all your life and one another with a true heart."[43] Forgiveness,[44] almsgiving,[45] purity,[46] humility[47] are inculcated and in language plainly reflected in the words of Jesus.[48]

We need not limit Jesus' reading to these four books. No doubt he read others he did not approve. He could scarcely avoid knowing the wild apocalyptic outpourings of his own day; the only proof that he knew them is the condemnation of their teachings.[49] Something of what he read may have been lost. Many of his parables find more or less close parallels in the stories of the later rabbis. Certainly they did not borrow from Jesus, therefore all must have had a common origin. This origin may have been literary, more probably it should be looked for in the common stock of popular folk tale. But Jesus' parables have a freshness which leaves no doubt that they came primarily from his own direct observation of actual life.

First of all his education came from the scripture, whether studied at home or heard sabbath by sabbath in the syna-

---

[42]R. H. Charles, *The Testaments of the Twelve Patriarchs,* 1908.
[43]Dan 5:3; *cf.* Mt. 22:37–39; Mk. 12:29–31.
[44]Gad 6:7; *cf.* Mt. 18:35; Lk. 17:3.
[45]Zebulon 7:2; *cf.* Mt. 5:42; 7:2.
[46]Benjamin 8:2; *cf.* Mt. 5:28.

[47]Joseph 17:8; *cf.* Lk. 22:27.
[48]Other examples: Zebulon 8:6; *cf.* Mt. 6:16; Issachar 3:4; 4:6; *cf.* Mt. 6:22; Asher 1:7, 9; *cf.* Mt. 12:35.
[49]Lk. 17:21; *cf.* Mt. 4:8–10; Lk. 4:5–8.

gogue. Its majestic rhythms moulded his style, his everyday
speech could not but have been affected by the Targums. In
the quiet of the synagogue service, he meditated on what he
had heard. There was more time for meditation in the joiner's
shop. There too was opportunity for discussion, for Jesus
learned from his fellow men.

Still more did Jesus learn from nature, as his parables and
sayings were to make clear. The countryside offered a quiet
beauty, the wider view was inspiring. Nazareth itself might
not be able to point out one single mention in the scriptures.
A sceptic might demand: "Can anything good be from
Nazareth?"[50] Judæans looked down on the Galilæans as
stupid. High priests were to challenge Jesus' defenders: Let
them search the scriptures and they would discover for
themselves that from *Galilee* no prophet arises.[51]

The men of Nazareth were fully prepared to refute the
base allegation. Galilee did have a prophet, recognized as true
by the scriptures. He was Jonah, son of Amittai, who eight
centuries before had encouraged that mighty king of Israel,
Jeroboam II (785-745 B.C.), to enlarge his kingdom at the
expense of Damascus, Israel's oppressor during the preceding generation. Unlike his contemporary, the stern Amos
from Judah, Jonah was no prophet of doom; he preached
hope for his crushed people and the Lord proved his words
true by wondrous victories.[52] What better forerunner could
be found for patriotic, militant Galilæans? Did he not come
from Gath Hepher of Zebulon, a short walk from Nazareth
on the road to Cana? Could not his inspiration still be felt if
one pilgrimaged to his tomb on its low rocky hill?

But that was by no means all. A whole book out of the

---

50 Jn. 1 :46.
51 Jn. 7 :52.
52 II Kings 14 :25; Josh. 19 :13.

twenty-two in scripture was devoted to this same Jonah, son
of Amittai! What other prophet made such journeys, from
Joppa on the way to Tarshish, then to far eastern Nineveh?
Of what other prophet was so marvellous an experience
recorded, three days and three nights in the body of the
great fish, then safe return to land? What other prophet enjoyed such overwhelming success in his preaching?[53] Yet the
wicked Judæans actually could deny any prophet at all to
Galilee and could bolster their denial by pointing out alleged
"tombs of Jonah" near Ashdod and near Hebron.[54] How
did they dare when all the time the true sepulcher was so well
known? Before the end of our fourth century, Saint Jerome
visited the hamlet of Geth and the tomb was pointed out to
him.[55] In the intervening centuries, the villagers have changed
their religion, but their tiny mosque still enshrines Jonah's
martyrium, which gives its name Meshhed to the modern site.[56]

Jerusalem took pride in its historic sites. How late they
were in comparison with those surrounding Nazareth! We
may stand where Jesus so often must have reposed, and view
with our own eyes from the hill back of Nazareth the same
wide landscape which inspired his soul with memories from
Israel's earliest history. Over the low hills in the foreground
rises the truncated cone of Tabor, consecrated by memories
of Deborah and Barak. On the slope of Little Hermon lies
Endor, where in his last extremity Saul consulted the witch.
Beyond the concealed road to the Jordan and the spring of
Harod, where Gideon chose out the brave three hundred before destroying the Midianites, stretches the bare backbone of
Gilboa on whose heights Saul and Jonathan met their fates
at the hands of the alien Philistines. On a platform reach-

---

[53]Mt. 12:39–41; 16:4, Lk. 11:29 f.
[54]F. M. Abel, "Le Culte de Jonas en Palestine," *Jour. Palestine Ex-*
ploration Soc., II, 1922, pp. 175 ff.
[55]Prolog. in Jonam, xxv, 1118.
[56]V. Guerin, *Galilée,* I, 165 f.

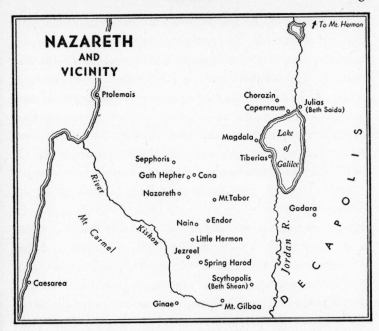

ing out into the Great Plain lies Jezreel, where Naboth had his ancestral estate until murdered through the wiles of wicked Jezebel and Jehu wrought a bloody vengeance. Into the blue distance extend the hills of Samaria between the fertile uplands and the low sunk Jordan.

To the east, the view is broken by the unseen Lake of Galilee, but we recognize the barren hills beyond the great break. Our gaze sweeps northward to the crowning glory of Hermon, almost ten thousand feet above the sea, its snow-capped head impressive even in summer. Our eyes pass along the line of hills forming the escarpment whose breakdown separates the high breezy plateau of Upper Galilee from the more irregular Lower. Seemingly at our feet to the northwest is a small but fertile plain whose center is Sepphoris on a low hill.

The Mediterranean and its broad bay swing into view just south of Ptolemais, the older Accho. Across the bay is Carmel, a long hog's back where Elijah contended with the priests of Baal. Behind Carmel another bit of the sea emerges to hint of the huge artificial harbor which has made possible the new Roman capital at Cæsarea. As Carmel sinks down, there are new glimpses of Samaria. Straight below us is the western half of the Great Plain, the narrow winding line of the Kishon brought out by the descending sun, in whose morasses Deborah and Barak completed the destruction of Sisera's army.

Nazareth was not on a main road, yet it was not so isolated as we might think. A trail over the hill less than half an hour long led to the main east-west road of Lower Galilee, and soon the traveller was at Sepphoris, barely three miles distant. Here was the "big city" of Jesus' boyhood, to which coins of Herod found on the spot yet bear witness. As a youth, Jesus had seen it destroyed by the Romans after Herod's death. In his young manhood, it was refounded by Herod Antipas as a Greek *polis* and made the capital of Galilee. A recently excavated theater testifies to the "Greek" character of Sepphoris in New Testament times.[57]

Along the same road by Cana Jesus might descend the long slopes to the Lake of Galilee, close to seven hundred feet below sea level. A not too fatiguing day's journey by foot would bring him down to Tiberias, newly walled and organized as a metropolis and after 14 A.D. named from the emperor Tiberius. Strict Jews refused to dwell within its walls because it was built over dead men's bones; Jesus appears to have shared their prejudices, though he often visited

---

[57]Leroy Waterman, *University of Michigan Excavations at Sepphoris,* 1937, 6 ff., 39; cf. S. J. Case, *Jesus,* 199 ff.

Capernaum farther up the lake. In honor of the emperor's mother Livia, Antipas refounded Beth Aramtha as Livias; lying across the Jordan from Jericho, it commanded the exit from the gorge coming down from Heshbon on the fertile Moabite highlands.

East of the Jordan outlet into the Lake of Galilee, Philip refounded the "House of Fish," Beth Saida, as Julias, so named from Augustus' daughter before Julia's disgrace in 2 B.C. At the Jordan source under Mount Hermon, where in Hellenistic times Paneas had supplanted once sacred Dan as Dan had supplanted Sidonian Laish, the settlement endured another change of name and became a city, Cæsarea of Philip.[58]

All these were turned into "Greek" foundations during the lifetime of Jesus. Larger and more distant cities had been Hellenized much earlier. Among the most important was Scythopolis, known to scripture readers as Beth Shean, on whose walls the Philistines hung the corpses of Saul and his sons. Along the seacoast were ancient Sidon and Tyre, Phœnician cities well on the way toward Hellenization at the very commencement of the Hellenistic period and now flourishing as never before. On the site of Phœnician Accho had been founded Ptolemais, just out of sight from the hill behind Nazareth. Across the Great Plain and beyond the long line of Carmel was concealed Herod's Cæsarea, founded during the childhood of Jesus, and since 6 A.D. the headquarters of Roman administration for the province of Palestine; its Greek citizens were constantly at war with their fellow Jews.

The visitor to Palestine is impressed by the sight of men always on the march. As a boy and a youth, Jesus must often

---

[58]Joseph. *Wars* ii, 168; *Ant.* xviii, 36 ff.

have walked the short distance to Sepphoris, learned something of its newly attained mask of Greek culture, even picked
up a little spoken Greek. As a man, he almost certainly visited
the other "Greek" cities, at most a tramp of a day or two.
Even had he, contrary to all probabilities, insisted on immur-
ing himself within Nazareth, there would have been now and
then Greek-speaking patrons of the joiner's shop.

From the opposite hill which separated the hamlet from the
Great Plain, Jesus could look down on the caravans traversing the Great Road of the more ancient orient. An hour's
steep descent and he was on the road itself. Beginning as a
track in the Sudan, it followed the Nile through Egypt and
crossed the desert to the Philistine coast. Avoiding Mount
Carmel, it traversed the Great Plain just out of sight of
Nazareth and climbed up the hills beyond Jordan to Damascus
or to Central Syria. In North Syria it divided, the older
branch leading eastward through Mesopotamia and Babylonia
and onto the Iranian plateau. Jesus might have heard rumors
that it ended in far distant India or followed the Silk Route
through the steppes of Central Asia to the almost mythical
land of the Seres. The other branch turned north and west
through Anatolia to reach Greece, Rome, and the far west.
During his own life time, much of this route was paved and
made an integral part of the great network of Roman com-
munications. There was more direct access to Rome by sea.

Jerusalem was the religious capital and as such conservative. Its conservatism might be slightly mitigated by pilgrim-
ages of Greek-speaking Jews, but those who visited the Holy
City would not be the most liberal of their Hellenized fellows.
Galilee was quite different. One of the later prophets had
called it "Galilee of the Gentiles"[59] because of its large non-

---

[59]Isaiah 9:1.

Jewish population. Judah the Maccabee had been compelled to evacuate all the loyal Jews from Galilee under military guard. After the conquests by John Hyrcanus, the Jews had flocked back and occupied the countryside, though the cities remained largely Gentile. From the standpoint of the strict Jerusalem hierarchy and of the Pharisees alike, the Galilæans were deplorably lax in their observance of the Law, but they could never deny that the Galilæans were ardent patriots. Revolt after revolt had already broken out. To the Romans the rebels were nothing but robbers; to the natives they were God's heroes who were about to restore the Kingdom to Israel.

Nazareth, however, was on the extreme verge of Galilee, surrounded by pagan cities, and just off the Great Road whose caravans would camp under its hill. Thus in many respects the tiny hamlet of Nazareth was more exposed to the outside Gentile world than was the Holy City Jerusalem. We shall not be surprised to find in the teaching of its most famous inhabitant a general universalism.

CHAPTER II

FORERUNNERS

IN the fifteenth year of Tiberius, the Roman Emperor, in the autumn of what we call the "year of our Lord" 28, a prophet appeared to the Jews. According to a life prepared by his disciples soon after his tragic death, his birth was accompanied by wonders. Yohanan, John to us, was the son of Zachariah, a priest from the class of Abijah, and Elisheba, from the "daughters of Aaron," who bore the name of Aaron's wife. Both were righteous before God, walking in all the commandments and ordinances of the Lord without blame. But there was not to them a child, because Elisheba was barren, and both were advanced in their days.

It came to pass in the days of Herod, King of Judah, that Zachariah was acting as priest in the order of his class before God, according to the custom of the priesthood. And he was chosen by lot for the highest honor, allowed a priest only once in a lifetime, of going into the Holy Place to offer incense. All the crowd outside was praying at the hour of the incense offering.

There appeared to Zachariah an angel, standing at the right of the incense altar. Zachariah was troubled at the sight, and fear fell upon him. But the angel said: "Do not fear, Zachariah, because your request has been heard and your wife Elisheba shall bear a son to you and you shall call his name Yohanan. And it shall be joy to you, and great gladness, and many over his birth shall rejoice. For he shall be great before the Lord, and 'wine and liquor he shall not drink,' and he shall be filled with Holy Spirit, even from his mother's womb, and many of the sons of Israel shall he turn back to the Lord their God. And he shall go before his face in spirit and power of 'Elijah, to turn hearts of fathers to children' and disobedient to wisdom of righteousness, to prepare for the Lord a people well fitted."

Zachariah replied: "In what way shall I know this? For I am an old man and my wife advanced in her days." He received the answer: "I am Gabriel, who stands before God, and I was sent to speak to you and to bring you these good tidings. And see, you shall be dumb and not able to speak until the day these things come to pass, because you did not believe my words, which shall be accomplished in their proper time."

The waiting people wondered why Zachariah was delaying so long in the Holy Place. When he came out, he should have blessed them, but he could not speak and they realized that he had seen a vision. Elisheba conceived and hid herself five months, saying: "Thus has the Lord done to me in the days in which he looked upon me, to take away my reproach among men."[1]

The words placed in the angel's mouth make perfectly clear his disciples' concept of John's mission. Ever since the prophetic canon had been closed by Malachi, Jewish nationalists had been looking forward to the coming of Elijah predicted in its closing verses. Only after the prophet had appeared could the "great and terrible day of the Lord arrive" when Israel's enemies would be destroyed.[2]

This was the hope of Jeshua, Sira's son, who looked in vain to the high priest Simeon II as the expected national Messiah:

---

[1] Lk. 1:5-25.   [2] Mal. 4:5 f.

There arose a prophet like fire,
  And his word like a furnace burning.
He broke for them the staff of bread,
  And by his zeal made them few in number.
By God's word he shut up the heavens,
  Fire also descended thrice.
How terrible were you, Elijah!
  And he who is like you can glory.
Who raised up a dead man from death,
  And from Sheol, by the word of the Lord;
Who brought down kings to the Pit,
  And those who were honored from thrones;
Who anointed kings in retribution,
  And a prophet as successor in your place;
Who heard rebukes on Sinai,
  And judgements of vengeance on Horeb;
Who was raised in a whirlwind of fire,
  And by horses of fire to the heavens;
Who by scripture is ready for the time,
  To still wrath before God's fierce anger,
To turn hearts of the fathers to children,
  And to restore the tribes of Israel.
Blessed who sees you and dies![3]

Jeshua was deceived in his hopes. Others continued to hope on. In the generation to which Jesus belonged, belief in the immediate coming of Elijah was almost universal.[4] This same belief is equally evident in a song of expected victory over Israel's enemies, written a generation or two earlier, and inserted piecemeal throughout the story of John's birth:

[3]Ecclesiasticus 48: 1–11.
[4]Mt. 11:14; 16:14; 17:3 f., 10–12; 27:47, 49; Mk. 6:15; 9:4 f., 11–13; 15:35 f.; Lk. 9:8, 17, 30, 33; Jn. 1:21, 25.

Magnifies my soul the Lord,
    Rejoices my spirit in God my Savior;
Since he looked on the lowliness of his slave,
    From henceforth all generations call me blessed.

Since for me he did great things,
    The Mighty and Holy is his Name;
And his mercy from generation to generation,
    To those who fear him.

He made strength with his arm,
    Scattered the proud in thought of their hearts,
Deposed petty rulers from their thrones,
    And exalted the lowly.

Those hungry he filled with good things,
    Those rich he sent empty away;
He helped Israel his servant,
    Mercy to remember.

Blessed is the Lord, God of Israel,
    For he visited and redeemed his people,
And raised for us salvation's horn,
    In the house of David, his servant.

Salvation from our enemies,
    And from the hand of all who hate us,
To do mercy with our fathers,
    And to remember his covenant holy.

The oath he swore to Abraham, our father,
    To grant us, from enemy hands freed,

To serve him in holiness and righteousness,
   Before him all our days.

To shine upon those in darkness,
   And sitting in the shadow of death,
To guide our feet into the path of peace,
   And to . . .

Release now your slave, O Lord,
   According to your word, in peace;
For my eyes have seen your salvation,
   Which you prepared before the face of all peoples,
A light for revelation to the Gentiles,
   And the glory of your people Israel.[5]

When her time was completed, Elisheba bore a son. The neighbors and her relatives heard that the Lord had magnified his mercy toward her, and rejoiced with her. On the eighth day, they came to circumcise the child and were calling him Zachariah after the name of his father, but his mother said: "No! Rather call him Yohanan." They objected: "No one of your relatives is called by this name," and made signs to his father to tell them what he should be called. Zachariah asked for a wax tablet and wrote: "Yohanan is his name." Immediately his mouth was opened and his tongue loosed and he blessed God. Fear came upon all those dwelling round about, and in all the hill country of Judah all these things were talked about. All who heard them laid them up in their heart, saying: "What now shall this child be?" For the hand of the Lord was with him.[6]

Thus beautifully our author has told the birth story of the Baptist. He goes on to tell how Zachariah was filled with

---

5Lk. 1:46–54, 68 f., 71–75, 79;   6Lk. 1:57–66.
2:29–32.

Holy Spirit and prophesied. A part of the prophecy associated
with a formerly expected national king was quoted and in it
was now inserted:

But *you,* also, child,
  Prophet of Most High shall be called,
For going before the Lord,
  To prepare his ways,

To give knowledge of salvation,
  To his people in remission of sins,
Through the loving mercies of our God,
  By which shall visit us dawn from on high.[7]

John's birth took place sometime between 37 and 4 B.C.,
during the reign of Herod. To understand the prophet to
come, we must understand his environment, the country and
town where lived his parents, the abode of his manhood, and
the history of his times.

Some seven miles south of Hebron lies the village of
Yatta, which is undoubtedly to be identified with the Juttah,
a city of the hill country, mentioned in the lists of Joshua. As
it was one of the cities assigned to the priests,[8] there is every
reason to identify it likewise with the city Juda, also located
in the hill country of Judah,[9] where John was born. Its
height above sea level, about 2800 feet, is much lower than
that of Hebron, for it lies well down a valley extending into
the dry river bed which swings around Beersheba in the
direction of the Mediterranean.

Juttah's location is significant, for it lies on the border of
"the desert and the sown." A few miles north are the vineyards

<hr>

[7] Lk. 1:76–78.
[8] Josh. 15:55; 21:16.

[9] Lk. 1:39; *cf.* 1:65.

around Hebron, then the forty-mile road straight along the crest of Judah to Jerusalem. On the south, however, a dozen miles of descent brought the traveller into the arid Negeb, the south country, where the Edomites had dwelt since their expulsion from the fertile breezy uplands east of the Dead Sea and their gorges around Sela, the "Rock," or Petra as the Greeks translated the name. Were not the Negeb in control of the routes from Palestine to Egypt and from the spice lands of southwest Arabia to the Mediterranean at Gaza, there could have been little settlement; as it was, each oasis boasted a small town for the traders.

A few miles to the east of Juttah brought one to the rim of the occupied hill country of Judah. From the rim, one could look down into the desert of Judah, not a desert of sand or gravel, but of huge gorges, blasted rock descending to the even more desolate shores of the Dead Sea. The view is magnificent, awe-inspiring rather than beautiful. Under such mingled influences, that of the desert predominating over that of the settled country, the child grew and became strong in spirit. As he reached maturity, the desert influences conquered; John was in the desert until the day of his showing to Israel.[10]

In the desert, John had ample opportunity to mourn over the sad fate of his people. Israel's golden age had passed with the mighty conqueror David and the rich builder Solomon. Their successors did evil in the sight of the Lord and the people suffered in punishment. Again and again God's prophets had summoned them to repentance but they were stiff-necked and turned their backs. At last the Lord's long-suffering was exhausted and first Israel and then Judah were carried into captivity.

---

[10]Lk. 1:80.

In Babylon, they sought and found the Lord, who by the hand of Cyrus the Persian permitted return to Zion. Patriotic hopes immediately revived. In glowing terms of apocalyptic, the prophets Haggai and Zechariah proclaimed that Zerubbabel, a descendant of the captive king of Judah, should resume the throne of his father David. The movement collapsed but the literature remained and was finally incorporated into the canonical prophecies of scripture.

In the days of Hebrew independence, the king himself had been head of the state religion and the chief priest was one of his subordinate officials. After the loss of independence, the "great priest" was the sole leader of the Jewish people. As such, he must represent Israel to the nations. The task required diplomacy and the high priest quickly lost his interest in religion as such and degenerated into a worldly official in a great empire. As quickly, he lost the confidence of his people, who continued to dream of a coming national ruler. In contrast to the worldly high priest, as Malachi insisted, this Anointed King (Messiah) would be righteous. Ezra the scribe thought otherwise; God Himself, through the Law of Moses now promulgated, would be their only monarch. Nehemiah on the contrary believed in direct action; the walls of Jerusalem were restored against the day when the Holy City should once more be free.

Two centuries passed with nothing for history to record except names of high priests clever enough to keep on good terms with Persian or Macedonian kings. Unnoticed by nobles and strangers, the followers of Ezra meditated on the Law of their God, fitting their lives to its demands, and pouring out their pious aspirations in beautiful, moving psalms. Jewish civilization remained little changed under the Persians, but the higher classes were seduced by the Greek culture introduced by the Macedonians. Jewish mercenaries fought in Ptolemaic and Seleucid armies, were assigned a special quarter in Alexandria for their residence with special rights, as soldiers in the reserve were granted lands for cultivation, and formed a regular part of Seleucid colonies. Jewish merchants found profitable business throughout the entire Hellenistic world. The Dispersion of the Jews had begun.

Jerusalem itself was affected. The high priests assumed Greek names, taken from Greek legend and mythology. Ordinary priests hurriedly abandoned their ritual duties in the temple when the sports of the palæstra were announced. Jerusalem was refounded as still another Antioch, its citizens were now treated as colonists, the aristocratic youth was enrolled as *ephebi,* the ancient representative of the Reserve Officers' Training Corps, and the enrollment guaranteed their later membership in the citizen body. The fashionable wore the Greek hat, always a sign of westernization to our own day. The national God of the Hebrews was identified with Zeus Olympius.

Nationalist hopes slumbered until the Roman destruction of the Seleucid Empire by the Battle of Magnesia and the Treaty of Apamea (190–189 B.C.). Jeshua son of Sira praised the high priest Simeon II as the coming independent king,[11] but Simeon died and his successor made a profitable arrangement with the Seleucid ruler. The time was not yet ripe, and Antiochus IV, to himself the God-made-manifest, to others the Man-gone-crazy, took advantage of open revolt by a pro-Ptolemaic high priest to desecrate the temple and to turn it into a Greek shrine. Deliberate religious persecution, rare enough in antiquity, soon followed; without doubt we must ascribe its inception to the Hellenized, irreligious high priests.

---

[11]*Cf.* p. 19.

The scriptures were destroyed wherever found. Those who followed the prescriptions of the Law were slain. Sacrifices to pagan divinities were compelled by force.

The Pious, followers of Ezra, bent to the storm, dying in their innocency rather than profane the sabbath by fighting. An apocalyptist, speaking in the name of the ancient hero Daniel, encouraged them to endure by promise of a Son of Man who should bring redress from heaven. Bolder spirits rallied to a simple country priest, Mattathiah of Modin, in armed resistance. After his death, his son Judah the Maccabee carried on the fight. The temple was recovered and cleansed from the Greek impurities; its dedication was each year thereafter celebrated by a much beloved feast, the Feast of Lights, beginning Chislev 25, December 24, 165 B.C.[12]

But Judah soon was killed in battle. His brother Jonathan was driven to the bandit's life. By skillful balancing between the contenders for the toppling Seleucid throne, he gradually recovered authority and ultimately was recognized as high priest. To this title he had no legal right, for he was only a descendant of Levi and not of Zadok, the Levitical family to which that office had belonged since the reign of Solomon. Nevertheless, so long as his family was successful in winning victories over the pagans, its right was not challenged. After Jonathan's treacherous capture and murder, his brother Simon carried on both line and title.

John Hyrcanus, Simon's son, began his reign in disaster. His father had been assassinated, he himself was besieged in Jerusalem by Antiochus VII Sidetes and forced to capitulate. Nevertheless, he was remembered as Judæa's most successful warrior. When the Parthians killed Antiochus in battle, Hyrcanus took advantage of Seleucid disintegration and con-

---

[12]Jn. 10:22.

quered the surrounding Greek cities, just winning a precarious independence from Seleucid misrule as their former masters granted them "freedom, holiness, and inviolability" because already too weak to protect them. The Edomites were subjugated in their southland home and were compelled to become Jews by force; thus the ancestors of Herod were introduced into the Israelite commonwealth. Shechem and Samaria were reduced and the national temple on Mount Gerizim was destroyed; any possibility of cooperation between these two rival followers of the Law of Moses was destroyed, and the hatred between Jew and Samaritan became traditional.[13] Under the mask of Hyrcanus' ancestor Levi, these marvellous victories were celebrated by a friendly Pharisee who composed the *Testaments of the Twelve Patriarchs;* this book Jesus read.[14]

All this time, the threat of the great republic of the west was coming closer and closer. Rome's story parallels our own. In the beginning a simple, practical, uncultured people, Rome had slowly but inexorably expanded from a few square miles about the Tiber crossing on the main north-south road of Italy until it had reached the boundary seas. Wisely the fathers had been generous in the grant of Roman citizenship. Many of the citizens of the former rival states had been granted full citizenship, others held the almost equally valuable citizenship without the suffrage, still others a lower grade but might be considered on probation for the gift of the higher.

Constant war with fellow Italians had toughened their spirits. A small army machine had been built up which, despite its temporary citizen character, its amateur commanders,

---

[13]*Cf.* Jn. 4:9, 20; Lk. 9:52–54;   [14]*Cf.* p. 20.
10:33, 37.

and the defeats their blunders constantly invoked, was proving terribly efficient in winning the wars in which their
dilatory and incompetent diplomacy so often involved them.
Constant struggles between the poor, the rich of plebeian
birth, and the patricians had been at last brought to a close
by the formation of a new aristocracy of patricians and
rich plebeians through which a few families controlled the
state and through the senate enforced a consistent foreign
policy.

Conquered Italians had become "friends and allies" by
one-sided treaties. Subjugation of Greek cities in South Italy
had decidedly increased Greek influence, which was reflected
in religion, art, and literature. Rome began to aspire to Greek
culture.

After a generation-long war had swept the seas of Car-
thaginian fleets in the first hostile contact with an oriental
power, the Romans found themselves burdened with their
first territory across the water, Sicily. Greek cities could be
made "friends and allies," but the serfs who tilled the great
estates or pastured the cattle on the ranches could never aspire
to citizenship, they were nothing but "war-surrendered," deprived of regular legal rights. The governor under whom
Sicily was "reduced to the form of a Roman province" proclaimed the fundamental provincial law which each succeeding governor modified at his discretion. At the same time, he
carried out the census, the basis for future taxation. It was
an ugly indication that Rome was beginning to savor the
taste of empire.

Stabbed in the back by a presumed friend while engaged in
the life-and-death struggle of the Second Punic War, Rome
must cross the Adriatic and enter with an army the world of
the Hellenistic empires. No one at Rome dreamed of the

significance of this first venture across the seas. When Hannibal was finally driven out of Italy and defeated in Africa, the senate forced a reluctant people, anxious to rebuild their cities and restore their farms, into a second war with Macedonia.

Still they did not realize the full import of their victories, but a certain Lycophron of Chalcis knew the truth. His *Alexandra* shows an obscure and contorted Greek and a wealth of recondite literary allusions which almost but not quite hide the fact that the poem is pure apocalyptic. Alexandra, more familiar to us as Cassandra, was the maid who refused Apollo's advances and was cursed by the gift of prophecy never to be believed. In apocalyptic detail, she presents the relations between east and west, from Io and Europa, through the Trojan War, the invasion of Xerxes and the return invasion of Alexander, to the race of her ancestors, the Phrygians from Troy, who under Æneas settled Latium and whose descendants had just conquered Macedonia. To them would be the future, as she predicts with genuine apocalyptic fervor.

As yet, the Romans had remained simple, deeply awed by the mighty contributions of the Greeks to literature and art. They were nevertheless deeply imbued with the conviction that they had been appointed by manifest destiny to set the world aright. At the Olympian Games which followed the war (196 B.C.), amid scenes of wildest enthusiasm for the barbarian liberators, the Roman commander announced that Rome decreed freedom to all the Greeks. Observers noted, however, that "freedom" did not extend to Greek subjects of Roman allies or to "allied" Greek cities at home.

Blundering diplomacy on the part of Rome no less than by the Seleucid Antiochus III, called by himself the Great, involved two reluctant states in another conflict. Antiochus was defeated (190 B.C.) at the battle of Magnesia and next year punished by the treaty of Apamea. In their innocence, the Romans took not an inch of soil for themselves. All their conquests were handed over to their "friends and allies," and they withdrew their troops back across the seas, hoping that now at last they might find time for the serious economic and social problems pressing for attention at home.

They were not permitted to remain in peace. Constantly their intervention was demanded to settle the squabbles incident to a decaying political situation. From those to whom they gave favorable decision, they received no thanks, they had made only a just award; from the losers they won bitter hatred. Reluctant to employ military force, they resorted to commissions of observers, a preferred junket for less able senators. These commissions threatened, promised, and cajoled. One such commission made great promises to Judah the Maccabee; before the formal treaty arrived, Judah was dead at the hands of his enemies. When realization came to the Hellenistic states how reluctant the Romans were to fight, disdain took the place of fear. Even when a member of a commission was assassinated in the theater of Laodicea in Syria and the assassin boasted of his crime, no action was taken.

But a new generation was growing up in Rome. Its aristocratic youth had travelled as tourists or as minor officials in Greece or in the Hellenistic orient. They had observed the political and social disintegration, the constant fighting on a petty scale, the flagrant dishonesty and graft, the servility of a people fast losing its freedom. At Rome itself, they had been bored by the vapidities endured from the lips of the hordes of "Greek" philosophers at their public lectures. They

found that the visiting philosophers considered them uncultured and did not hide the fact, even while energetically
hunting for a wealthy and powerful patron. No wonder they
concluded that all the great Greeks were dead.

They had lost their elders' sense of world responsibility.
They knew that the world lay at their feet. With the responsibility and the ill will, they would take the gain. So when
Macedonia started a third war, it was quickly smashed and
quartered. Greece and Corinth revolted. In one terrible year
(146 B.C.), Corinth and Carthage, two of the most populous
and wealthy capitals in the civilized world, were literally
razed to the ground and remained thereafter unoccupied
under a curse. The peoples around the Mediterranean had
been taught their lesson; they cowered before a new and
savage Rome.

The Romans were slow to take formal possession of their
heritage. For the time being, they were content to permit disintegration to carry on its deadly work. Native states were
encouraged or at least not prevented from taking advantage
of the opportunity; John Hyrcanus and his Jews were among
the chief beneficiaries of the policy. In addition, there were
good pickings for Italian merchants and money lenders in
the states of the Hellenistic orient, chronically bankrupt despite ruinous taxation.

A forged will of the last king of Pergamon gave his rich
territory to Rome, which promptly reduced it to the province
of Asia. Wealth beyond their wildest previous dreams was
at the disposal of a horde of legalized plunderers. That same
year (133 B.C.), Tiberius Gracchus introduced at Rome his
"reforms." Thus began the century and two years more of
the "Roman Revolution," which deluged the empire with
blood, caused untold misery and destruction of property, and

fortunately ended with the Roman aristocracy a suicide through repeated "proscriptions."

When, therefore, Aristobulus declared himself a king, no thinking Jew could persuade himself that it meant true independence. Aristobulus was merely claiming a higher rank among the vassals of Rome.

Roman "knights," members of the merchant class, fell upon the new province of Asia like a swarm of locusts. Their extortions were almost incredible; then if ever publicans deserved inclusion among the worst sinners. Mithradates, the Iranian ruler of Pontus, took advantage of the universal hatred to obtain Asia, where thousands of Italians were brutally massacred on a single agreed day. Oracles in limping Homeric verse and ascribed to one or another of the Sibyls savagely predicted the imminent and violent fall of Rome. The predictions were proved false, for Mithradates was driven out and the last state of Asia was worse than the first.

Palestine rapidly decayed under the later Hasmonæans, whose right to the high priesthood was now repeatedly challenged. Graft and rapacity characterized the Jewish nobility, bitterly anti-Roman and looking for aid from the Parthians now approaching the Euphrates. So far as they had a religion, these nobles with the high priests belonged to the reactionary sect of the Sadducees. Against them thundered a great unknown prophet, whose poems in the manner of Amos are preserved in the collections ascribed to Enoch.

The Pious had by this time been organized into "Associations" and had been nicknamed Pharisees, the "Separated." Their meditations were still devoted to the Law, whose prescriptions were explained in minute detail by a series of distinguished rabbis. While the priests carried on the temple ritual and the chiefs of the synagogues controlled the activities of the congregations formed to bring together Jews for worship when far from the temple, the rabbis were simple teachers, without official status save as individuals were members of the Sanhedrin. They were highly reverenced by the great mass of the people and their influence was outstanding.

Pharisees differed among themselves as to the degree of literalness with which the Law should be observed, but in general their influence was thrown on the side of mercy, to the best of their ability the harshness of the ancient codes was mitigated; the Sadducees are to be blamed for insisting on the letter of the Law. Under Queen Alexandra Salome, widow of Alexander Jannæus, the Pharisees were in favor. After her death, they lapsed into their normal pacifism, paying no attention to international affairs or to internal politics unless their religious sensibilities were challenged.

Two sons of Alexandra, Hyrcanus and Aristobulus, contended for the supremacy. By this time it was obvious who would give the decision. Pompey had for the moment cleared the sea of the pirates, whose ravages had so long disgraced the Roman name. He had then been given the war against Mithradates and had brought it to a successful conclusion. He had refused to recognize the rights of the last claimant to the Seleucid throne and had reduced Syria to a province.

Then Pompey took up the problem of Judæa. Almost day by day we may trace the progress of events through the hymns of a minor psalmist whose works have been preserved only because they were attributed to Solomon himself. He tells how the Roman was received by Jerusalem with joy, how the supporters of Aristobulus held out in the temple against him, how the temple was captured and its defenders slaughtered while himself and his fellows escaped the storm, and how Aristobulus and his adherents were carried off into captivity at Rome. Pompey entered the Holy of Holies and henceforth the world knew that there was nothing inside.

One calumny was removed, that of the ass worshipped by the Jews, but plenty of others remained. For Judaism was now brought face to face with a terrible danger, one which has reached its worst in our own day. Anti-Jewish feeling first developed in Egypt. Its first trace is the destruction of the rival temple set up by the mercenaries at Elephantine when the native Egyptians revolted against the Persian masters those Jewish soldiers served. It finds literary expression in the history of Egypt written in Greek by the priest Manetho to inform the second Ptolemy of the past glories of the country he ruled. The siege of Jerusalem by Antiochus Sidetes gave occasion for the spread of the slanders over the Near East. Cicero's speech in defense of Flaccus contains as vicious examples of anti-Semitism as of unfair depreciation of Greeks.

Author after author repeated the same stories. Moses was a renegade Egyptian priest, who led Egyptian lepers into Palestine. As might be expected from such ancestry, the Jews had always been robbers, haters of all strangers. Their religion was a weird and disgusting superstition, made up of fragments of alien cults, inviting the odium of the human race.

Certain Jews retorted by claiming for their own people all useful inventions. Even Egyptian religion owed its form to Moses. Other writers attempted to familiarize Greeks with a highly idealized picture of their own history. Some proved that Hebrew religion and Greek philosophy were the same, the latter of course borrowed from the former.

Missionaries preached the one true God with conspicuous success, especially with women. For the reception of proselytes, the rite of baptism was introduced. Other converts were satisfied with the status of God-reverencers; they worshipped the God of Israel and attended the synagogue but did not announce themselves openly as Jews or take upon themselves the whole yoke of the Law. Even the nationalists must make terms with the Greek culture and express their detestation of Greeks and Romans in the Sibylline Oracles, which imitated Homer, though the more extreme confined themselves to Aramaic or Hebrew.

By the reorganization of Pompey, Hyrcanus was permitted to continue to rule the Jews in Palestine, though only as high priest and as subordinate to the governor of Syria. Shortly thereafter, the people were granted their wish, a theocracy, under the supervision of a council, the Sanhedrin, which took its name from the Greek *synedrion*. The experiment was a disappointment to all concerned. Hyrcanus was weak, the power behind the throne was the Edomite Antipater, whose ancestors had but recently been converted through conquest.

Disappointment with the theocracy, the collapse of the Hasmonæan monarchy, a half-veiled Roman control through an Edomite tool brought fresh dreams of a national Savior. Near the end of his life, the psalmist who has since been masked as Solomon predicted the glorious advent of the Messiah. A few years later, two more prophets appeared; one told of the coming Elect One, the other of the Son of Man. "In that day," the day of vengeance and of national independence, became the slogan. Learned scribes penned in the margins of their Bibles reminders of God's promises to David, for whom a lamp would ever burn; the whole of the later literature was interpolated with brief sayings promising a king to Judah.

But Judah's king never arrived. The Roman revolution was nearing its climax. A political deal, the so-called first triumvirate, brought together the former enemies, the rich Crassus and the victorious Pompey, with Caius Julius Cæsar as intermediary. Crassus sought to balance the triumphs of his colleagues by the conquest of Parthia; he died at Carrhæ. Cæsar and Pompey fought for control of the Roman world; our psalmist celebrated the miserable death of the hero once called the "Great" who had destroyed the Jewish monarchy. Cæsar was murdered and the "Liberators" who for their own selfish purposes had killed him looted Palestine with the remainder of the Near East. Antipater's son Herod won the good will of the "Liberators" by proving himself a good tax collector; he did not endear himself to a people already bled white by his exactions. When Mark Antony suppressed the "Liberators," only to show himself even more ruthless, again Herod was found zealously aiding the Romans.

The orient was desperate and when the Parthians from across the Euphrates invaded Syria the orientals flocked to their standards. Parthian cavalry swept into Palestine; despite the comforting promises of the prophet who had predicted the coming of the Elect One as Messiah, Jerusalem was taken (41 B.C.). Four years Judæa was ruled by "King Antigonus," as his Greek coin legends said, but in the Hebrew it was "Mattathiah the High Priest and the Community of the Jews." Under Parthian suzerainty, the Jewish theocracy was re-established, under the rule of another Hasmonæan.

Herod was a fugitive through the desert and across the winter sea. Perils surmounted, he arrived at Rome where he found Antony and Octavian for the moment in agreement and quickly returned with the title of king granted by the senate. Three years more were needed to make the title good, then Mattathiah was driven out, but the nationalists never forgot the promise of aid from the great rival empire beyond the Euphrates.

Judæa once more could boast a king, but he was not the Messiah from Judah. He was neither truly Jewish nor was he powerful, his royal title depended on the whim of the man who held Rome. When Octavian conquered Antony, Herod was in grave danger but he weathered the storm and retained the kingdom, though not the full confidence of Octavian.

The pro-Parthian nationalistic higher classes had been largely killed off in the constant wars. The influence of Babylonian Jewry had declined. Herod kept tight in his own hands the nomination of the constantly changing high priests. The temple was restored and enlarged and thus the priests were won. Until almost the end of his reign (37–4 B.C.) the Pharisees were well disposed.

Augustus, as Octavian was now known, was the unchallenged master of the Roman state. Nobles at Rome might still delude themselves into thinking that Augustus was only the chief magistrate of the republic he claimed to have restored. Orientals could recognize the naked truth in the formula which they could read in every rescript, on every inscription, on the very coins they handled daily.[15] It was "Imperator Cæsar Augustus" in Latin, or in the more common Greek "Autokrator Kaisar Sebastos." First of all he was General, Supreme Commander-in-Chief, for the world realized perfectly well that his power rested solely on the might of the Roman legions. As General, he ruled the so-called imperial provinces through his legates or military lieutenants. He was Cæsar; the least of Roman nobles was greater than an ordinary king, was not the greatest of all Romans greater by far

---

[15]Mt. 22:20 f.; Mk. 12:16; Lk. 20:24.

than the Parthian king of kings? He was Augustus, worthy of reverence; to the oriental he was a god-king.

Augustus was no benign ruler of provincials. The line between Roman citizen and mere "war-surrendered" was sharply drawn, the more so as too many orientals had already been given citizenship. But one gift he made to the provinces, the greatest of all possible, peace. The much advertised Augustan Peace may have been exaggerated but it was a reality and prosperity returned in its train. Herod devoted himself to restoring this prosperity, and with considerable success. Despite his elaborate building schedule, the temple at the head, taxation was not abnormally heavy, and the common people were satisfied.

Herod was a typical petty prince of the Augustan period. As it happens, we know more of him than of any other such contemporary. His crimes and his follies are described for us in minute detail. His "massacre of the innocents" as described by the Evangelist has forever damned his memory in the popular mind. Despite his terrible family tragedies, he must be considered one of the ablest and most successful rulers of his time. Herod stands out almost alone among the petty rulers as a man who after a long, prosperous reign died in his royal bed.

Herod had been fortunate in his death (4 B.C.). Subservient as he had proved, his kingdom was too large, his power too great for a king on so dangerous a frontier and ruling a people so turbulent. Augustus divided his kingdom among his sons. Archelaus was permitted to retain his father's title of king but only over Judæa. With the lesser title of tetrarch, "ruler of a quarter," Herod Antipas was installed over Galilee and Trans-Jordan, the Decapolis cities excepted, and Philip over a narrow strip along the north border of Galilee and south of the tetrarchy ruled from Abila and Chalcis by a second Lysanias.[16]

Ten years after the death of Herod, Archelaus was deposed and the Judæan kingdom ended. Judæa was made an imperial province of the second rank, under a procurator directly responsible to the emperor. Herod's new foundation of Cæsarea on the coast was made the capital and was garrisoned by a legionary cohort of time-expired veterans, probably already the Second Italian Cohort.[17] Quirinius, legate of Syria, assessed the census,[18] on which was to be based the tribute henceforth to be paid by Judæa to Rome. At once a revolt broke out, the first of many against the direct authority of the Romans.[19] In place of the high priest chosen by the populace, the first procurator appointed a newcomer named Hanan or Ananus. After a few years, Annas, as he is called by the Evangelists, gave way to others, but, through five sons and one son-in-law, he generally contrived to remain the power behind the high-priestly throne.

Augustus was followed by Tiberius (14–37 A.D.). In due time, Pontius Pilate arrived as procurator of Judæa (26 A.D.). Pilate was no lover of the Jews and determined to test at once the strength of their "superstition." Previous and wiser procurators had kept the peace during the last two decades. Among their precautions against undue irritation of their suspicious subjects had been the leaving behind in Cæsarea of the military standards when it was necessary for troops to enter Jerusalem lest it be asserted that the Holy City had been polluted by idols. Pilate, however, ordered their retention, and next morning after the entrance the Jerusalem populace

[16]Lk. 3:1; cf. Mt. 2:22.
[17]Cf. Acts 10:1; Corpus Inscriptionum Latinarum, III, 13483a; VI, 3528; XI, 6117.
[18]Lk. 2:1 f.
[19]Acts 5:37.

discovered these idolatrous symbols profaning the very court
of the temple. Crowds immediately rushed down to Cæsarea
and begged Pilate to rescind his order. For six days he held
out and finally threatened the mob with the troops he had
concealed around the judgement seat on which he sat. The
crowds threw themselves to the ground, bared their necks,
and dared him to kill them for the sake of their Law. Pilate
realized that it was not safe to take the dare. Wholesale
massacre was no way for a new procurator to begin his term
of office, especially when his emperor was as determined to
protect his subjects as Tiberius. If their past history was any
criterion, such martyrdom would be revenged by fresh out-
breaks. The hierarchy would protest to Rome and to a just
and politic emperor. Pilate would be recalled in disgrace. So
the procurator unwillingly made promise, and on the second
of December the crowds might see the offending standards
carried out of the Holy City though the soldiers themselves
remained for the winter.[20]

But the damage had been done. Through its representative,
Rome had lost face, always in the orient a matter of serious
concern. The Roman standards had been compelled to slip out
of Jerusalem in disgrace. All this had been accomplished by
mob action; more organized pressure might be equally successful again.

The tense atmosphere of the "ten days of repentance"
leading up to the solemn Day of Atonement, October 18,
28 A.D., brought the word of God to Yohanan, son of Zachariah, in the desert.[21] Clad in the rough camel's hair garment
worn by Elijah and thus identifying himself as Elijah's successor, with a leather girdle about his loins and his food

---

[20]Joseph. *Ant.* xviii, 55 ff.; *Wars*
ii, 169; *Megillat Taanit,* Chislev 2.

[21]Lk. 3:2 b; so Rabbi George Fox.
[22]Mt. 3:4; Mk. 1:6.

locusts and wild honey,[22] he was a strange apparition when
he suddenly appeared in the Circuit of Jordan, just north of
the Dead Sea.

The spot where he had appeared was as strange, appropriate background for a proclamation of coming woe. Behind him lay the Dead Sea, its bare shorelands uncultivated,
its springs of hot water nauseous. Under its oily waters, flat
in the sun and destitute of fishy life, lay Sodom and Gomor-
rah, destroyed by fire and brimstone from heaven for their
sins. Close by, Lot's wife stood eternal guard; she had looked
back when escaping from the doomed cities of the plain and
in punishment had been turned into a pillar of salt.

John had taken up his abode at Bethany beyond Jordan.[23]
The site is otherwise unknown. Perhaps it consisted merely
of a few huts around the salt pans to evaporate the intensely
saline waters; the huts may have belonged to fishermen attempting to make a catch before the fish were swept to their
watery death in the Dead Sea. The surrounding view was
sheer desolation.

At his feet twisted and turned the Jordan in its narrow,
deep-sunk trough. No longer was its water bright clear green,
as when it left the Lake of Galilee; its rapid flow deeper and
deeper into the earth, to which it owed the name of "De-
scender," had charged its waters with mud to the point of
saturation. A few streams coming down from the hills
through deep-cut gorges showed a thin line of green. On the
western side, one small mass of verdure marked out the palms
and the precious medicinal balsams which clustered around
Jericho's copious spring. Elsewhere, the valley terraces
showed bare alkaline soil, baked and cracked by the sun, horrible for walking with unshod feet.

---

[23]Jn. 1:28; *cf.* 1:6.

To either side, valley and sea were shut in by lines of un-scalable hills, broken rarely by gorges through which trails climbed up to the plateau. The rocks were almost unbelievably barren, thrown about in wild confusion, tilted, contorted, and overturned by the titanic earth movements which produced this long double fault, extending, we have learned, one sixth of the distance around our globe. Closer in, the marl cliffs add a ghostly effect by their pale tints. In winter, winds passed over snow-covered Hermon at the valley head and whistled down the narrow trough; in summer the hills shut in to an intolerable heat the few unfortunate peasants who tended Jericho's balsam wealth for absentee landlords. To the heat and to the ever-present malaria was added the unrealized but not unfelt atmospheric pressure, which makes mere breathing a misery, for the spot is actually the lowest open to the sun on earth, almost thirteen hundred feet below the level of the sea.

To John's proclamation: "Repent! For near is the King-dom!"[24] excited crowds streamed out from Jerusalem and Judæa. There was reason for their excitement, especially so soon after Pilate had failed in his attempted desecration of the Holy City. There could be no misunderstanding of what Kingdom John was preaching; it was definitely Messianic.

To the crowds John gave harsh greeting: "Generation of vipers, who warned *you* to flee from the coming wrath? Produce therefore fruit worthy of repentance. Also, do not say to yourselves: 'As father *we* have Abraham!' For I tell you that God is able from these *stones* to raise up *sons* to Abraham! Already the ax is being laid to the root of the trees; every tree therefore not producing fruit is hewn down and thrown into the fire," the fire of the coming judgement.[25]

---

[24]Mt. 3:2. [25]Lk. 3:7-9; Mt. 3:7 b-10.

When the crowds inquired: "What therefore shall we do?"
John answered: "Let him who has two shirts give to him who
has not," the judgement will come before the second is needed,
"and let him who has food do the same." Tax collectors were
warned: "Exact nothing more than has been prescribed." Soldiers were ordered: "Intimidate no one, do not accuse any
one falsely, be content with your rations."[26]

Impressed by his fiery preaching, the crowds were baptized
in Jordan and confessed their sins.[27] Baptism of proselytes
had become a common Jewish practice but baptism of Jews
by birth was a novelty, which gave John his title of the Baptist. Not all accepted the practice, for we hear of a debate
between a Judæan and John's own disciples about purification.[28] Repentance was an ancient theme of the scriptural
prophets, the Kingdom on earth was a more recent revival.
Like the Pharisees, the disciples of John fasted.[29] He taught
them a simple prayer.[30] Like most of the prophets of old, he
did no signs,[31] no miracles to authenticate his mission.

Repentance and judgement—what was to follow? Some
further announcement was to be expected. The people were
debating in their hearts whether John himself might not be
the Messiah.[32] The perturbed Jerusalem authorities sent
priests and Levites to ask: "Who are *you?*" John at once admitted that he was not the Messiah. To further questioning
he admitted that he was neither Elijah nor the Prophet. Again
they demanded an answer to bring back to those who had sent
them: "What do *you* say about *yourself?*" John's only reply
was: "I am the voice of one calling in the desert: Make

---

[26]Lk. 3:10–14; Joseph. *Ant.* xviii,
117, gives the preaching in terms
of Greek philosophy.
[27]Mt. 3:5 f.; Mk. 1:5.
[28]Jn. 3:25.

[29]Mk. 2:18; Mt. 9:14; Lk. 5:33.
[30]Lk. 11:1.
[31]Jn. 10:41.
[32]Lk. 3:15.

straight the Lord's Road."[33] "Why then are you baptizing, if you are neither the Messiah nor Elijah nor the Prophet?" they insisted.[34] John was now ready to announce the secret: "*I* baptize you with water, but a mightier is coming after me, the thong of whose sandal I am not fit to loose; *he* shall baptize you with fire; his winnowing shovel is in his hand to cleanse thoroughly his threshing floor and to gather the wheat into his granary, but the chaff he will burn in fire unquenchable."[35] The coming Messiah had been proclaimed.

To John, while still baptizing across Jordan, came a certain Jesus from Nazareth. He did not realize it, but this was the high point of the Baptist's career.

---

[33]Isaiah 40:3, already referred to by anticipation in Zachariah's canticle, Lk. 1:76 b, and quoted in full, doubtless from the original Life of John, Lk. 3:4-6; Mk. 1:2 f.; Mt. 3:3 b.

[34]Jn. 1:19 b, 20 b-23, 25.
[35]Lk. 3:16 b-17; Mt. 3:11 f.; Mk. 1:8; Jn. 1:26 f.; *cf.* Acts 1:5; 11:16.

CHAPTER III

JERUSALEM

NAZARETH for close to half a century remained the home of Jesus. Here unnoticed he spent his childhood, youth, and middle age. Joseph died and Jesus succeeded to his father's trade of joiner.[1] Mary continued to live with her son. At least two of his brothers, James and Jude, grew up to maturity, married, and had children.[2] Two grandsons of Jude were living near the end of the century; arrested by the emperor Domitian (81–96 A.D.) as suspected pretenders to the Davidic kingship, they were contemptuously released when he discovered that they were nothing but simple peasants.[3] Jesus himself never married. When his return as Messiah was awaited, there was only his oldest surviving brother James to act as regent in the interval.

To seek reasons for this failure to marry is quite futile.[4] It cannot be explained as due to consciousness of a future mission, for this consciousness did not come to Jesus until decades after he had reached the normal age of marriage. Work in the joiner's shop demanded and developed physical hardihood, especially when the carpenter must hew out his own timber. Long climbs under a blazing sun over the rocky trails of Palestine required stamina. Courage was needed for a mere provincial to face the representative of Roman might.

---

[1]Mk. 6:3.
[2]I Cor. 9:5.
[3]Hegesippus, in Eusebius, *Church History,* iii, 20, 32,

[4]Explanations based on the unauthentic saying in Mt. 19:12 are absurd.

Men and women alike loved and admired him. Children cuddled in his open arms. Strangers were drawn by his magnetic powers. There was none of the selfishness and coldness often associated with the confirmed bachelor; Jesus was always tender and sympathetic with the poor and the oppressed. Injury to the weak, however, could bring to the surface a blazing and thoroughly healthy indignation. We are reminded of friends, vigorously masculine among men, attractive to women, clean and simple in their life, yet quite content to exist without closer feminine relationship. Looking back, we realize that Jesus unconsciously was freeing himself from mundane cares in preparation for a mission not yet recognized.

News of John's preaching reached Nazareth. Jesus was interested and determined to hear the new Prophet. From Nazareth he would descend to the Great Plain and so by Scythopolis down to the Jordan where it left the Galilee Lake. The time was about December 1, 28 A.D. and the winter rains would have cooled the air and have produced a film of green in the valley. John was found at Bethany beyond Jordan.

Possibly John recognized Jesus as a fellow Prophet. However that may be, Jesus was baptized by John.[5] Later, when the followers of Jesus were contending with those of John for converts, baptism of their Master by the Baptist became embarrassing, and could be explained only by the claim that John was merely the Forerunner, but the fact of the baptism remained. At the moment of baptism, there descended upon Jesus the consciousness that he too had been summoned to carry on God's work.

Two of John's disciples had overheard their Master conversing with the stranger; one was Andrew of Beth Saida,

---

[5]Jn. 1:29; Mk. 1:9; Mt. 3:13, 16; Lk. 3:21.

the other can be only the author of the account, John, the future apostle. Out of curiosity, they followed Jesus, who turning demanded: "What are you seeking?" They answered: "Rabbi, where are you staying?" and were invited to "Come and see." They remained with him that day; it was about the tenth hour, at that time of the year nearing dusk. Thus simply John recalls the memories of his first meeting with the Master.

We are told nothing of the tenor of the conversations. Andrew was so impressed that early next morning he sought out his own brother Simon and excitedly informed him: "We have found the Messiah!" Simon was brought by Andrew to Jesus, who looking at him announced: "You are Simon, son of Jonah; you shall be called Kepha," Aramaic for "Rock"; in Greek, the form would be Cephas, though more often the Greek translation Petros would be employed and from this came the English Peter.

The day after, Jesus decided to return to Galilee. Finding Philip, also from Beth Saida, he bade him: "Follow me." In turn, Philip found Nathaniel, and told him: "Him whom Moses in the Law and also the Prophets wrote of we have found: Jesus, son of Joseph, who is from Nazareth." Nathaniel objected: "Can anything good come from *Nazareth?*" Philip retorted: "Come and see!" As Jesus noticed Nathaniel approaching, he commented: "See! An Israelite truly, in whom there is no craft." "From where did you recognize me?" asked Nathaniel; Jesus answered: "Before Philip called you, under the fig tree I saw you."[6] Perhaps John's memories were tinged by later knowledge of his Master, the simplicity and vividness of the recital give ample witness to the essential accuracy of the conversations. So far as we can see, none

---

[6] Jn. 1:35–36a, 37–48.

of these followers became open and formal disciples at this time.

Like John and the prophets of old, Jesus must have his time of meditation in the desert.[7] It was also to be a time of self-examination. He had been called of God, of that he was convinced, but just what did this call imply? Jesus would explain his mental experiences in the metaphorical terms in familiar use by teachers of his time. Inevitably the thoughts which tormented his mind would be explained as temptations of the Satan, who through the influence of Persian dualism had advanced from a position as the "Accuser," a sort of prosecuting attorney in good and regular standing at the divine court,[8] to be the Evil Spirit himself.

The stories of these temptations must represent Jesus' own teaching. They agree fully with his actual practice, as they do not with what his disciples expected of him; and they flatly contradict what the early church believed of the Son of God. He was fasting, and as the fast neared its end visions of food would flash through his wearied brain. The stream-rolled stones in the gorge took on the appearance of round flat loaves of bread. Why should he not test his new-found authority as God's prophet by attempting the actual miracle? The authors of the Lives tell us of spectacular miracles, even the usually objective John has them, one a resurrection from the dead! We cannot doubt their honesty, though sometimes the line between the convinced eyewitness and the literary improver may be difficult to draw. Not a few of the miracles may be explained by psychical phenomena, to-day well recognized if not fully understood. But we cannot avoid the evidence of the Lives that Jesus was most reluctant

---

[7]Mt. 4:1–11; Lk. 4:1–13; Mk. 1:12 f., placed by all immediately after the baptism. [8]Job 1:6–12.

to perform these healing miracles, that he refused to offer them as proof of his divine mission, and that he repeatedly warned the recipients of these favors to keep quiet about them. Such was *not* the attitude of the early church.

How could a simple artizan from out-of-the-way little Nazareth in despised Galilee convince his people that he spoke the word of God? Why not do something spectacular to attract their attention such as throwing oneself from the high corner tower of the temple enclosure? Would not God, as He had promised in scripture, send His angels to buoy up His messenger? No! That would be deliberately testing out God, like a doubting servant; who knew in what fashion the Lord would bring His word to success? Throughout his ministry, Jesus made no attempt to draw attention to himself. More often he concealed himself from public view. The word of God he preached must grow from within.

John the Baptist had preached a coming Messiah. Some of John's disciples had recognized in Jesus the Messiah he prophesied. Through John's baptism made aware of his call as God's Prophet, Jesus must ask himself in all modesty whether the recognition attested the actual fact. As from an exceeding high mountain, he saw in vision all the kingdoms of the world and their glory. All this might be his if he declared himself the Messiah, for no loyal Jew could doubt that his God was all powerful, that if He wished He could destroy the Gentiles from off the earth. But Jesus felt in himself no Messianic consciousness. The dream, he recognized, was only one more temptation of the Satan. As he understood God's mind, the Kingdom he had been called to preach was something far different.

Again his disciples misunderstood him. During his lifetime, they waited in vain for the day to come when he should manifest himself as the Messiah. After his execution they waited once more for the return of their Lord, and once more in vain. The picture of their Master they give in the Lives is colored by the Messianic expectations, but here and there the true greatness of Jesus' teaching shines forth, and confirms the story of the temptation.

Returning to Galilee, Jesus arrived in Nazareth, where he had been brought up. Here in his home town he would announce his ministry.[9] On a sabbath, he entered the synagogue, the traditional site of which is pointed out with a certain plausibility.

We are to think of the Nazareth synagogue as a modest replica of the magnificent structure of some two centuries later excavated recently at Capernaum; perhaps we secure a better impression from the smaller synagogues of that time from Upper Galilee. In the court outside would be the basin in which the hands must be washed before the services inside. Within we should observe first the platform, whose Greek name of *Bema* was indication that the synagogue originated in Gentile lands. At its rear was the Ark, a niche closed by folding doors, in which the sacred rolls were preserved. To the front was the reading desk and to the side a chair for the preacher. Before the platform were seats for the elders, facing the congregation, which occupied rude benches and fixed their eyes in the direction of the Holy Temple. The women sat apart; in the more elaborate structures, they were assigned a gallery.

Service began with the recitation in unison of the *Shema,* the "Hear, O Israel," which confessed the unity of God. Introduced by and interspersed with blessings, the high point of

---

[9]Mk. 1:14; Mt. 4:12, postpone the beginning of the ministry until after the Baptist's imprisonment.

the service was reached, the reading of the Law, which must already have been carried on according to a three-year cycle. Verse by verse this was followed at once by an oral recitation of the authorized Targum so that every soul might hear the word of God through Moses in the Aramaic, alone fully understood by the majority. After this came a selected passage from one of the Prophets and its Targum, this time after each three verses.

The returned traveller was invited by the synagogue chief to read the lesson and perhaps add a word of exhortation. In the triennial cycle of readings the sixty second week had been reached, and the sabbath was December 18, A.D. 28. It was therefore the roll containing the writings assigned to the prophet Isaiah which the attendant placed in Jesus' hands. Jesus unrolled the scroll to the passage which was to be read for the day, Isaiah 60:17–61:6, and found the place where it was written:

The Spirit of the Lord is upon me,
> Because of which he anointed me to preach good news to
> the poor;
He has sent me to proclaim release to war prisoners,
> And to the blind recovery of sight;
To send forth the crushed into freedom,
> To proclaim the favoring year of the Lord.[10]

Rolling it up again to the beginning, for unlike the Law the prophetical scrolls had a roller at only one end, Jesus handed it to the attendant and sat down to give the exposition. Sensing something out of the ordinary, the eyes of all in the

---

[10]Isaiah 61:1 f.; Luke's version differs enough from our present Hebrew text that we suspect its origin in a now lost Targum. The extract is no longer read in the synagogue.

synagogue were fixed on him. He began: "This day this scripture has been fulfilled in your ears." As he went on, his fellow
townsmen wondered at what he was teaching and especially
at his ability to speak in public: "Where did this fellow get
these ideas? What sort of wisdom would be given *him?* Is
not this fellow the joiner, Mary's son, and brother of James
and Joseph and Judah and Simon? And are not his sisters
right here among us?" And they were scandalized at him!

Sensing the hostility of the congregation, Jesus struck
back: "A Prophet is not unhonored—except in his own fatherland and among his own relatives and in his own house![11]
But in truth I tell you: Many were the widows in the days of
Elijah in *Israel,* when the heaven was closed tight three
years and six months,[12] when there came to pass a great
famine over all the earth, and to not one of *them* was Elijah
sent, but only to Zarephath in the land of Sidon, to a widow
woman. Many too were the lepers in *Israel* at the time of
Elisha the prophet and not one of *them* was cleansed but
only Naaman the Aramæan."

The point could not be missed and Jesus was not permitted
to finish the exposition. At these words, the entire congregation, filled with anger, jumped up and rushed him out of
town as far as the brow of the hill on which the city was
built, intending to throw him down headlong. But Jesus
passed through their midst and escaped.[13]

Over the hill to the north and down the road eastward toward the Lake of Galilee, Jesus, his mother, and the few
disciples he had already made reached Cana. A wedding was
in progress, and as Mary was acquainted with the family, she

---

[11]*Cf.* Jn. 5:44.
[12]Reminiscence, Jas. 5:17; perhaps based on a lost Targumic expansion.

[13]Lk. 4:14, 16–22, 24–30; *cf.* Mt.
4:13a; later account, Mk. 6:1–6a;
Mt. 13:54–58.

was invited and with her Jesus and his disciples. John remembered how the wine failed and how Jesus' mother told her son the bad news; he replied: "What is there in common between me and you, woman? Not yet has come my hour!" As always, Jesus was reluctant to claim miraculous powers. Despite this rebuke, despite also the failure at Nazareth, the trusting mother bade the servants: "Whatever he says to you, do." Then Jesus commanded: "Fill the water jars with water," for placed there according to the Jewish purification custom were six stone water jars, holding about two or three *baths*. The servants filled them to the top after which Jesus gave order: "Draw out now and carry to the ruler of the feast." He tasted the water become wine and did not know from where it came—but the servants who drew the water knew—and calling the bridegroom he chided him: "Every man sets out first the fine wine and, when people are drunk, the poorer, but *you* have kept the fine wine until just now." A charming idyl, no doubt improved by memory, but justifying the apostle's comment: "This beginning of the signs Jesus made in Cana of Galilee."[14]

Cana was on the road to the Lake of Galilee. Avoiding Tiberias as a pagan foundation, Jesus, accompanied by his mother, brothers, and disciples, went down to Capernaum, in the native tongue Kaphar Nahum, "Village of Nahum," from the supposed tomb of that prophet. Capernaum and the Lake of Galilee have been consecrated in our minds by the presence of the Master. Even without the memories, there would be a certain austere beauty. Seen as Jesus first beheld it from the slopes above, the harp-shaped lake whose form gave it the name Chinnereth is attractive, the more so in contrast to the bare hills beyond. At harvest, the nearer slopes

---

14Jn. 2:1-11.

would show the ripe wheat. Directly ahead, the new city of Tiberias would be rising. Farther to the north, an occasional palm, a few olives, some gardens would indicate the site of Magdala or Capernaum. Where the Jordan entered the lake would be seen the patches of swamp green even in summer, and beyond that Beth Saida, the "House of Fish," proud of its new city status under the name of Julias.

There was little enough reason for agricultural settlement about the lake; it is doubtful if the region was ever self-supporting. Its location, almost seven hundred feet below sea level, meant heavily increased atmospheric pressure which must be felt to be appreciated. The near-by swamps, still the most dangerous in Palestine, produced swarms of mosquitoes which passed on the dreaded fevers. Hot springs might give hope of cure to the sick, they would scarcely please the taste of the well.

But all was compensated by the lake, whose waters furnished an amazing wealth of fish. There is reason for the frequent mention of the lake, of boats, of fishing in our Lives of Jesus. The formal call of the four leading disciples, Simon Peter and his brother Andrew, James and John, sons of Zebedee, took place, we are told, while they were fishing; they belonged to well-to-do fisherman families, whose boats were their own property. Their last fishing trip was rewarded by a miraculous catch; they left and followed Jesus only to become fishers of men.[15] Another outstanding disciple, Matthew, earned his living by collecting taxes on the fish caught or on their transport and export.[16] In the worst of summer, the oppressive heat might be tempered by a cool breeze from the lake, though this kindness might be more than counterbal-

---

[15]Mk. 1:16–20; Mt. 4:18–22; Lk. 5:1–11. [16]Mk. 2:13 f.; Mt. 9:9; Lk. 5:27.

anced by the winds sweeping down into the confined bowl
and stirring up the sudden storms whose violence too often
brought the fisherman's career to a sudden end.

In Capernaum, Jesus remained not many days.[17] There he
abode with Simon Peter and Andrew, for his first disciples
were already married. The next sabbath he entered the synagogue. Its site we may still visit, though the over-ornate
structure excavated in our own day was to wait nearly two
centuries more before construction.[18] Again Jesus preached;
again his auditors were struck with astonishment that he
taught by his own authority and not like the scribes to whom
they were accustomed, who could cite a precedent of a master
for every statement.

In the synagogue was a man with an unclean spirit, who
on seeing Jesus shouted: "What is there in common between
us and you, Jesus of Nazareth? Have you come to destroy us?
We know who you are, the Holy of God!" Jesus rebuked
him: "Be muzzled! Come out from him!" The spirit threw
him into convulsions but obeyed. In amazement, the spectators
inquired of one another: "What is this Word? For with
Authority and Power he commands the unclean spirits and
they obey him!"[19]

The story breathes the atmosphere of contemporary demon
lore. Jesus is recognized by the evil spirits as a wonder worker,
a holy man of God like the prophets Elijah and Elisha. "Be
muzzled!" is employed in incantations of the period. The
Memra or Word is used by the Targums as surrogate for
God Himself; it has descended from the most ancient Shumerian Inim Enlila, the Divine Command of the first Lord
of the Gods, Enlil of Nippur. Translated into the Babylonian

---

[17]Jn. 2:12.
[18]G. Orfali, *Capharnaum et ses*   *Ruines*, 1922.
                                        [19]Mk. 1:21-28; Lk. 4:31-37.

Amat Enlil, it influenced the creation story of Genesis with its "And God said : 'Let there be Light.'" As late as 163 B.C., a hymn to the Divine Command was copied in Babylonia, both in Shumerian original and in Akkadian translation, and it indicates the path along which the Creative Word passed to become the basis of the Christian Genesis in the prologue to the Fourth Gospel.[20] Authority and Power we should also capitalize; in current thought they had become almost independent entities.

Despite the literary form, there can be no doubt that Jesus did cure mental diseases. The phenomena of present-day mental healing may suggest the process. Undoubtedly such cures did secure Jesus a hearing. Equally undoubted is the fact that Jesus himself laid little stress on the cures. So far as possible, he avoided the exercise of his healing powers and the unwise enthusiasm which they invoked.

On the return from the synagogue, Jesus found Peter's mother-in-law lying abed and burning with fever—no uncommon occurrence on the malarial shore of the lake. He lifted her up by the hand and the fever left her; at once she proceeded to wait on the company, in flat defiance of rabbinic precept.[21] Similar examples of sudden release from fever, followed by intense activity, have been witnessed by the author in the present-day Near East. At sunset, the sabbath ended, they brought to the door of Peter's house many sick and demoniac, and Jesus cured them.[22]

After these few days at Capernaum, Jesus arose before dawn and went out to pray in a deserted spot. Peter and his

---

[20]A. T. Olmstead, "Intertestamental Studies," *Journal of American Oriental Society,* LVI, 1936, 248.
[21]Mk. 1 :29–31; Lk. 4 :38 f.; Mt. 8 :14 f., misplaced. Contrast Babylonian Talmud, Kiddushin, 70a, 81b.
[22]Mk. 1 :32–34; Lk. 4 :40 f.; Mt. 8 :16.

fellows pursued after him, urging a return: "All are seeking for you." Jesus replied: "Let us go into the near-by village-cities," current usage for the larger towns, "so that I may preach there also, because it was for this reason I came out."[23]

This preaching tour brought Jesus to the synagogues of Judæa,[24] by this time of the year more comfortable and more healthy than Capernaum, far below sea level and already producing its deadly fevers. Passover, which came this year April 18, 29 A.D., was nearing, and Jesus went up to Jerusalem.

Had Jesus paused a moment by the ruins of Gibeah, Saul's ancient capital, he would have caught a fine glimpse of the Holy City and of the Temple. For the next three miles he would have lost the view amid the masses of olive trees which clothed the scant rocky soil and gave to the northern suburb just building up the name Beth Zatha or Bezatha, "House of Oil."[25] Fifteen years were to elapse before King Agrippa brought Bezatha within his new wall; Jesus therefore would have missed the line of the present north wall of the city, he could not have entered by the modern Damascus Gate.

On his left, the view to the eastward would have been shut off by the houses of Bezatha. Some two hundred yards east of the road the Pool of Beth Hesda could be recognized. Between the suburb Bezatha and the city wall the road led down into the Kidron, up the steep slopes of the Mount of the Olives, and shot down to Jericho, the Dead Sea, and Trans-Jordan. The road from Galilee through Samaria taken by Jesus met this road and also the road along which Pilate

---

23Mk. 1:35–38; Lk. 4:42 f.; cf. Mt. 4:23.
24Lk. 4:44, correct manuscript reading; Galilee, Mk. 1:39 cf. Mt. 4:23.

25It was called in Greek Cænopolis, the "New City," Joseph. Wars ii, 503; 504.

had led up his cohort from Cæsarea just before the Gate of the Fish, also known as the Gate of Benjamin.

The rejoicing pilgrims entered the Holy City; the inhabitants met them with quite different emotions. From its earliest beginnings straight down to our own day Jerusalem always has been, in an economic sense, a parasite city. The Jebusite hill fort protected the countryside—and the peasants handed over their surplus for the protection. David's Town was the capital of the united Hebrew tribes, which paid the expenses of court and army; Solomon's "improvements" of the tax system brought new revenues to embellish the city. He also built a new royal shrine to bring religion under tribute.

Revolt of the more wealthy northern tribes destroyed the prosperity of the upstart town, the Temple fell into ruins. The bold effort of Hilkiah to confine formal worship to the Jerusalem Temple alone, even though bolstered by a law ascribed to Moses, was in his own day a complete failure—in fact, a few years after the promulgation the promises assigned to Moses were falsified by the destruction of city and Temple alike.

Where Hilkiah failed, Jeshua and the high priests who followed him succeeded. That same "Mosaic" Law which had contributed to its destruction became the proof that the Temple would be rebuilt. Orthodox post-exilic Judaism, as it evolved in Babylonia, accepted the one unique Temple as part of its faith. To be sure, the actual Temple when restored was small and mean, but it was the one symbol which could hold together the Jews, as time went on more and more scattered throughout the Hellenistic and Parthian world.

The Jerusalem Temple was fortunate. One rival, at Elephantine by the Nile cataract, was destroyed by revolting Egyptians and never restored. Desecration of the Jerusalem

Temple by Antiochus Epiphanes led to the foundation of a small replica at Leontopolis in the Nile Delta, but it did not flourish. The desecration in Jerusalem was followed by the renewed Dedication, and the danger to which the old Temple had been exposed only strengthened the universal love for it.

After the collapse of the Hasmonæan dynasty, Jerusalem had nothing on which to live except its reputation as the Holy City. After the organization of Palestine by the Romans, it was not even the provincial capital. Its reputation must be carefully guarded. Fortunately, this was the great period of ancient "tourism." Athens, deprived of the very shadow of power, prospered again from the crowds of tourists, armed with their guidebooks, and from other crowds of the gilded youth of Rome, seeking a quick application of "culture" in schools located on the very spot where great authors wrote or performed their plays, great sculptors set up their statues, great architects built their temples, and great events took place. No man could boast himself properly travelled until he had beheld the Pyramids, the Labyrinth, the ruins of Egyptian Thebes, until he had fed the sacred bull, the sacred ram, and the sacred crocodile. All this demanded guides, transportation, lodging, and it brought money into the country.

The farther away the Jew, the stronger the sentimental appeal of the Temple. At every feast, and especially at Passover, crowds would appear in Jerusalem. The Holy City might slumber in the short intervals between feasts; the advance guard of the pilgrims quickly awakened it. Shops would be dusted out, new souvenirs exhibited, food must be brought in. Greek, Latin, the oriental languages must be brushed up. There was profit in the air.

Jerusalem was badly prepared to receive the pilgrims. It was true that Herod had rebuilt the Temple in new splendor and had increased the area devoted to religion. New and massive towers adorned its walls, new buildings its interior. Synagogues were available for each group of pilgrims, where services would be conducted in a language they understood. But all this new building, so impressive to the tourist, only subtracted from the scant space available for ordinary housing. Even under conditions to be expected in an oriental city, narrow streets and minute houses, it is doubtful if as many as 40,000 permanent inhabitants could have been accommodated within walls which had not been extended since the years of the Judæan kingdom.

Nehemiah might have found the walls enclosing too great a space to be easily filled by the returned Zionists, but by the first century of our era the Holy City was densely crowded. When to the permanent inhabitants were added hordes of pilgrims, every inch must have been occupied; prices must have soared sky high and only the rich could have purchased relative comfort. A few may have found cheaper accommodations outside the walls in the Bezatha suburb, others might climb the Mount of the Olives to find lodging in the villages of Bethphage and Bethany, or in even more distant towns, but their number was strictly limited by the barrenness of the surrounding countryside. Doubtless many beside Jesus and his disciples spent the night in the open, under the trees of the gardens; in case of inclement weather, they might sleep in the porticoes or doorways.

If in imagination we would wander through Jerusalem in the footsteps of Jesus, we must in the first instance turn to the accounts, not of Josephus,[26] born seven years after Jesus'

---

[26]Joseph. *Wars* v, 136 ff.; *cf.* Tacitus, *Histories,* v, 11.

death, but of Nehemiah,[27] for the general outline of the city
as formed by the walls was the same as in the days of Hezekiah. We have entered the city through the Gate of the Fish
(Dagim),[28] where in the time of Nehemiah's governorship
Tyrians sold their sea food,[29] still earlier known as the Gate
of Benjamin, which Manasseh once restored.[30] Its situation
was fixed by the depression which entered the city about
where the Church of Our Lady of the Spasm now stands.
Within the city, the depression rapidly deepened into a valley
called by the natives the Maktesh,[31] the "Mortar," but by those
who spoke Greek the Tyropœan,[32] named from the "Cheesemakers" who prepared the curds today so well-known under
the name of *lebben*. We are now within the Mishneh,[33] the
"Second City," once a suburb but after the invasion of Sennacherib brought within the fortifications by "the other wall
outside" which Hezekiah constructed.[34]

We shall not take the street down the Mortar which runs
almost due south to the Gate of the Ash Heap at the south
side of the city. Instead, we shall follow the line of the wall
and thus make the complete circuit of the city. A short distance west of the Fish Gate, the wall turns directly south to
the Gate of Ephraim[35] which seems to have taken the name
of the older Gate of Ephraim in the center of the north
stretch of the older first wall. Soon after, the wall made an
angle west and south to avoid a knoll and a garden cemetery;
did the sight of Golgotha send a premonitory chill over Jesus?

Where the second wall joined the first stood the old Gate
of the Corner (Pinneh).[36] After his capture of Jerusalem,

---

[27]Neh. 2:13-15; 3:1-32; 12:31-39.
[28]Zeph. 1:10; II Chron. 33:14.
[29]Neh. 13:16.
[30]Jer. 37:13; II Chron. 33:14.
[31]Zeph. 1:11.
[32]Joseph. *Wars* v, 136, 140.
[33]Zeph. 1:10; II Kings 22:14; II Chron. 34:22.
[34]II Chron. 32:5.
[35]Neh. 12:39.
[36]Jer. 31:38.

Jehoash of Israel broke down two hundred yards of the city wall from that gate to the older Gate of Ephraim.[37] Soon after Jerusalem's recovery, Uzziah erected a tower to command this Corner Gate.[38] Nehemiah seems to call it the Gate of the Old . . .,[39] but by changing one letter we make Gate of the Second City, which is far more appropriate.[40] Still later was the name First Gate;[41] in the time of Jesus it was the Gate of the Garden (Genath).[42]

At this Gate of the Garden, a trifle east of the present Jaffa Gate, the second wall joined the first. Before the gate branched roads leading west to Japho or Joppa on the sea and south to Bethlehem, Hebron, and through the desert to Egypt. It guarded the street down the steep gully which descended due east to join the Cheesemakers' Valley at the point where it passed under the newly extended Temple walls. By this time, the street level had been raised on underground arches to provide a secret access to the Temple from the palace of Herod. Just before reaching the Temple wall, this east-west axial street was crossed by the north-south axial street from the Fish Gate, which had followed down the Cheesemakers' Valley, by means of an arch forty-two feet long and twenty-one high.

From the Garden Gate eastward the northern wall of the earlier city had run along the south slope of this gully. About the middle, at the highest point, had stood the first Gate of Ephraim.[43] Close by and no doubt on the site of still earlier royal buildings stood the Palace of the Hasmonæans; from its southeastern corner extended a viaduct ending in a great

---

37II Kings 14:13.
38II Chron. 26:9.
39Neh. 3:6; 12:39.
40This is the reading of the Syriac version.

41Zech. 14:10.
42Joseph. *Wars* v, 146.
43II Kings 14:13; II Chron. 25:23.

stone arch fifty feet wide and forty long over the Cheesemakers' Valley to connect the palace with the Temple at its
southwest corner.[44] Even today we may examine the spring
of the arch tied into the Temple wall, for the debris of ages
has so filled the once deep valley that it is now within reach
of the present surface. Forty-two feet below, the pavement
of the street from the Fish Gate as relaid by Herod has been
excavated; below that is an earlier arch, going back to Hasmonæan times. To the east of the palace on a lower slope lay
the "polished" Xystus, the gymnasium built by the renegade
high priest Jason at the height of Hellenistic influence. To
pious Jews, the gymnasium was a place of shame, where
Jews exposed their nude bodies to the public gaze. But it was
not always thus. Close by the Xystus and yet directly under
the Temple cloisters was the Senate House, where the Sanhedrin met; its nearness to the gymnasium dates its construction to the days when the priests hurriedly interrupted
the Temple sacrifices to respond to the proclamation that the
discus games were about to begin. On its site is the so-called
Judgement House.[45]

Where the second and first walls came together was the
Broad Wall. Farther south, on the west side of the older
wall, was the Tower of the Ovens (Tannurim), so named
from the near-by street of the bakers.[46] As contrasted with
the Temple fortifications, this was the most commanding spot
in the city and naturally Herod constructed here his most
impressive fortifications.

Defence was based on four huge towers irregularly spaced.
All were set on solid bases. To the north-northwest of the

---

[44]Joseph. *Wars* i, 143; ii, 344; *Ant.* xx, 189 f.

[45]II Macc. 4:14; Joseph. *Wars*, ii, 344; iv, 581; v, 144; vi, 191, 325; *Ant.* xx, 189.

[46]Neh. 3:11; Jer. 37:21.

Garden Gate was the isolated octagonal Psephinus, whose summit, over a hundred feet high, afforded a magnificent view over the Dead Sea into Arabia to the east and on the west down to the Mediterranean; its massive piers may be viewed in the School of the Christian Brothers. Facing to north and to south of the Garden Gate were the Towers of Hippicus and of Phasaëlus. The solid foundation of Hippicus, probably on the site of Uzziah's Tower, was thirty-seven by thirty-seven by forty-five feet. Above it was a reservoir thirty feet deep. A two-storied palace brought the total height to one hundred and twenty feet. Phasaëlus on the south was yet taller, its one hundred and thirty-five feet of height divided between a solid base of sixty-five feet, a fifteen-foot portico defended by parapets, the remainder devoted to a palace with bathing facilities. The solid base may be examined in the so-called "Tower of David." There are sixteen courses, whose average height is four feet two inches. The individual blocks weigh from five to ten tons and gleamed snow-white when new; the bedding and jointing are of extraordinary fineness. They may be distinguished from the older Hasmonæan blocks of the wall whose courses the tower breaks, not alone by their more massive size but even more strikingly by their peculiar dressing, chisel pick for the narrow drafted edges and comb pick for the finishing.

As befitted a lady, Mariame, the fourth tower, so named from Herod's wife, was only seventy-five feet high, its base a cube of thirty feet; naturally the palace was far more luxurious. This tower was on the first wall, but no certain traces have been uncovered.[47] Two other towers continued the line

---

[47] Joseph. *Wars* v, 159 ff.; vii, 1; Psephinus, *Wars* v, 55, 133, 147; Hippicus, *Wars* ii, 439; v, 134, 144, 147, 284, 304; Phasaëlus, *Wars* i, 418; ii, 46, 439; *Ant.* xvi, 144; xvii, 257; Mariame, *Wars* ii, 439.

of the older wall to the south.[48] Not far from this group of towers was the Pool of *the* Towers (Amygdalon), where now tourists visit the "Pool of Hezekiah."[49]

South of the tower group, within its own towered wall, extended Herod's palace, which still further cramped the space available for general housing. While the mass of the population huddled in their tiny houses and overflowed the alleys, the guests occupying Herod's hundred beds might saunter along broad porticoes facing courts where the grass was always kept green by water brought in deep runnels. They might amuse themselves beside the pools, watching the water spout from prohibited bronze statues, or stroll along the shady walks and listen to the cooing doves whose picturesque cotes provided the fertilizer.[50] The gardens of the Armenian monastery give us a pale reflection of the ancient beauty.

Recent excavations afford us no trace of a gate to the south of the great tower group, and indeed we should expect none along the line of Herod's palace and gardens. The gardens probably extended to the south line of the modern wall, but for the days of Jesus all recollection of this modern south wall should be wiped from our minds, since it corresponds to nothing in the ancient history. We must think, then, of the ancient wall as continuing straight on due south to the rock-hewn base of the great southwestern tower under the English School which is well known to all visitors. By the time of Jesus, the site of the traditional Zion, David's Town, had been transferred from the original Ophel to the southwest hill. Here was situated the Upper Agora, the business cen-

---

[48]C. N. Johns, "Excavations at the Citadel, Jerusalem: Interim Report," *Quarterly of the Department of Antiquities in Palestine*, V, 1934, 127 ff.; "Excavations at the Citadel, Jerusalem," *Palestine Exploration Quarterly*, LXXII, 1940, 36 ff.
[49]Joseph. *Wars* v, 468.
[50]Joseph. *Wars* v, 176 ff.

ter.[51] Here also must be sought the official residence of the high priest;[52] the traditional House of Caiaphas is approximately correct.

To the west of the wall, below the Garden Gate, the ravine sinks rapidly and sweeps around the base of the great southwest tower to become the deep Ravine of the Son of Hinnom. The wall descends southeast to approach the Ravine. This whole southern side of the city wall has been excavated,[53] and here and there for our guidance the excavators have left significant bits of the old fortifications. We may differentiate the poorer remains which perhaps date back to Solomon, the better work of the Hasmonæans crowned by the impressive blocks of Herod's reconstruction, and the smaller but well-trimmed stones of early Christian rebuilding. Just around the corner of the great southwest tower, we reach a gate, the Gate of the Essenes[54] as it was called in the time of Jesus. From it a paved street runs northeast into the city. In all probability, here is to be located the earlier Gate of the Ravine,[55] while the tower erected by Uzziah to guard this gate[56] would have been the predecessor of that whose ruins impress us southeast of the exit of the paved street.

Fifteen hundred feet by the lost Fountain of the Monster (Tannin) brought the rapidly descending wall over the contours of the Ravine to the Gate of the Potsherds (Harsith)[57] or of the Ash Heaps (Ashpoth),[58] a name which suggests that in sanitation Jerusalem was not Rome. It also explains a more recent name for the Ravine of the Son of Hinnom, the Gehenna, for the ever-burning piles of refuse

---

[51] Joseph. *Wars* v, 137.
[52] Joseph. *Wars* ii, 426.
[53] F. C. Bliss and A. C. Dickie, *Excavations at Jerusalem*, 1898.
[54] Joseph. *Wars* v, 145.
[55] Neh. 2:13, 15; 3:13.
[56] II Chron. 26:9.
[57] Jer. 19:2.
[58] Neh. 2:13; 3:13 f.; 12:31.

afforded lurid parallel to that Hell-fire into which sinners
were to be thrown at the last judgement.

The Gehenna opens into the still more deeply sunk Gorge
of the Kidron, which descends down to the Spring of the
Fuller (En Rogel), and on its way to the Dead Sea enters
what the Arabs well name the Canyon of the Fire of Hell.
From the Gate of the Ash Heaps, we reach a great projecting
tower at the southeast corner of the city, and turn north
across the Cheesemakers' Valley along an unusually broad
wall. In the valley and now dammed by the wall is Solomon's
Pool, once known only as the King's Pool near the King's
Garden and the King's Winepresses.[59] A little higher up is
the Pool of Siloam (Shiloah), whose rock-cut basin was
extended to fifty feet square by Herod and adorned with
porticoes. On another occasion we shall visit it by the steps
descending from the city; to our own day its water is still
conducted from the Gihon spring outside the east wall of
Ophel through the winding rock-cut tunnel whose excavation
by the men of Hezekiah we may learn from the inscription
once carved in the tunnel mouth.[60]

If we wish to visit the oldest Jerusalem, we climb the
"ascent of the wall," the steps from the Gate of the Fountain
(Ain) straight up the Knoll (Ophel), a long spur extending
south from the Temple Mount. Dwarfed though the Ophel
is by the superior height of the Temple Mount, dwarfed today much more by the cutting down of the crest and by the
filling-in of the depression to either side by the accumulated
debris, we can realize still how strong must have appeared
this position to the earliest occupants. By the first century
of our era the old western wall of Ophel along the Cheese-

[59]Joseph. *Wars* v, 145; Neh.
2:14; Jer. 39:4; Zech. 14:10.
[60]Isaiah 8:6; II Chron. 32:30;
Neh. 3:15; Jn. 9:7; Joseph. *Wars*
ii, 340; v, 140, 145, 252, 410 f., 505;
vi, 363, 401.

makers' Valley had lost all meaning, but that to the east along the Kidron Gorge remained an integral part of the city's defences. Even thus late, there were to be recognized incorporated stretches of the wall built by David, when he changed the name of his new acquisition from Jerusalem to David's Town.

As we labor up the steep hill, over the hidden aqueduct, we pass the Tomb of David, opened in search of treasure by John Hyrcanus and by Herod, the latter of whom built a white stone monument at the entrance to atone for his sacrilege.[61] The "Made Pool" mentioned by Nehemiah may have survived, but the House of the Mighty Men,[62] the barracks of David's bodyguard, had disappeared when the summit which marked the ancient City of David had been cut down by Hyrcanus so that it should no longer endanger the Temple by its citadel.[63]

We look down on the Spring of Gihon, the cause of the original choice of this site. On another occasion, we may visit the spring itself and note the sudden rush of water through the unseen siphon which gave it the name of the "Bubbler." If we do not fear this sudden rush, we may follow the galleries which brought the waters together, look up the steep scarp down which buckets could be let in time of siege from within the safety of the walls, or even crawl through Hezekiah's tunnel to its exit at the Pool of Siloam.

With the destruction of the Citadel went also the Ascent of the Armory (Nesheq), but excavation has shown the Turn (Miqsoa) of the wall, where Uzziah erected a tower[64] to stand guard over the spring below. The official house of the

[61]Neh. 3:16; Joseph. *Wars* i, 61; *Ant.* vii, 393 f.; xiii, 249; xvi, 179 ff.
[62]Neh. 3:16.
[63]Joseph. *Wars* v, 139 in i, 50;
Ant. xiii, 215 wrongly ascribed to Simon.
[64]II Chron. 26:9.

high priest has been transferred to the southwest hill in the vicinity of Herod's palace. The massive Projecting Tower has been found; set beyond another Turn of the wall, it protected the gate leading to Gihon. Jeremiah called it the Gate of the Sons of the People by which the kings of Judah enter and leave,[65] later it was only the Gate of the Water, whose site is indicated by the path yet taken by the women to the spring. The wall of the Ophel seen by Nehemiah, the Jebusite foundations destroyed by David, had disappeared in the debris which filled the draw separating the Knoll from the Temple Mount, to be excavated only in our own day.

The continuation of the wall to the north was quite different from that described by Nehemiah, since Herod had rebuilt the whole Temple Area and had doubled its extent.[66] Solomon's Temple was impressive only to Israelite peasants and herdsmen. The Second Temple, refounded on the old lines by Zerubbabel, was even meaner than the first. The first great improvement came near the beginning of the second century before our era when the high priest Simeon, in preparation for an anti-Seleucid revolt which never took place, repaired the breaches of the House, fortified the Temple with towered walls, and excavated the great reservoir.[67] Already the Temple was taking on again its ancient function as a great fortress.

The desecration by Antiochus Epiphanes was not unconnected with this fortress character but it was temporary. After the rededication by Judah the Maccabee, its military character was again emphasized. Early in the reign of Simon the Maccabee, the unknown Greek traveller who enthusiastically described Jerusalem noted especially the three walls

---

[65]Jer. 17:19.
[66]Joseph. *Wars* i, 401.

[67]Ecclus. 50:1–4.

over a hundred feet high which enclosed the Temple.[68] Already rebels had shown the Romans that the Temple made a good fortress.

About the very year of Jesus' birth,[69] Herod began a complete rebuilding of the whole Temple area. Priests, specially trained for the task, were alone permitted to work on the House, which was completed in a year and a half; eight and a half more years were needed before the other portions were virtually finished, though work continued until just before the outbreak of the great revolt.[70]

To the sophisticated Gentile tourist, who with his own eyes had looked upon the Rome of marble left behind by Augustus, the chaster beauties of Athens, the strange enclosure at Baalbek with its stones of unparallelled size, and the huge agglomeration of gloomy temples at Egyptian Thebes, the little Jewish shrine must have appeared poor and even tawdry, worthy a visit only because of the bizarre practices of its worshippers. The pilgrim from the Dispersion may have been disappointed. Even the Galilæan peasant might have compared it in disparagement with more ornate structures at a near-by Greek polis. But it was not the actual building, richer but more pagan since the reconstruction by Herod, which thrilled the pilgrim's heart. He was about to visit in very truth the House of God.

From the Ophel he would enter the Temple area through the two double gates of Huldah; the present triple and double gates are closed, but we can reach them from inside the Haram and then reascend nearly forty feet, following the steps

---

[68]Aristeas 84.

[69]Our most precise datum is found in Jn. 2:20, from which we learn that in 29 A.D. the Temple had been forty-six years under construction; this would bring back the beginning to 17 B.C. Josephus contradicts himself, year 15 in *Wars* i, 401, year 18 in *Ant.* xv, 380, either 23–22 B.C. or 20–19 B.C.

[70]Joseph. *Ant.* xv, 420 f.; xx, 219.

of Jesus. In his day, these stepped passages would have brought him under and into the Royal Portico, which Herod had erected where once extended Solomon's palaces. Huge new constructions had brought the south end of the Temple enclosure far out over the Valley of the Cheesemakers to join the new arch leading to the Hasmonæan Palace and to the southeast pinnacle,[71] from which he could look down into the Kidron gorge one hundred and seventy feet below, until, as Josephus tells us, one would grow dizzy. Since then, the Kidron gorge has been half filled, but we are still impressed by the splendid masonry, characteristic of Augustan building, whose drafted blocks are three feet high and up to twenty-two in length, fitted without mortar almost microscopically tight.[72]

Looking back at the Royal Portico, we should have noticed how it stretched a little over a hundred feet along the southern wall and how its roof of sweet-smelling cedar was upheld by a hundred and sixty-two monolithic Corinthian columns, requiring three men to span, and arranged in four rows. To the west, a gate led to the viaduct across the Cheesemakers' Valley and thus to the Palace of the Hasmonæans. From the portico, we should have enjoyed fine views over the valley to the Holy City on the west and south.

Eastward in the Kidron gorge we should have observed below us a group of tombs constructed within the last century or two in somewhat degenerate Greek style, not unmixed with foreign elements. One showed a partially rock-cut cube faced by Ionic columns and crowned by a weird flowerlike pinnacle. Another, the tomb of the sons of Hezir, as we learn from a

---

[71]Mt. 4:5; Lk. 4:9.
[72]For the Temple area, cf. Joseph. Wars v, 184 ff.; Ant. xv, 396 ff.; Mishna tractate Middoth; F. J. Hollis, The Archæology of Herod's Temple, 1934.

Hebrew inscription in the characters of Jesus' day, consisted of a series of rock-cut chambers from which extended narrow shafts for the individual bodies, the vestibule upheld by Doric pillars. A third was a rock pyramid with Ionic columns and half columns but Egyptian cornice.

The colonnades around the other three sides of the Temple had but two rows of columns. That to the east was Solomon's Portico,[73] hung with trophies of Herod and his predecessors. From it a fine view was afforded of the gardens and orchards, such as Gethsemane, which clustered up the steep ascent of the Mount of the Olives and gave the whole scene an olive-green tone. The Gate of the Horses,[74] still commemorated by the Stables of Solomon in the southeast corner, and the Gate of the Sunrising had disappeared, but the Gate of the Guard (Miphqad)[75] had become the Gate of the Lily (Shushan), from the decoration of its capitals; it led to the Kidron, which it crossed on a viaduct, and then to the Mount of Olives. Its position is approximately indicated by the Golden Gate of Christian times. Under the north portico was the Gate Todi. In the west Temple wall were four more gates. That of Qiponos was named from the procurator Coponius and so must have been nearest Antonia. One of the next two was the Gate of Jeconiah. The last led to the viaduct and the Hasmonæan Palace.

Within these irregularly oriented porticoes rose the Mount of the House. A large section, the Outer Court or Court of the Gentiles, paved with varicolored stones, was open to tourists. Its limits were marked by a balustrade (Soreg) to whose pillars were affixed warning notices, picked out in glaring red paint in sharp contrast to the gleaming white limestone; two

---

[73]Jn. 10:23; Acts 3:11; 5:12;   [74]Jer. 31:40; Neh. 3:28.
Joseph. *Ant.* xx, 210 ff.   [75]Neh. 3:31.

extant inscriptions preserve the very words by which the Greek visitor was informed that it was not permitted "any foreigner to enter within the balustrade around the Temple and the enclosure. But whoever is caught shall be responsible to himself for the death to follow at once."[76]

Fourteen steps led up to a fifteen-foot-wide terrace (Hel) beyond which had been erected a wall, sixty feet high on the outer face, which made the Inner Temple a veritable fortress in itself. Beyond this was the Court of Israel; while the outer Temple walls and porticoes were irregularly oriented, following the contours of the native rock, the Inner Temple was carefully oriented to bring the sun's rays directly into the House on the annual equinoxes.

Recently the eastern portion of the Court of Israel, fifteen curving steps lower down, had been partitioned off as a Court of the Women. This was entered by the largest of all the ten temple gates, the Gate Beautiful,[77] covered with gold and silver. Around the court were the rooms devoted to Temple finance, forming the Treasury. In it stood the "trumpets" into which the pilgrims threw their coins;[78] seven were for the obligatory dues, six for free-will offerings. Beyond this, women were not permitted to go, but in compensation balconies reserved for them alone permitted an excellent view of the Temple ceremonies.

Men however passed into the Court of Israel through the Gate of Nicanor, presumably named from the Seleucid general over whom Judah the Maccabee won his most noteworthy victory. It was a huge affair, requiring twenty men to close the gate at nightfall and to shoot the iron-covered bars into

[76]J. H. Iliffe, *Quarterly of the Dept. of Antiquities*, VI, 1938, 1 ff.
[77]Acts 3:2.
[78]Jn. 8:20; Mk. 12:41-44; Lk. 21:14; Joseph. *Wars* v, 200; vi, 282; *Ant.* xix, 294; Mishna, Shekalim vi, 1, 5.

the wall and the bolts into the monolithic threshold. But its greatest claim to remembrance was that it was covered by the famous Corinthian bronze while the other nine gates had only the less esteemed gold and silver.

Jesus could not penetrate beyond the Court of Israel, but he might gaze upon the performance of the sacred ritual from behind the low barrier wall, only a foot and a half high, which marked off the Court of the Priests. In the center of this court stood the Great Altar of Burnt Offering. According to the foundation story, David had first built the altar, saying: "This is the House of the Lord God and this is the Altar of Burnt Offering for Israel," at the threshing floor of Ornan the Jebusite, where the angel of destruction had ceased his deadly work.[79] The threshing floor would be at the point where the most breeze for the threshing would be found; we must therefore look for the site of the altar on the bare rock summit, now protected by the exquisite early Islamic Dome of the Rock.

The original altar of Solomon was of bronze,[80] a disquieting fact demanding editorial explanation when it was later discovered that the original Law of Moses required that it be made of unworked stones. Now it rose on a square base forty-eight feet on a side in a series of steps to a height of thirteen and a half feet and to a hearth forty-two feet square. Through two openings in the great white unhewn blocks and then through a rock-cut channel the sprinkled blood ran off to a pool and then into the Kidron.[81]

From a distance, the vast clouds of smoke billowing up from the altar would have appeared to us picturesque. A nearer view would probably have nauseated us by the stock-

[79] I Chron. 21:15–22; I.
[80] I Kings 8:64; II Kings 16:14 f.
[81] Cf. the descriptions of Hecatæus of Abdera, Joseph. Apion i, 198 f.; unknown geographer, Aristeas 87 f.

yard sights and smells, for unlike the ancients our eyes and nostrils are not habituated to bloody sacrifices. North of the altar, the cattle to be sacrificed were tied to rings in the pavement until they were slaughtered according to the ritual still employed by our own Chicago packers in the preparation of *kosher* meat. In the House of the Slaughterers were four stone tables for skinning and washing, and the pillars and hooks on which the carcasses were hung. Two other small structures of three chambers each afforded storage for skins, salt, and wood; permitted washing of the entrails before examination for omens, quite along the line of Babylonian liver divination; or housed the bucketed water wheel which drew from the huge underground cisterns, filling so large a part of the substructure and so exciting the admiration of pagan visitors,[82] what was needed to flush the sloping pavement of the court. The pools of blood from the slit throats, the offal odor which must have persisted despite the constant flushing, and the stench of the burning flesh would have been to us rather sickening.

But the pious Israelite ignored all this as he lifted up his eyes to the ultimate goal of his pilgrimage, the House where his Lord abode. Yet at that, he did not behold the actual House, unless he viewed it from an acute angle within the Temple courts; it could be better seen from the city proper or from the Mount of Olives. Sight of the House proper was shut off by the Porch, to which, after passing the Laver which had been substituted for Solomon's Bronze Sea, twelve broad steps led up.

We must envisage the Porch, not from the well-known Propylæa on the Athenian Acropolis, still less from the entrance to Solomon's Temple, a true Porch flanked on either

---

[82]Aristeas 89; Tacitus, *Histories* v, 12.

side by a huge column in the Phœnician style; now it resembled most a Pylon from Egyptian Thebes. Plated as was
also the true House[83] with solid gold, it rose a hundred and
fifty feet high and was the same distance broad, but its depth
was only thirty feet. So shallow a structure needed further
provision for stability and was therefore joined to the main
building by tie beams. The thirty-foot wings "like shoulders,"
otherwise called "crowns," indicate a double-towered gateway
like the Egyptian Pylon. The Egyptian effect was further
strengthened by the tall narrow opening, one hundred and five
feet high but only thirty-seven broad. Over this doorway,
five oak beams were inserted between the stone courses; it
was an antique practice, for the same technique has been
found in one of Solomon's buildings excavated recently at
Megiddo.

From the Porch, doors on either side gave access to a row
of three-storied structures which surrounded the House to a
height of ninety feet and still further masked the Temple
proper. Through the main Pylon entrance, closed by no doors
during the day, could be seen the doorway of the House,
whose gold-plated double valves were hidden by an enormous
curtain. It had been manufactured by the Babylonians, the
most famous textile workers of the day, who into it wove
heavenly figures, purple flowers, and pillars. The colors represented the cosmic elements—the scarlet: fire; the byssus:
earth; the blue: air; and the purple: sea; so at least declares
Josephus. Under the cornice twisted the golden vine, the
height of a man.[84]

The Holy Place (Hekal) must have the traditional ground
plan of sixty feet by thirty, though the ceiling was raised to
ninety. This was also the height of the surrounding struc-

---

[83]Mt. 23: 16 f.   [84]Cf. Tacitus, Histories v, 8.

tures, but above the Holy Place was a second story which brought its total height to one hundred and fifty feet. Within the Holy Place were the Altar of Incense, the Table of the Show Bread, and the ever-burning seven-branched Lampstand, all of solid gold and weighing up to two talents. Once before they had been looted, by Antiochus Epiphanes;[85] a generation later their more beautiful substitutes were to be carried to Rome, never to be returned; we may see them depicted on the Arch of Titus in the imperial capital. Jesus could hear of them only through the priests.[86]

The smaller woolen curtain, adorned with Assyrian weaving and the Phœnician purple and let down by cords between the Holy Place and the Holy of Holies (Debir), had also been looted by Antiochus Epiphanes and presented to the temple at Olympia.[87] A new curtain had taken its place[88] and shut off the cube of thirty feet on the side. The thick darkness in which the Lord Himself abode was violated but once a year, on the Day of Atonement, when the High Priest ventured alone to face his God for the sins of his people. The Ark of the Covenant with its attendant Cherubs, human-headed bulls imitated from Assyria, was long since gone; after Pompey had desecrated its sanctity, the whole world knew that the Holy of Holies was empty.

Over the huge stones of the House, up to thirty-seven feet by twelve by eighteen, and set in walls twelve feet thick, was the flat roof of beaten clay. Stone rollers kept it in shape and passages down the sides drained its rain waters into cisterns. Spikes along the roof prevented defilement by birds.

The whole complex of structures which formed the Tem-

[85]Pausanias v, 12, 4.   [88]Hebr. 9:3; Mk. 15:38; Mt.
[86]Cf. Hecatæus, l.c.   27:51; Lk. 23:45.
[87]Pausanias l.c.

ple proper was oriented due east in accordance with general oriental practice.[89] Such orientation was easy to secure; we still may recognize today the lines drawn on the foundations of Egyptian temples by the use of the split stick and the line held taut by the plumb bob when sighted at the North Star. A similar system was employed in Assyria. That the rear of the Inner Temple Complex did not abut in an exactly straight line against the west portico would be no objection in Jewish eyes: already the orientation of the outer complex had been forced into irregular lines by the slope of the rock.

As the pilgrim departed from the holy site through the northern gate, his pious meditations were rudely challenged. In the days of the kings, two towers, that of the Hundred (Meah) and that of Hananeel, had guarded the city wall on the north of the Temple.[90] By the time of Nehemiah, the second had been named Birah, the Fort.[91] Throughout the Maccabæan wars of liberation, it had been held by the Seleucid garrison, and the Jews had learned how dangerous it was to the Temple. After its surrender to Simon, that canny ruler promptly refortified it; a contemporary Greek visitor marvelled at its elevated position, its height and its huge stones. He noted the view it afforded over the temple ceremonies and the care with which it was garrisoned. He possessed an official pass, but the oath-bound five hundred soldiers honored it reluctantly, "even though we were but two unarmed men."[92] After the destruction of the city walls by Antiochus VII, the Baris, to give it its Aramaic name, was quickly rebuilt.[93]

---

[89] Aristeas 88.
[90] Jer. 31:38; Neh. 3:1; 12:39; Zech. 14:10.
[91] Neh. 2:8; 7:2.
[92] Aristeas 100 ff.; I Macc. 13:52.
[93] Joseph. Ant. xviii, 91; cf. xiii, 307; xv, 403, 409; Wars i, 75, 118.

When Herod extended the limits of the Temple on the north, the northwest angle was brought close under the tower, which he rebuilt and named Antonia in honor of his patron Mark Antony. It now extended five hundred feet from east to west and two hundred and sixty-five from north to south. So thorough was the restoration that all traces of the former structures were completely obliterated. Its base was solid rock, whose scarped south face under the former Turkish barracks may be observed from the Sacred Area. On the north, it was cut off from the hill of Bezatha by a fosse and a counterscarp, while the whole slope of the rock was covered by a revetment of stone slabs to make escalade impossible.

Within a parapet four and a half feet high rose Antonia, with its palaces, baths, and barracks, another sixty feet. The great quadrilateral was crowned by four towers, one at each corner; three were seventy-five feet high, that at the southeast reached one hundred and five. From it, the Roman garrison commanded a better view of the Temple than the pilgrim, for Antonia dominated the Temple area as did Herod's Palace and the three great towers of Hippicus, Phasaëlus, and Mariame the Upper City.[94]

From Antonia, two "descents," ramps or steps, led down, one into the north portico, the other into the west. After Judæa became a Roman province, Antonia was garrisoned by a detachment of Roman troops, always prepared to dash down into the Temple courts at the least sign of trouble.[95] At the festivals, the fortress would be jammed with soldiers, who in case of more serious riots could be rushed through underground passages constructed by Herod under the plat-

---

[94]Joseph. *Wars* v, 238 ff.; *cf.* i, 118; *Ant.* xv, 292; xx, 110; *Life* 20; Tacitus, *Histories* v, 11. [95]Acts 21:31 f., 35.

form and into the very heart of the Temple precincts; one came out at the East Gate, the other at Strato's Tower.[96]

Aside from the rock scarp, the few scanty remains are now below the present surface. Thanks to repeated excavation, thanks even more to the exceptionally skillful interpretation of the great Dominican scholar Père Hughes Vincent, from the few disunited bits of Herod's masonry and a larger area over which the rock has been scarped we may reconstruct with almost miraculous precision the mighty edifice and, though the merest tourist, may check this reconstruction by the remaining traces.[97]

Roman oversight of their holy Temple could not be avoided, it must be endured. Another insult to the pilgrim's meditation was capable of immediate amendment. Inside the Gate of the Flock (Zon), in the court to which Gentiles were admitted and so before profane eyes, were shops in which everything needful for sacrifices might be purchased. Not content with the profits which flowed more or less legitimately from the crowds of pilgrims through priestly ownership of inns and bazaars in the city, the nobility exercised what amounted to a monopoly of the supplies needed for temple worship. Cattle must be officially inspected; if bought elsewhere, there might be danger of rejection. There could be no doubt of the ritual purity of cattle, sheep, doves, wine, oil, salt purchased within the Temple itself, and we may be sure that the pilgrims paid well for the certainty. Even the doves allowed by the kindly Mosaic Law as substitutes for the very poorest must pay their share of priestly graft. Then there was the sacred half shekel which each Jew must every year

---

[96]Joseph. *Ant.* xv, 424; xiii, 309; *Wars* i, 75.
[97]L. H. Vincent, "L'Antonia et le Prétoire," *Revue Biblique*, XLII, 1933, 83 ff.

pay into the Temple treasury. Only the proper coins must be used, the Temple must not be profaned by idolatrous heads of earthly rulers; the imperial currency must be exchanged for what the priests would accept. The Greek word *kollybos* was transliterated into the Aramaic *qolbon* for the commission demanded for the exchange.[98]

Shocked by this "bandit's den," Jesus twisted a whip of ropes and threw out of the temple area all these harpy bazaar keepers with their animals. The small change of the discounters was poured out, and the tables, *trapeza* in Greek, which to contemporaries gave the name to "trapezite bankers" were overturned. A law had prescribed that a man "may not enter into the Temple Mount with his staff or his sandal or his wallet or with the dust upon his feet, nor may he make of it a short cut."[99] It was being violated, for the way around the Temple was long; Jesus prevented any one from carrying an object through the courts. To those selling doves he ordered: "Take them away from here! Do not make my Father's House a trading post!"[100]

To the excited visitors at the feast, this and "other signs he did"[101] of which we have no further information could have only one meaning; the overturned tables of the bankers portended social and economic if not political revolution. Many, especially of his fellow Galilæans, were prepared to become his followers, but Jesus did not trust himself to them.[102] He did, however, make one influential if timid recruit, the Pharisee Nicodemus, who had been accepted as one of the ruling aristocracy through his membership in the

---

[98]Mishna, Shekalim 1:6 f.
[99]Mishna, Berakot 9:5; Tosephta, Berakot 7:19.
[100]Jn. 2:13–16; strangely placed in Passion Week, Mk. 11:15–17; Mt. 21:12 f.; Lk. 19:45 f.
[101]Jn. 3:2; 4:45.
[102]Jn. 2:23–24a.

Sanhedrin.[103] He visited Jesus by night and confessed: "Rabbi, we know that you are a teacher come from God, for no one could be able to do these signs which you do, if God were not with him."[104] Jesus and the Pharisees had much in common; Nicodemus is one witness to this feeling of solidarity which was to be manifested again and again.[105]

Sale of animals for sacrifice within the temple precincts was perfectly normal for heathen shrines. Similar prebends, income from daily sacrifices, were daily bought and sold on the open market in Babylonia and Egypt, and we can show the documents. To Jesus, it was profanation of his Father's House.

To Annas, the powerful ex-high priest, such attack on priestly perquisites was outrageous. Seriously injured by loss of business at the height of the pilgrim season, Annas and his fellows would not have been slow to appeal to the procurator, following his usual practice in Jerusalem for the feast and with his legionary cohort watching the disturbance from the Tower of Antonia. Pilate's innate fear of revolution could easily be turned into suspicion of the new Prophet. Already the stage was being set for the tragedy of the crucifixion.

103Jn. 7:50; 19:39.
104Jn. 3:1 f.

105Cf. e.g., Lk. 13:31; Mk. 12:28–34; Acts 5:34, 38 f.; 23:6–10.

CHAPTER IV

TAX COLLECTORS AND SINNERS

BEFORE the storm he had raised by his temple cleansing, Jesus must retire to the Judæan countryside where he spent some time baptizing. Meanwhile John also continued baptizing, but now in Ænon near Salim. We are told that he did so because there were many waters there; eight miles south of Scythopolis, the bare Jordan Valley is cheered by a fine group of springs, five in number, a few minutes' walk one after the other.[1] But the location indicates something else: it is *west* of the Jordan, that is, within the limits of the Roman province. There was a reason for the change in locale.

Herod Antipas was only a petty tyrant, "Herod the tetrarch" as he calls himself on his coins. "Son of King Herod" is all the claim that could be made for him to give a slightly higher status.[2] His rule as a Roman vassal was therefore exceedingly precarious. Hitherto he had managed to remain on good terms with Tiberius, but nothing could more quickly raise the suspicions of the Emperor than great crowds listening to proclamations of a coming Kingdom, to be ruled by a national Messiah, when revolt might already be sensed in the air. Antipas must take action at once or risk the loss of his uneasy thronelet.

To fear of revolution was now added in the mind of An-

[1] Jn. 3:22 f.; Eusebius, Onomasticon, 40; F. M. Abel, "Exploration de la Vallée du Jourdain," *Revue Biblique*, NS.X, 1913, 222 f.

[2] G. F. Hill, *Catalogue of the Greek Coins of Palestine*, 1914, xcvii, 229 f.; W. Dittenberger, *Orientis Græci, Inscriptiones Selectæ*, no. 416 f., honorary dedications from Cos and from Delos in return for gifts. Mark 6:14 is accordingly wrong in assigning him the title of king.

tipas a sense of personal grievance. He had long been married to a daughter of the able Nabatæan king, Aretas IV to the Romans, "Harithath, loving his people, king of Nabat" (9 B.C.–39 A.D.) to his willing subjects. The two rulers remained on cordial terms until Antipas found it necessary to visit Rome, probably on the accession of the new Emperor in 14 A.D. On the journey he stopped over with his half-brother Herod, whose mother was the daughter of the former high priest Simon. There he fell in love with the half-brother's wife, Herodias, daughter of another brother, Aristobulus, and sister of the king-to-be, Agrippa I. On promise of divorcing his first wife, Antipas persuaded Herodias to agree to marriage after his return from Rome.

Aretas' daughter however got wind of the proposed marriage. To forestall the divorce, she begged permission to retire to Machærus on the Nabatæan border and from there was forwarded to her father, who promptly started war with Antipas. Nevertheless, the tetrarch carried out his bargain and married Herodias about the year 15 A.D.

According to the Mosaic Law, the marriage was clearly incestuous; marriage with a brother's wife was allowed only when the brother was deceased and the survivor must raise up seed to the dead. Furthermore, Herodias was his niece. Herodias and Antipas no doubt considered themselves Greeks, emancipated from the shackles of ancestral law; John however kept on denouncing the illegal marriage: "It is not lawful for you to have her."[3]

Not only was this a minor sort of *maiestas*, personal in-

---

[3]Joseph. *Ant.* xviii, 109 ff.; *cf.* 148; Lk. 3:19 and the original of Mt. 14:3 had only "his brother's wife"; Mk. 6:17 incorrectly makes the brother Philip, who actually married Herodias' daughter Salome, and in the majority of manuscripts the passage in Matthew has been corrected from Mark.

sult of a ruler, however petty, in view of the war now raging between Antipas and Aretas over this very marriage, it was actually treason. Tiberius had taken the side of Antipas, therefore it was also treason against the Roman state. No wonder that John felt it wise to escape the tetrarch's dominions and to retire into the scarcely more safe Roman province.

While John's disciples were debating with the Jewish orthodox about his new practice of purification,[4] Jesus left Judæa and set out for Galilee. If he traversed the direct route, he must pass through Samaria, often avoided by Galilæan pilgrims because of the constant danger of attack from the Samaritan heretics. After its capture by John Hyrcanus, Shechem had almost disappeared and its place was taken by Sychar, a little village around a spring farther out in the plain, some two miles northeast of the ancient ruins. Just before the track reached these ruins, was the site of the "Tomb of Joseph," marking the plot, Jesus was told, which Jacob gave to his son Joseph. A tiny modern structure still commemorates the traditional tomb. A mile southeast of the tomb was Jacob's Well, a spring well, rock-cut and at least a hundred feet deep, from which cold, clear water to this day is drawn for the tourist. Wearied by the journey, Jesus was sitting by the well; it was about the sixth hour.

A woman from Sychar appeared and prepared to draw water. Jesus requested: "Give me to drink." In surprise she replied: "How can you, a Jew, ask a drink from me, a Samaritan woman?" Jesus answered: "If you knew the gift of God, you would have asked of me and I would have given you living water." "Master, you have no bucket," said the woman, "and the well is deep; from where do you have the

---

[4] Jn. 3 :25.

living water? Are you greater than our father Jacob, who gave us the well? He drank from it and his sons and his flocks." "Every one who draws from *this* water," replied Jesus, "shall thirst again, but whoever drinks from the water which *I* shall give him shall never thirst again." She demanded: "Master, give me this water so that I may neither thirst nor come here to draw."

Her attention awakened, Jesus commanded: "Go, call your husband and come here." Shamefacedly she answered: "I have no husband." This was the opportunity: "Rightly you say: 'I have no husband,' for you have had five husbands, and he whom you now have is *not* your husband! Thus you have spoken truly." Now the woman admitted: "Master, I realize you are a prophet." But he was a Jewish prophet and she had a question to propound: *"Our* fathers worshipped in this mountain." Gerizim was straight above them where the tourist may yet, if he is fortunate, watch the diminished Samaritan community slaughter the Paschal Lamb together with all due ceremony. If he waits patiently under the glorious full moon on the flat mountain top, he may see the pits opened, the food snatched one from another amid realistic shouts of "Curse the faith of your father," and eaten with indecent haste. "You," as a Jew—continued the woman, "say that in Jerusalem is the Place where one must worship." Jesus retorted: *"You* worship what you do not know; *we* worship what we know, for restoration is from the Jews." She said: "I know that Messiah comes," for the Messianic hope was just as strong with Samaritans as with Jews and was in future to lead to bloody revolts against the Roman power until the community was almost destroyed. *"He,* when he comes, will proclaim everything." Jesus' reply has been edited and we do not know what he said.

Upon this came his disciples. They were surprised that he was talking to a woman, for this was contrary to proper rabbinic custom. Nevertheless, no one said: "What are you seeking?" or "Why are you speaking with her?" Here we have reported the impressions of the eyewitness. The woman left her water jar and went off into the city and told the men: "Come, see a man who told me all that I have done; is not *he* the Messiah?"

The men came out of the city and were approaching Jesus as the disciples were begging him: "Rabbi, eat!" But he said to them: "I have food to eat of which *you* do not know." In surprise, the disciples asked one another: "Has any one brought him something to eat?" Jesus explained: *"My* food is to do the will of him who sent me and to accomplish his work." Gazing out over the little plain from the knoll through whose rock the well had been dug, he continued: "Are you not accustomed to say in proverb: 'Yet four months and harvest comes?' Behold, I say to you: Lift up your eyes and note how they are white for harvest already." The time was May.

Many of the Samaritans from that city believed on him because of the woman who testified: "He told me all that I had done." When therefore the Samaritans came to him, they requested him to remain with them and he remained with them two days. Many more believed through his word and said to the woman: "No longer do we believe on account of your talking, for we ourselves have heard."[5]

After the two days' visit, Jesus continued on to Galilee, where he was received hospitably because the Galilæans had seen what he had done at Jerusalem during the feast.[6] Next we find him a second time at Cana, again on his way to

---

[5]Jn. 4:3–42, much revised by the editor.   [6]Jn. 4:43, 45.

Capernaum. From there came a royal official, who had heard that Jesus had returned from Judæa. The term "royal official" is quite appropriate in Antipas' tetrarchy; the evangelist Mark follows common usage when he incorrectly gives the tetrarch the honorary title of king.[7] Not improbably he was Kuza, the tetrarch's steward, whose wife Johanna was among the women who later followed Jesus on his journeys and contributed to his support.[8] His son was about to die and he begged Jesus to come down and heal him. Jesus answered: "Unless you see signs and portents, you will not believe"; the answer was characteristic of Jesus' attitude. "Master, come down before my little son dies," was the only reply made.

Touched by his faith, Jesus bade the official: "Go, your son lives." In full belief, the man turned back, but as he was descending the slaves met him and reported: "Your son lives." Then he inquired from them the hour when the child began to improve and was told: "Yesterday at the seventh hour the fever left him." The father therefore knew that it was at the very hour in which Jesus said to him: "Your son lives," and he believed and all his house.[9]

Jesus travelled on to Capernaum. Word was passed: "He is in a house," no doubt again that of Peter. So great a crowd collected as he spoke to them the Word that even the space about the door could not hold them. Four men approached carrying a paralytic on his pallet. They could not reach Jesus on account of the crowd. Accordingly they took the paralytic up the outside stairs to the roof of mud rolled down over the

---

[7]Mk. 6:14.
[8]Lk. 8:3.
[9]Jn. 4:46–53; in Mt. 8:5–10, 13; Lk. 7:1–10, the son of the royal official is turned into the slave of a cen-turion, whose presence in Galilee is extremely unlikely until after it had been incorporated into the Roman province.

tree trunks and brush which served as rafters, and dug it up. Through the hole thus made they let down the paralytic so that he lay before Jesus. "Arise, lift up your pallet and go to your house," the paralytic was ordered; he obeyed and all the beholders glorified God, declaring: "Like this did we never at all see anything."[10]

Going out from the house, Jesus walked by the seashore; as a crowd collected, he taught them. Strolling along, he came to the custom house on the beach, where officials of Antipas collected tolls from the boats crossing the lake from the independent Greek cities of the Decapolis or from the territory of his brother Philip, as well as imposts on the fish caught in lake waters. At the custom house Jesus found the tax collector Levi, son of Halphai (Alphæus), better known to us by his alternative name Mattathiah or Matthew. Jesus gave the invitation: "Follow me!" Rising up, the tax collector followed.

As a tax collector, Matthew scarcely would be poor. His house would be commodious enough for the good-sized dinner party he gave in honor of his new master. To it fellow tax collectors and those considered by the pious to be "sinners" were invited. Tax collectors never have been popular. Nationalists hated them as representatives of the barely concealed Roman dominion. The orthodox declared their testimony in court of no value.[11] After the dinner, the scribes in surprise asked of Jesus' disciples: "Does he actually eat with tax collectors and sinners?" Overhearing the question, Jesus answered: "No need have those who are strong for a physician, but rather those unwell; I did not come to summon the righteous but rather sinners."[12]

---

[10]Mk. 2:1-4, 11 f.; Mt. 9:2a, 6b-7; Lk. 5:18 f., 24b-26.

[11]Babylonian Talmud, Sanhedrin 25b, a Baraita and so of early date.

[12]Mk. 2:13-17; Lk. 5:27-32; Mt. 9:9-13.

The orthodox continued to mutter: "This fellow receives sinners and eats with them!" To them Jesus told a story: "What do you think? If it happens that a man has a hundred sheep, and one wanders from them, does he not leave the ninety-nine on the mountains and going, seek the wanderer? And if he happens to find it, he rejoices over it more than over the ninety-nine who had not wandered. I tell you: Thus there shall be more joy in heaven over the repentant sinner than over ninety-nine righteous who do not need repentance."[13]

"Or what woman, having ten coins, if she loses one, does not light a lamp"—her little house had no window—"and sweep the house" with its packed clay floor, "and search carefully until she finds it? And having found it, she calls together the friends and neighbors, saying: 'Rejoice with me, for I have found the coin I had lost.' So, I tell you, there shall come joy before the face of the angels over one repentant sinner."[14]

Thus, at the very beginning of his ministry, Jesus enunciated a great principle, which marked a significant innovation in religious thought. To many of his contemporaries, his fellow Galilæans in particular, God was primarily a God of vengeance, whose strong right arm would soon destroy Israel's pagan oppressors and restore the Kingdom to Israel. To John the Baptist, this God of vengeance would extend His punishment to those Jews, sons of Abraham though they might be, who had shown themselves disloyal. Even the gentle Pharisees, who repeatedly insisted that their God was forgiving, stopped at this point. For them the responsibility lay with the sinner; he must repent and seek God before God could forgive. Jesus thought of God as far more loving; so

---

[13]Mt. 18:12 f.; Lk. 15:2-7, with correct content and moral.   [14]Lk. 15:8-10.

anxious was He for erring man to repent that He actually went out Himself in person to recover him. And what joy was the reward of God and His holy angels when the wanderer was returned to the fold. Jesus had given to erring man the ultimate picture of God.

Jesus was always on good terms with the Pharisees, who recognized their mutual kinship in thought. Now and then he was invited by one to dinner.[15] On one such occasion, they were at meal when a woman of the city, a sinner, slipped in and took her stand at his outstretched feet. Wetting them with her tears and wiping them with her hair, she kissed them repeatedly and anointed them with myrrh from an alabastron. This was too much for the hitherto friendly Pharisee and his face showed what he was thinking: "This man, if he were a prophet, would have realized who and what sort was the woman who touched him, for she is a sinner." Jesus answered his unspoken thought: "Simon, I have something to tell you." "Rabbi, tell me," Simon replied.

"There were two debtors to a certain creditor; the one owed him five hundred denarii, the other fifty. As they had nothing with which to repay him, he forgave them both; which therefore of them will love him the more?" Simon answered: "I suppose that it is he to whom he forgave the most." "Rightly you judge" was the reply. Turning toward the woman, Jesus told Simon: "Look at this woman! I entered your house. Water on my feet you did not pour, but *she* with tears has wet my feet and with her hair has wiped them. A kiss you did not give me, but *she,* from the time I entered, has not left off kissing my feet. With oil my head you did not anoint, but *she* with myrrh has anointed my feet. Because of this, her many sins are forgiven her, for she

---

[15]Other examples, Lk. 11:37; 14:1.

loved much, but he to whom little is forgiven loves little."[16]

Recently Jesus had been reading the stories of Ahiqar and of Tobit, and certain expressions yet clung in his mind.[17] It seems close to sacrilege to mention their origin, for on Jesus' lips they were transformed into one of the most beautiful of his parables:

"A certain man had two sons. And the younger of them said to his father: 'Father, give me the part of the property which falls to me.'" This he had no right to ask before his father's death, but nevertheless "he divided to them his possessions. And after not many days, collecting all"—it would be the younger son's allotment, one third—"the younger son went abroad into a distant country. And there he squandered his property, living in debauchery.

"But having spent his all, there arose a terrible famine throughout that country, and he himself began to be in want. And going, he joined himself to one of the citizens of that country, who sent him into his fields to pasture swine." For a Jew, this meant the deepest degradation; Jesus had remembered the incident from his reading. "And he would have been glad to fodder himself from the carobs which the swine ate, but no one gave anything to *him*. But coming to himself, he says: 'How many hired day laborers of my father have more than enough of food, but I am perishing here from famine. Rising up, I will go to my father and will say to him: "Father, I have sinned against Heaven and before your face; no longer am I worthy to be called your son. Make me one of your hired day laborers."' And rising up, he went to his father.

"But being yet far distant, his father saw him and was moved to compassion. And running, he fell upon his neck

---

[16]Lk. 7:36–47.　　　　　　　　8:19, 21; 10:10; 11:9.
[17]Ahiqar 8:34, Syriac; Tobit

and kissed him repeatedly. But the son said to him: 'Father, I have sinned against Heaven and before your face; no longer am I worthy to be called your son. Make me one of your hired day laborers.' But the father said to his house slaves: 'Quick! Bring the best robe and clothe him, and place a ring on his hand and sandals on his feet. And bring the fatted calf; kill it, and, eating, let us make merry. For this my son was dead and lives again, he was lost and has been found.' And they began to make merry.

"But his elder son was in the field. And as, coming, he neared the house, he heard music and dancing. And summoning one of the servants, he inquired what all this might be. But he said to him: 'Your brother has arrived and your father has killed the fatted calf because he has received him safe.' But he was angry and would not enter. But his father, coming out, besought him. But he, answering, said to his father: 'Look! So many years I have served you as slave and never did I transgress a command of yours; yet never did you give *me* even a kid, that *I* might with *my* friends make merry. But when this son of yours, who has gulped down your possessions with harlots, came along, you killed for *him* the fatted calf!' But he said to him: 'Child, *you* are always with me, and all that is mine is yours. But it was proper to make merry and rejoice, for this *brother* of yours was dead and is alive, and he was lost and is found.' "[18]

There was no need to add a formal moral. The story of the forgiving Father was indeed beautiful, but it would not have been complete without the contrast. The attitude of the righteous brother who never needed repentance is presented with understanding, but the great principle remains unchanged: There *is* more joy in heaven over a repentant sinner.

---

[18] Lk. 15:11b–32.

The disciples of John the Baptist, still a free agent, were fasting. They demanded of Jesus why his own disciples did not follow their example. He replied by one of his homely comparisons:

"No one sews a patch of an unshrunk rag on an old cloak,
> For the new insert pulls away from the garment, and the tear becomes worse.
No one pours new wine into old wineskins,
> If he does, the new wine bursts the wineskins and the wine is lost."[19]

One sabbath day, Jesus and his disciples were walking through the sown fields; it was about the end of May and the grain was ready for the harvest. As they passed along, the disciples plucked the ripe grain and ate. This was contrary to the strictest rabbinic law, which prohibited plucking on the sabbath. It might even be argued that they were doing still worse—by their plucking they were reaping, they were grinding by the rubbing to cleanse from chaff, and they were making bread.[20]

His opponents demanded why his disciples were doing what was unlawful on the holy day. Jesus based his answer on scripture: "Did you never read what David did, when he was in need and hungry? He entered into the House of God and ate showbread, which was unlawful to eat except for the priests, and he gave it also to those with him!"[21] This was a poser, which long was to trouble the interpreters. "Or have you not read in the Law how on the sabbath the priests in the temple profane the sabbath and are without blame?"[22] There

---

[19]Mk. 2:18, 21 f.; Mt. 9:14, 16 f.;
Lk. 5:33, 36 f.
[20]Tosephta, Shabbat 9:14; *cf.*
Mishna, Shabbat 7:2.
[21]I Sam. 21:1–6.
[22]Num. 28:9 f.

was permission in the Law itself for plucking the neighbor's grain by hand,[23] and to this appeal is made; "the sabbath came into being for the sake of man and not man for the sake of the sabbath, so that the son of man," that is, man himself, "is master even of the sabbath."[24]

Thus began a whole series of disputes over sabbath observance. On another sabbath, Jesus was again in a synagogue and there appeared a man with a hand withered. Deliberately Jesus posed the challenge: "Is it lawful on the sabbath to do good or to do evil, to save a life or to kill?" His auditors did not answer. It was a problem which troubled the Pharisees; had they made answer, it would probably have been: "That depends on the immediacy of the danger; in this case it is not necessary." Angrily looking around at them, Jesus bade the man: "Stretch out your hand!" and the hand was restored.[25]

Teaching in one of the synagogues on yet another sabbath, Jesus observed a woman who had suffered eighteen years from a spirit of weakness. She was bound together and unable to raise herself up at all. She was summoned, told: "Woman, you are loosed from your spirit of weakness"; hands were laid on her; immediately she was made straight and she glorified God. But the synagogue ruler, moved with indignation because she had been healed on the sabbath, declared: "Six days are there in which men ought to work; in them you should come and heal and not on the sabbath." Jesus made reply: "Hypocrites! Does not every one of you on the sabbath loose his ox or his ass from the manger"—the animal was tied to a hole in a low stone manger such as we may yet see in Solomon's stables in recently excavated

---

[23]Deut. 23:25.
[24]Mk. 2:23-28; Lk. 6:1-5; Mt. 12:1-5, 8.
[25]Mk. 3:1-5; Lk. 6:6-10; Mt. 12:9 f., 13.

Megiddo[26]—"and leading him away, water him? But ought not she, being a daughter of Abraham whom the Accuser has bound, lo, eighteen years, to have been loosed from this chain on the day of the sabbath?" Pharisees of the school of the stricter Shammai would probably have said no, those of the milder Hillel would have agreed. At any rate, as Jesus was saying this, all his opponents were put to shame and all the crowd rejoiced for all the glorious deeds carried on by him.[27]

One sabbath day he had entered the house of one of the rulers to eat bread. There appeared before him a man suffering from the dropsy, and the legists were watching to see what he would do. To their unspoken question, Jesus answered with another: "Is it lawful to heal on the sabbath or not?" When they remained silent, he healed the man and let him go. Then Jesus asked another question: "What man shall there be among you who shall have one sheep, and if it falls on a sabbath into a pit, will he not take hold of it and lift it out? By how much therefore is a man worth more than a sheep? So it *is* lawful to do good on the sabbath." And they could return no answer.[28]

However we may attempt to explain these cures, the evidence is overwhelming that Jesus deliberately went out of his way to challenge popular opinion on the proper observance of the sabbath. Why he should take this attitude we cannot explain; it alienated many of the best spirits in contemporary Judaism and ultimately it was to lead to his exclusion from synagogue teaching.

The excitement caused by these debates drew the attention of the Herodians, the followers of Herod Antipas, the Latin

---

[26]A. T. Olmstead, *History of Palestine and Syria*, 1931, 345.
[27]Lk. 13:10–17.

[28]Lk. 14:1–6; Mt. 12:11 f., inserted in the story of the man with the withered hand.

form of whose name indicated their pro-Roman leanings.[29] Antipas began to suspect that Jesus might be even more dangerous to the peace than John the Baptist. Jesus realized the false position into which he had been forced and cryptically warned his disciples against the "leaven of Herod."[30] This new danger may have been responsible for Jesus' withdrawal to the lake shore, where a skiff was ordered always to be waiting for him; in our sources the reason is the thronging crowds; we may suspect it was actually for hasty escape across the water and out of Herod's reach. Already we hear the ominous note: "And he ordered those healed not to make him known."[31]

With this danger threatening, Jesus determined to spread his teaching more widely while it was yet possible. As he had travelled about, still carrying on his own teaching ministry, he was moved with compassion for the crowds because they were troubled and cast down "like sheep not having a shepherd." To his disciples he observed: "The harvest is great but the workers few; beseech therefore the Master of the Harvest that he hurry out workers into his harvest."[32] Seventy-two "apostles," messengers, were selected; among them almost certainly was Joseph, son of Sabba, whose Roman name was Justus, and Matthiah, the successor of Judas among the Twelve.[33] And he began to send them out two by two before his face into every city and place into which he himself was to come. These were his instructions:

"Lo, I send you out as lambs in the midst of wolves; become therefore prudent as the serpents and guileless as the

---

[29]Mk. 3:6; Herodians at Jerusalem, Mk. 12:13; Mt. 22:16.
[30]Mk. 8:15.
[31]Mk. 3:7-12; Mt. 12:15 f.; cf. Lk. 6:17-19.

[32]Mt. 9:37 f.; Lk. 10:2.
[33]Acts 1:23; Eusebius, *Church History*, i, 12.

doves. Provide no gold or silver or bronze for your girdles, no haversack for the road, no two undergarments or sandals or staff, and salute no one on the road. And into whatever city or village you enter, search out in it who is worthy, and there remain until you leave.

"But, entering into the house, first say: 'Peace to this house.' And if a son of peace should be there, your peace shall rest upon him; but if not, it shall return to you again." The peace is thought of as a living reality in itself, capable of being recalled. "And in that very house remain, eating and drinking what comes from them, for the worker is worthy of his food; do not wander about from place to place.

"And into whatever city you enter, and they receive you, eat what is set before you. And heal the sick who are in it, but going, proclaim: 'Near is the Kingdom of Heaven!' Heal the sick, cleanse lepers, cast out evil spirits; freely you have received, freely give.

"But into whatever city you enter, and they do not receive you, going out into its streets, say: 'Even the dust clinging to us from your city on our feet we wipe off against you;' " it is a pagan city, its dust should not pollute true Israelite soil. " 'Nevertheless, know that the Kingdom of God has been near you.' I tell you: It shall be more tolerable for Sodom on that day than for that city."[34]

The Seventy-two returned with joy, boasting: "Master, even the evil spirits are becoming subject to us." As usual, Jesus depreciated these manifestations; ironically he recalls the fallen Watchers of the book of Enoch: "I saw the Accuser like lightning fallen from the heaven! See, I have given you the authority to tread upon snakes and scorpions and over all

---

[34]Lk. 10:1–12; Mt. 10:16, 9a, 10a, 11–13, 9b, 1b, 7 f., 14 f.; transferred to the sending out of the Twelve,

Mk. 6:7–11; Lk. 9:1–5; Mt. 10:1. Possibly the last sentence is not authentic.

the power of the Enemy, and nothing shall at all harm you. Nevertheless, do not rejoice in *this,* that the spirits are subject to you, but rejoice that your names are written in the heavens."[35] He had read what was said in the Testaments of the Twelve Patriarchs: "Then shall all the spirits of deceit be given to be trodden down and men shall rule over the evil spirits." "And He shall give Power to His children to tread upon the evil spirits."[36]

Next Jesus chose out twelve of his disciples to be his especially close associates; the number was symbolic, one for each of the twelve tribes of Israel, as the preceding seventy-two was six for each. After his death, they were to be known as *the* Disciples or as the Twelve.[37]

The most outstanding of the Twelve was Simon, a half-Hellenized form which tended to supplant the old tribal name Simeon, the son of Jonah,[38] whom Jesus at the beginning of his ministry had surnamed Kepha, the "Rock." In Greek he appears as Cephas or in translation Petros, our English Peter.[39] With him is regularly mentioned his brother Andreas, English Andrew, whose Greek name is sometimes turned into the Semitic Andrai.[40] Next we have listed the two brothers Jacob (James) and Johanan (John), sons of Zabdai (Zebedee), a moderately well-off fisherman,[41] and of Shalomith (Salome) his wife.[42] Them Jesus called "Sons of Thunder," Bne Regez, because no doubt of their violent, impetuous disposition.[43] These four are once represented as forming an

[35]Lk. 10:17–20; *cf.* [Mk.] 16:17 f.
[36]*Testaments of the Twelve Patriarchs,* Simeon 6:6; Levi 18:12.
[37]*Cf.* I Cor. 15:5, 7, where the Twelve are distinguished from "all the apostles."
[38]Jn. 1:42; 21:16; Mt. 16:17.
[39]Jn. 1:42; *cf.* Mt. 16:18.
[40]Jn. 1:40, 44; 6:8; 12:22; Mk. 1:16, 29; 13:3, Mt. 4:18.
[41]Mk. 1:19 f.; Mt. 4:21 f.
[42]Mk. 15:40; 16:1; Mt. 20:20; 27:56.
[43]Mk. 3:17. The original spelling of the word transliterated into Greek as Boanerges is uncertain.

inner group within the Twelve,[44] otherwise it is made up of Peter, James, and John, with Andrew excluded.[45]

The other eight played a less important part. Like Andrew, Philip is known by his Greek name, Hebraized as Pilipi.[46] Bartholomaeus (Bartholomew) is remembered only through his father, for he is "Talmai's Son," if that father was named for the biblical son of Anak or the biblical king of Geshur;[47] more probably, as the Greek form suggests, he is merely Ptolemy's son, for Jewish fathers did not hesitate to name their sons after pagan monarchs. As Nathanael was summoned to discipleship by Philip,[48] with whom Bartholomew is bracketed in the lists, the identification of the latter with Bartholomew Mattathiah is plausible. Thomas is for Teoma, the "Twin," as we learn from his translated Greek name Didymus.[49] This again is a byname; presumably his true name was Judah, the other Judas, not the man of Karioth, of whom we hear later.[50] With him is paired Mattai (Matthew) the tax collector, no longer given his alternative name of Levi, son of Halphai.[51] Another son of Halphai was Jacob (James), otherwise called the Little;[52] the name of his partner is uncertain, either Taddia (Thaddæus) or Libbai (Lebbæus). Next to the last is Simon the Canenæan (Qanan), the byname properly translated as Zealot; this should mean in these days only that he was zealous for religion, not that he belonged to the party of fanatic assassins, its meaning half a century later. In the place of dishonor is listed Judah

[44] Mk. 13:3.
[45] Mk. 5:37; 9:2; 14:33; Mt. 17:1; 26:37; Lk. 8:51; 9:28.
[46] Jn. 1:44 ff.; 6:5 ff.; 12:21 f.; 14:8 f.
[47] Num. 13:22; II Sam. 3:3.
[48] Jn. 1:45.
[49] Jn. 11:16; 20:24; 21:2.
[50] Jn. 14:22; so also the Acts of Thomas, cf. Eusebius, op. cit. i, 13.
[51] Mk. 2:14.
[52] Mt. 27:56; Mk. 15:40; Jn. 19:25.

(Judas), the man of Karioth, son of Simon, who was to betray his Master.[53]

Now that this more intimate group of disciples had been formed, Jesus was prepared to begin more regular instruction.

---

[53]Jn. 6:71; Mt. 10:2–4; Mk. 3:16–19; Lk. 6:14–16; Acts 1:13b.

CHAPTER V

PREACHING THE KINGDOM

JESUS was an oriental in the truest sense of the word. In no slightest degree had his thought been infected by Hellenism. For him, the beauties of Greek literature were non-existent. The clarity of Greek logic was repellently cold and impersonal. He could not understand a philosophy without a personal God. Greek sophistic was as dark to his mind as would have been the theology worked out in succeeding centuries by his Gentile followers. We cannot ourselves understand his teaching until we recover something of his oriental point of view. Only for our dull western minds is it necessary to arrange his sayings in what we call formal order.

Like all great oriental sages, Jesus employed prose, but even in prose his preaching tended to fall into a definite rhythm which often makes it difficult for us to make up our minds whether to present it as poetry. In his more pregnant sayings, the evidence of carefully thought out poetical structure is unmistakable.

To understand his form of poetical expression, we must first go back to the psalms of the most ancient peoples of Babylonia. These psalms, whether in the older Shumerian or the Akkadian translation or adaptation, are regularly written on clay tablets line by line. Rarely we may find examples of two metrical lines crowded into one or one expanded into two; prose passages may be inserted, but normally the line on the tablet is the guarantee of the metrical structure. One

tablet even indicates the "feet" by vertical lines.[1] Unlike the
Greek, this poetry is not based on a regular alternation of true
longs and shorts, but on simple stress accent, quite like our
own. Thus, when we make a literal translation, what we
write falls almost automatically into English meter; the
famous rhythm of the King James version is not due primarily to the learned translators, it is due to literal translation from the Hebrew original, for Hebrew metrics naturally
followed Babylonian.

Babylonian poetry may be quite elaborate. One of their most
famous poems, the tale of the goddess *Ishtar's Descent to
the Land of No Return* in search of her dead lover Tammuz,
is in the same meter as Isaiah's Taunt Song against the
Assyrian invader Sennacherib. In Hebrew, it was called the
qina or "mourning" meter; in both literatures, the line con-
sists of two stress accents, cæsura, and three accents; or three
accents, cæsura, and two. Numerous variations on these more
elaborate metrical forms, often displaying a genuine ingenuity, have been detected. Generally, however, we have a
sort of blank verse, again like that of the Hebrew prophets,
where the line may be three three, three two, two three, or
even two two. All these sounded poetical to the Semitic ear.

Almost equally important in Semitic metric is the verse.
Sometimes the verse is perfectly regular, the same number of
lines to each, but the poet is never troubled if it is not. The
most significant phenomenon, however, is what is traditionally called "parallelism of members," but might be more
appropriately named balance.[2]

Already in a bilingual inscription from Egypt, dating from

---

[1]H. Zimmern, "Weiteres zur baby-
lonishcen Metrik," *Zeitschrift für
Assyriologie*, X, 1895, 1 ff.

[2]Illustrations of Biblical poetry
may be found in the author's *History of Palestine and Syria*, 1931.

the fifth century before Christ, the Aramaic version shows this poetic structure.[3] It is probably to be detected in an Aramaic incantation text of the Seleucid period written in cuneiform characters.[4] In more elaborate metrical schemes, not untouched by Greek metrics, it is found in Syrian Christian hymns. Even in English translations based on our extant Greek Gospels, it is perfectly recognizable.[5] To give adequate representation of one of Jesus' outstanding characteristics, we accordingly must report many of his most striking sayings in verse form.

In our childhood days, our unlearned Sunday School teachers persuaded us to memorize selected verses from the Gospels. Their natural instinct was often wiser than were the scholars. Not a few of the sayings we are happiest to recall are quite without context. To employ the simile so beloved of the oriental, they are uncut jewels strung irregularly on a necklace, but jewels of great price.

Now and then, we find more elaborate sermons. Too often they are interpolated, at times with authentic sayings which demand another context, again with alleged sayings produced to meet the needs of the early church, but when at last we have them in their original carefully constructed form, we can generally find the appropriate occasion.

As an oriental, Jesus inevitably used the comparison. His own Bible was filled with examples, and he found more in the books he read. They were employed in daily conversation.

In its simplest form, the comparison was merely a special category of the proverb or wise saying, and many of Jesus'

---

[3]C. C. Torrey, "A Specimen of old Aramaic Verse," *Journal of the American Oriental Society*, XLVI, 1926, 241 f.

[4]Cyrus Gordon, "The Aramaic Incantation in Cuneiform," *Archiv für Orientforschung*, XII, 1937–39, 105 ff.

[5]C. F. Burney, *The Poetry of Our Lord*, 1925.

so-called parables are of this type. What we call the parable proper was a more developed form, the story. To be acceptable, it must have three elements, the occasion on which the anecdote was told and the point it was intended to make, the story itself, and the moral, which might later circulate as an independent saying. An anecdote without an explicit moral was rare. It was told to make a single point and one alone; to seek for double meanings in a single story is to misunderstand Jesus' purpose. Nor must we seek for allegory; the anecdote is to be understood in its plain literal sense.

A few of these comparisons or stories are to be found in books which Jesus must have read. Following this clue, we detect his use of individual phrases and ideas which struck his imagination. None too close parallels in the language of later Jewish Fathers prove that Jesus employed certain stock motifs. But how superior they sound in his telling! On his lips, they are transformed by genius and give us life itself.[6]

A former Jesus, the son of Sira, had in pompous, rather stuffy fashion issued an elaborate prospectus, inviting would-be students to attain instruction in his own Academy.[7] Jesus had read it; his own invitation is far more appealing through its sheer simplicity:

> Come to me, all who labor and are burdened,
>   And I will refresh you;
> Lift my yoke and learn of me,
>   For meek am I and lowly in heart;
> And you shall rest your souls,
>   For easy my yoke and my burden light.[8]

---

[6]Cf. W. O. E. Oesterley, The Gospel Parables in the Light of Their Jewish Background, 1936; B. T. D. Smith, The Parables of the Synoptic Gospels, 1937.

[7]Ecclesiasticus 51:23–30.
[8]Mt. 11:28–30; for the yoke of the Kingdom, cf. Mishna, Berakot, 2:2, 5; the yoke of God, II Enoch, 34:1.

Like other contemporary teachers, the author of Second
Enoch for example,[9] Jesus enunciated a series of blessings and
curses :

> Happy the poor, for yours is the Kingdom,
> Happy those hungering, for you shall be filled,
> Happy those mourning, for you shall find comfort.
> But woe to you rich, for you have your comfort,
> Woe to you sated, for you shall hunger,
> Woe to you laughers, for you shall mourn and weep.[10]

These blessings and woes deal specifically only with social
classes; the religious implications behind the terms "poor,
hungry, mourners," is more clearly brought out in another
group of blessings:

> Happy the humble, for the earth they inherit,
> Happy the merciful, for they have mercies,
> Happy the pure in heart, for they see God,
> Happy the peacemakers, for God's Sons are they called.[11]

Humble too must be his followers :

> A disciple is not above the teacher,
>   Nor the slave above his master;
> Enough for the disciple to become as his teacher,
>   And the slave as his master.[12]

During these early months, when the chosen disciples were
being given their preliminary instruction, Jesus taught them
by a series of brief, pregnant sayings. They were simplicity
itself and required no elaborate commentary. To be more
easily remembered, they were expressed in metrical form.

---

[9] II Enoch 42:6–14; 52:1–14.
[10] Lk. 6:20b–21, 24 f.; *cf.* Mt.
5:3 f., 6.
[11] Mt. 5:5, 7–9.
[12] Mt. 10:24–25a; *cf.* Lk. 6:40;
Jn. 13:16.

The extent of Jesus' success may be measured by the fact that to this day they are among the most treasured of the sayings.

By a series of metaphors, the disciples are warned of their new responsibilities:

> Good is salt;
>> You are the salt of the earth.
> But if the salt has lost savor,
>> With what can it be salted?
> For nothing is it longer good
>> But to be thrown out and trampled by men;
> Have salt in yourselves,
>> And be at peace with one another.[13]

To the oriental, salt was precious; for the poor man, it was the one available condiment to give savor. It was terribly expensive, every state enforced the salt tax. Taken from the Dead Sea salt pans, it was poorly cleansed and it might be disappointingly adulterated.

The metaphor changes:

> You are the light of the world!
>> Nor can a city be hid
>> Which on top of a hill is set;
> And they do not light a lamp
>> To place it beneath a grain measure,
> But rather upon a light stand,
>> And it shines upon all in the house.
> So let your light shine before men,
>> That they may see your works good,
>>> And glorify your Father in the Heavens.[14]

---

[13]Mt. 5:13; Mk. 9:50; Lk.   [14]Mt. 5:14-16; *cf.* Mk. 4:21; Lk.
14:34 f.   8:16; 11:33.

The house in which they live is small, it has but a single room; Palestine is a tiny land among the great nations. Yet if only the disciples permit the light within them to shine forth freely, the world will glorify their God.

This metaphor leads to another:

> The lamp of the body is the eye.
> If then your eye is sound,
> All your body is light;
> But if your eye is bad,
> All your body is dark;
> If then the light in you is dark,
> How great is that dark![15]

They must understand that the dark is the darkness of sin. It is the Satan, the Accuser, who is responsible for this darkness. The infected eye symbolizes the sin itself; let the disciples rid themselves of the infection before it destroys them utterly.

To the south of the city walls of Jerusalem lay the "Valley of the Son of Hinnom." In it were the dump heaps, foul-smelling from their ever-burning fires. The "Valley of Hinnom," Ge Hinnom in the Hebrew, had in its Aramaic form Gehenna become the symbol of that eternal Hell Fire the Jews had learned from the Persians. Here, if the Satan had his will, the unfortunate sinner would spend eternity. Against this dire fate they must be on guard:

> If your right eye makes you stumble,
> Pluck it out and hurl it from you!
> Better for you that one member be destroyed
> Than your whole body hurled into Gehenna.

---

[15]Mt. 6:22 f.; Lk. 11:34-36; cf. Ahiqar, Syriac II, 48; *Testaments of the Twelve Patriarchs,* Issachar, 3:4; 4:6.

And if your right hand makes you stumble,
   Cut it off and hurl it from you!
Better for you that one member be destroyed
   Than your whole body hurled into Gehenna.[16]

Do not fear those killing the body,
   But cannot kill the soul;
Fear rather him who is able
   Soul and body to kill in Gehenna![17]

Freedom from sin is not easily attained. When the disciples struggle to attain this freedom, they must not expect to be popular; they will find themselves in the minority:

Enter through the narrow gate.
   For broad is the gate and wide the road
Which leads away to Destruction,
   And many are those who pass through.

How narrow is the gate
   And troubled the road,
Which leads to Life,
   And few are those who find it!"[18]

They must remember that they are being trained to service. Some day they must carry on the work of their teacher:

What I tell you in the darkness,
   Speak in the light;
And what you hear in the ear,
   Proclaim upon the house tops;[19]
For nothing covered shall not be unveiled,
   And hidden, shall not be made known.[20]

---

[16]Mt. 5:29 f.; 18:8 f.; Mk. 9:43, 47.
[17]Mt. 10:28; Lk. 12:5.
[18]Mt. 7:13 f.; Lk. 13:24.
[19]Mt. 10:27; Lk. 12:3.
[20]Mt. 10:26; Mk. 4:22; Lk. 8:17; 12:22.

But they should look forward to disbelief, and should act accordingly:

> Give not the holy to the dogs,
>   Nor throw your pearls before the swine,
> Lest they tramp them with their ·feet,
>   And turn about and rend you.[21]

After these preliminary instructions, Jesus was prepared to expound his deeper teaching. The core of that teaching was the Kingdom. It might be called the Kingdom of the Heavens, by a usage common for three centuries[22] substituting Heaven for the Divine Name, now become too sacred for open pronunciation. More rarely it might be simply the Kingdom of God.

To many of his auditors, as to John the Baptist, mention of the Kingdom implied that earthly kingdom which was to be ruled by the coming Messiah. To guard against misunderstanding, Jesus must resort to "comparisons." "To what shall we compare the Kingdom of God or by what figure shall we explain it? It is like a seed of mustard which a man took and sowed in his field. It is smaller than all the seeds but when it grows up it becomes larger than the garden herbs and is a tree so that the birds of the heavens enter into its branches."[23] The life history of the lowly mustard should give hope to the discouraged: "If you have faith as a grain of mustard seed, you shall say to this mountain: 'Remove from here to there,' and it shall remove; and nothing shall be impossible for you."[24]

Once proclaimed, the Kingdom will inevitably grow

---

[21] Mt. 7:6; cf. Didache 9:55.
[22] Already used in Pirqe Aboth I, 3; I Maccabees 3:18 f., 60.

[23] Mt. 13:31 f.; Lk. 13:18 f.; Mk. 4:30–32.
[24] Mt. 17:20; cf. 21:21; Lk. 17:6; Mk. 11:23; I Cor. 13:2.

through natural increase: "Thus is the Kingdom of God:
As a man casts the seed upon the ground, and should sleep
and rise up each night and day, and the seed should sprout
and grow tall, how he does not himself know. For the earth
of herself bears fruit, first green blade, then ear, then full
grain in the ear. But when the fruit yields, at once he sends
out the sickle because the harvest has come."[25]

This simple comparison is reinforced by a story: "The
Kingdom of the Heavens is like a man sowing good seed in
his field. But while men were sleeping, his enemy came and
sowed darnel in the midst of the wheat and went off." So it
would be in the earlier stages of the Kingdom's growth, good
and bad could not be distinguished. "But when the blade
sprouted and made fruit, then appeared also the darnel." By
this time, there could be no doubt as to which was wheat;
the darnel would be the higher. "But the slaves of the estate
owner came and said to him: 'Master, did you not sow good
seed in your field? From whence then has it darnel?' But he
says to them: 'A hostile fellow has done this.' But they say
to him: 'Do you wish that we should go and pull them up?'
But he says: 'No, lest by chance in pulling up the darnel
you root out along with them the grain,'" for by this time
the roots of the two are close locked together. "'Let them
both grow together until the harvest. And in the time of the
harvest I shall say to the reapers: "Gather up the darnel first
and bind them into bundles to burn them as fuel, but the
wheat gather into my storehouse."'"[26] This prediction of the
coming world conflagration is quite in the temper of the
Baptist.[27]

His followers should not be disappointed if not all to

---

[25]Mk. 4:26–29; *cf.* Jas. 5:7 f.   [27]Mt. 3:12.
[26]Mt. 13:24b–30.

whom the Kingdom is preached accept it, if some of those
who do accept it cannot endure: "See what happened when
the sower went out to sow. And it came to pass in his sowing
that some seed fell along the path, and the birds came and
ate it. And another part fell on the rocky places, where it
did not have much soil. And at once it sprang up, because it
did not have depth of soil. And when the sun rose, it was
burned up, and because of not having root it withered. And
another part fell into the thorns, and the thorns grew up and
choked it, and it did not give fruit. And others fell on the
good ground and gave fruit, growing up and increasing.
And it bore up to thirty fold and to sixty fold and to hundred fold."[28] Those who heard Jesus knew only too well the
thin rocky thorn-covered soils of their own Galilee; too
often they had envied the depth of soil around Sepphoris
or in the Great Plain.

From homely agricultural "comparisons," Jesus turned for
subject matter to the neighboring lake: "Again, the Kingdom of the Heavens is like a drag net, cast into the sea and
collecting from every kind. When it was filled, dragging it
to the beach and sitting down, they collected the good into
vessels but the inedible they threw away."[29] We can have
no doubt that in this period of his teaching, thoughts of the
Last Judgement bulked largely in Jesus' mind.

Little attention may now be paid to the good news of the
Kingdom, but at the last it will permeate the world: "To
what shall I compare the Kingdom of God? It is like leaven
which a woman took and hid in three *sata* (seah) measures
of wheat meal, until the whole is leavened."[30] Would-be members of the Kingdom must, if needful, abandon everything to

---

[28]Mk. 4:3–8; Mt. 13:3b–8; Lk. 8:   [29]Mt. 13:47–48.
5–8a; *cf*. IV Esdras 8:41 f.; 9:31.   [30]Lk. 13:20 f.; Mt. 13:33.

win the supreme prize: "The Kingdom of the Heavens is like treasure hid in the field, which a man, finding, hid and in his joy goes and sells all that he has and buys that field."[31] This is a typical "comparison"; there is no question as to the morality of the concealment; the one point to be made is the determination of the finder to retain the treasure he has accidentally discovered.

Nazareth lay just off the Great Road. Caravan travellers must have stopped over to visit the joiner's shop and must have told marvellous tales of the wonders seen on their trips to the farther orient. Among them would be stories of the divers at Bahrein in the Persian Gulf and how they secured the pearls, so highly valued by the beauties at Rome, and celebrated by the Roman poets. Perhaps among them was a dealer in jewels, for one of Jesus' comparisons ran thus: "Again, the Kingdom of the Heavens is like a merchant man, seeking fine pearls. But having found one pearl of great value, going, he sold all, whatever he had, and bought it."[32]

His earlier followers must not feel themselves superior to those who later entered the Kingdom: "The Kingdom of the Heavens is like an estate owner who went out early in the morning to hire day laborers for his vineyard. But having agreed with the day laborers for a denarius the day, he sent them into his vineyard." In the ancient orient, the position of the day laborer was most miserable; quite literally he was at the bottom in the economic scale, for even the slave was at least sure of his daily bread, while the hired man was at the mercy of irregular seasonal employment. Under the circumstances, all were most fortunate in being offered a full day's work and the pay was good.

"And going out about the third hour, he saw others sitting

---

[31]Mt. 13:44.   [32]Mt. 13:45 f.

in the market place without work. And to them he says : 'You too go into the vineyard and whatever is right I will give you.' But they went. And again, going out about the sixth and the ninth hour, he did the same. But about the eleventh, going out, he found others standing, and to them he says: 'Why have you stood here all the day without working?' They say to him : 'Because no one has hired us.' He says to them : 'You too go into the vineyard.' " The pitiful condition of the chronically unemployed could not be more truthfully presented.

"And when it was evening, the owner of the vineyard says to his steward : 'Call the day laborers and pay the hire, beginning from the last to the first.' But those coming who were hired about the eleventh hour received a denarius each." This was nothing but qualified almsgiving to men who had shown themselves willing to work when opportunity was offered. "And the first comers expected that they would receive more and they too received a denarius each. But having received it, they muttered against the estate owner, saying : 'These, the last, worked one hour, and you made them equal to us, who bore the burden of the day and the hot eastern wind !' But he, answering, said to one of them : 'Friend, I am doing you no wrong. Did you not agree with me for a denarius? Take what is yours and go! It is my intention to give to this latest arrival just the same as to you. Is it not allowed me to do what I wish with my own? Or is your eye wicked because I am good? So the last shall be first and the first last.' "[33]

Truth has many aspects and must be presented under many forms. This his disciples must remember in their own teachings : "Every scribe who has been made an apprentice to the

---

[33]Mt. 20:1–16; *cf.* 19:30; Mk. 10:31; Lk. 13:30, moral.

Kingdom of the Heavens is like a man, an estate owner, who brings out of his treasures things new and old."[34] "Not everyone saying to me: 'Master! Master!' shall enter into the Kingdom of the Heavens, but he who is doing the will of my Father in the Heavens. Everyone therefore who hears my words and does them shall be compared to a sensible man who built his house on the rock. And the rains poured down and the rivers came and the winds blew and struck that house and it did not fall, because it was founded on the rock. And every one who hears my words and does not do them shall be compared to a man, a fool, who built his house on the sand. And the rains poured down and the rivers came and the winds blew and struck that house. And it fell and its fall was great."[35] James his brother understood the meaning when years after he declared: "Faith without works is dead!"[36]

Jesus was praying, as so often he did, for he felt the need of constant communion with his Heavenly Father to renew his strength. As he ended, a disciple requested a form of prayer similar to that which the Baptist had taught his own disciples. Jesus remembered a prayer in which he had often joined as he had worshipped in the little synagogue at Nazareth:

> Magnified and made holy
> Be his Name great,
> In the world he created
> According to his Will;
> May his Kingdom be reigning
> Through your life and your days
> And the life of all House-Israel,
> Soon and in near time.

---

[34] Mt. 13:52.
[35] Mt. 7:21, 24–27; Lk. 6:46–49.
[36] Jas. 2:17.

To this day, the prayer is still recited in its original Aramaic within the Kaddish; we may read it in the authorized Prayer Book. At the close is added: "And you shall say: Amen."

From this ancient synagogue prayer as model, Jesus composed the beautiful "Lord's Prayer":

> Our Father in the Heavens,
>> Holy be your Name;
> May your Kingdom come,
>> May your Will be done,
> As in the Heavens,
>> So upon the earth.
> Our bread for today
>> Give us this day;
> And forgive us our debts
>> As we forgive our debtors;
> And lead us not into trial,
>> But free us from ill.
> For yours is the Kingdom and Power,
>> And Glory to the ages.
>>> Amen.[37]

Crowds still flocked to listen and to witness his healing, but Jesus made few converts. Even his family turned against him. One day, while Jesus was preaching to crowds so great that he was unable to find time even to eat, his relatives attempted to seize him, declaring that he was out of his head.[38]

No wonder that when his mother and his brothers made him a visit and sent in to announce their presence, he refused to go out and meet them. Dramatically he asked: *"Who is my mother and my brothers?"* Then, pointing to the crowd clus-

---

[37]Mt. 6:9b–13; Lk. 11:1–4.   [38]Mk. 3:20 f.

tered around him, he continued: "See my mother and my brothers! For whoever does the will of God, *he* is my brother and sister and mother!"[39] All the bitterness of rejection by his fellow townsmen, all the disappointment of unbelieving mother and brothers is concentrated in this pathetic admission of loneliness.

One day as he was preaching, a woman in the crowd enthusiastically lifted up her voice and in good biblical language called out: "Blessed the womb bearing you and the breasts you sucked!" We can feel no surprise that Jesus answered: "No! Blessed rather those hearing God's word and keeping it!"[40]

But Jesus found compensation. Little children were brought to him that he might touch them. The too officious disciples chided the parents. Jesus, however, cuddled them in his arms and blessed them, laying his hands on them. The disciples were rebuked: "Allow the little children to come to me! Do not dare to forbid them! For of such is the Kingdom of God. In truth I tell you: Whoever does not receive the Kingdom of God as a little child shall not at all enter into it."[41]

---

[39] Mk. 3:31–35; Mt. 12:46–50; Lk. 8:19–21.

[40] Lk. 11:27 f.; quoted Jas. 1:22–25.

[41] Mk. 10:13–16; Mt. 19:13–15; Lk. 18:15–17; *cf.* Mk. 9:36 f.; Mt. 18:2–5; Lk. 9:47 f.

CHAPTER VI

DANGER

JOHN the Baptist had found even the outskirts of the Roman province too dangerous. About the middle of summer, he returned east of the Jordan and was arrested, through the personal spite of Herodias all his friends were certain. So strong was the popular belief that John indeed was a prophet that Antipas did not dare to put him to death at first. He was therefore imprisoned at Mkaur (Machærus), a grim fortress built by the tetrarch's father east of the Dead Sea to defend the Nabatæan frontier.[1]

In his prison, John heard of Jesus' activities and sent two disciples with the query: "Are you the Coming One or another do we await?" Jesus refused a direct answer, but after the messengers had departed he commented:

Why went you out in the desert? To behold a reed by wind
    shaken?
If not, why went you out? To behold a man clothed in rich
    raiment?
Behold! Those wearing rich raiment are in the houses of
    kings!

But why went you out in the desert? A prophet to behold?
I tell you there has not arisen among women-born a greater
    than John;
But he who is least in the Kingdom of the Heavens is
    greater than he![2]

---

[1] Mk. 6:17 f.; Mt. 14:4–5; Lk. 3:19 f.; cf. Mk. 1:14; Mt. 4:12; Joseph. Ant. xviii, 119; cf. xiii, 417; xiv, 83 ff.; xviii, 111 f.   [2] Mt. 11:7b–9a, 11b; Lk. 7:24b–26a, 28.

John has been preaching an earthly Kingdom; this has in part vitiated his preaching of repentance:

From the days of John the Baptist till now,
    The Kingdom of the Heavens suffers violence,
And men of violence take it by force,
    For all the Prophets and the Law prophesied until John.[3]

Thought of John leads Jesus to consider the difference between that prophet and himself. They have been poles apart in their conduct yet both have been severely criticised. Surely this is a wicked and unreasonable generation:

    To what shall I compare this generation?
      And to what are they like?
    Like children sitting in the markets
      Who are calling to the others:
    "We piped for you, you did not dance,
      We wailed and you beat not the breast."

Nothing can please such people:

For John came neither eating nor drinking,
    And they say: "He has a demon!"
The son of man came eating and drinking,
    And they say: "Look, a man gluttonous and winebibber,
Friend of tax collectors and sinners!"
    But Wisdom has been approved by her children![4]

The excitement caused by John's imprisonment soon quieted down and Antipas mistakenly thought that it would be safe to execute him. The Baptist was therefore beheaded in the

---

[3]Mt. 11:12 f.; Lk. 16:16.
[4]Mt. 11:16-19; Lk. 7:31-35; *cf.* Jas. 3:13.

grim fortress of Machærus, where the daughter of Aretas some time before had stopped on her flight to her father.[5]

His death soon became the subject of folklore. According to the less improbable account, the daughter of Herodias danced before Herod on his birthday; actually, Salome the daughter had already married Antipas' brother Philip,[6] and was doubtless with her husband in his own tetrarchy. The story goes on that her dancing so pleased the tetrarch that he swore an oath to give her whatever she asked. Instigated by her mother, she demanded the head of John the Baptist on a platter. Because of his oaths and the presence of his fellow banqueters, Antipas unwillingly gave order that John should be beheaded in prison. The head was indeed brought in on a platter and the girl handed it over to her mother, but the body was placed by his disciples in a proper tomb.[7]

In a much later and more developed form of the tale, the whole blame was laid on Herodias. Antipas feared John as a righteous and holy man and kept him safe. He listened to him gladly, even though he was much disturbed by what he heard. Herodias' opportunity came when Antipas on his birthday gave a dinner to his nobles, military tribunes, and the most important men in Galilee, where our author thinks John had been imprisoned. "King Herod" (another mistake for Herod Antipas was only a tetrarch) offered the girl even the half of his kingdom to redeem his promise, but in vain; to his exceeding regret, he must order John's execution.[8]

Such tales illustrate how John's tragic death brought him again to public attention. His martyrdom fully convinced the populace that he was a genuine prophet. It was not safe, even for the hierarchy, to deny publicly the divine authority of the

---

[5]Lk. 9:9; Joseph. *Ant.* xviii, 116, 119; *cf.* 111 f.
[6]Joseph. *Ant.* xviii, 136 f.
[7]Mt. 14:6–12a.
[8]Mk. 6:19–29.

Baptist.[9] There was universal rejoicing over the severe defeats suffered by Antipas at the hand of Aretas, which were considered as divine retribution for John's murder.[10]

John the Baptist would have been for us only a minor prophet mentioned among many by Josephus had he not baptized Jesus of Nazareth. Even before his imprisonment, certain of his own disciples, John, Andrew, Peter, Philip, Nathanael, had abandoned him for a new Master.[11] Others came over to Jesus during the imprisonment, still others after John's death.[12] Until the middle of the century, we may trace his followers as a minor sect, for example, at Alexandria and at Ephesus; some of his adherents, like Apollos, ultimately became Christians.[13]

They produced a Life of their Master, parts of which were incorporated into the Gospels when the Baptist came to be recognized as the Forerunner of the Messiah. Their story of John's birth was imitated for the yet more wonderful story of the Messiah's birth. That Jesus received baptism from John and that through it consciousness of his own mission was awakened, that following his preaching Jesus proclaimed "Near is the Kingdom," that from his example came the "Lord's Prayer" and the rite of Christian baptism; these are the truly significant facts in the life of the Baptist.

Antipas' troubles were not ended by the execution of John. Excited crowds were now saying that Jesus was John risen from the dead. Others were convinced that he himself was the Forerunner, Elijah, still others that he was one of the former prophets returned to earth.[14] "Herod sought to see

---

[9]Mk. 11:30–32; Mt. 21:25 f.; Lk. 20:4–6.

[10]Joseph. *Ant.* xviii, 116.

[11]Jn. 1:35 ff.

[12]Mt. 14:2.

[13]Acts 18:24 f.; 19:1–4.

[14]Lk. 9:7 f.; Mt. 14:1 f.; Mk. 6:14 f.; *cf.* Mk. 27b–28; Mt. 16:13b–14; Lk. 9:18b–19.

him," but with no kindly purpose. There was reason for
Jesus to be alarmed at the attitude of the crowds. The alarm
was increased by the warning of friendly Pharisees: "Get
out! Go away from here! For Herod wishes to kill you!"
Jesus answered: "Go tell that fox: Look! I am casting out
evil spirits and performing cures today and tomorrow, and
on the third day I have finished"; in other less proverbial
words, Jesus announces that he will continue his work during
the short time remaining to him, then he is willing to die. But
he does not fear Antipas: "However, I must go my way today
and tomorrow and the next, for it is not possible for a prophet
to perish outside of Jerusalem."[15] His estimate of the situation was indeed prophetic.

No profitable teaching was possible with the crowds in this
excited state. Jesus therefore determined to withdraw for a
time from the tetrarchy, hoping that the excitement would
abate and he might resume his proper teaching in quiet. We
may follow his wanderings over the same landscape, but
Jesus we see dimly through the mist of the miracle stories,
which are almost all that our sources have preserved from
this period of his life.

First Jesus and his faithful disciples crossed the Lake of
Galilee to its southeast corner and took refuge in the territory
of Gadara, one of the "Ten Cities" of the Decapolis, which
since the days of Pompey's visit had enjoyed local autonomy
and freedom from Jewish control.[16] Here, in definitely pagan
territory, he should be safe from the tetrarch's hostile inten-
tions. On the voyage, he warned the disciples against "Herod's
leaven."[17] A great wind storm suddenly arose, the waves beat
into the boat and were filling it. Jesus was asleep on a pillow

---

[15]Lk. 13:31–33. [17]Mk. 8:15; cf. Lk. 12:1.
[16]Joseph. *Wars* i, 155 f.; *Ant.*
xiv, 75.

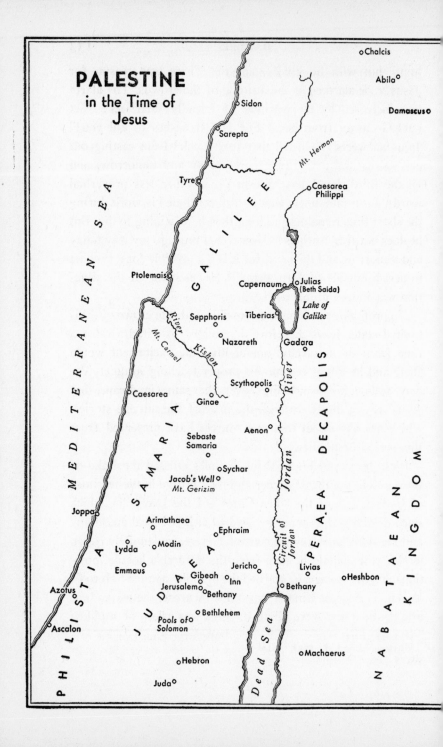

in the stern; his disciples awakened him, complaining: "Rabbi, do you not care that we are being destroyed?" Jesus rebuked the wind and bade the sea: "Silence! Be muzzled!" By this incantation, there was brought about a great calm. Jesus demanded of them: "Why are you frightened? Have you not yet faith?" They feared a great fear and said to one another: "Who then is he that even the wind and the sea obey him?"[18] We have entered the domain of the miraculous.

As they were landing, the story goes on, a man with an unclean spirit rushed out from the tombs where he was living; repeatedly he had been given the usual treatment for the insane, binding in chains, but he had always broken asunder the fetters and no one had strength to tame him. Night and day he remained in the tombs and hills, shouting and cutting himself with stones.

Jesus commanded: "Come out, unclean spirit, from the man!" "What is there in common between you and me?" responded the demon, "I adjure you by God not to torture me." Jesus demanded his name, since knowing the name gave power over the owner; "Legion" was the reply, for there were many evil spirits possessing the demoniac. In return for this essential information, the demons begged that they should not be expelled from the country; "send us into the swine," they asked.

Gadara was proud of an unusually long period of Hellenization. Already in the early third century before Christ, Gadara had produced its famous satirist Menippus, who had recently been imitated by that even more famous example of Roman conservatism, Varro, and in future was to be immortalized by that greatest of satirists, the "Greek" oriental

---

[18]Mk. 4:35–41; Mt. 8:18, 23–27; Lk. 8:22–25; perhaps only a late version of Jn. 6:14–21; Mk. 6:45–52; Mt. 14:22–33.

Lucian from Samosata on the Euphrates. Two centuries after
Menippus, Gadara had boasted Meleager, the first to collect
the finest of Greek verse into a "chaplet," and himself no
mean poet. Meleager had satirized his neighbors the Jews as
"sabbath keepers," he ridiculed their "cold sabbaths";[19] the
citizens ate pork to emphasize their Hellenic culture. From
the standpoint of the Jewish story teller, nothing could be
more appropriate than for Jesus to assent and to permit the
unclean spirits to take refuge in the swine; rushing down the
steep cliffs along the shore, the two thousand possessed pigs
were choked in the sea. The swineherds fled to report what
had happened in the fields and in the city, six miles distant.
The irate citizens poured out, insisting that Jesus leave their
frontier.

Like the majority of stories told of this period of flight,
we may be sure that it has become more picturesque than
reality. We can be certain only that Jesus visited the border
of Gadarene territory, that he cured a man of unstable men-
tality, and that the Gadarenes, bitterly anti-Semitic since the
destruction of their city by Alexander Jannæus and intensely
patriotic after its refoundation by Pompey,[20] would not allow
the Jewish miracle worker to remain within their boundaries.
As Jesus was leaving, the recovered demoniac expressed his
desire to become a disciple; a Gentile disciple at this time
would be a heavy liability, and Jesus refused, bidding him
go home and spread the news.[21]

Jesus must accordingly return to the western shore, to
Galilee and therefore to danger. But our stories go on with
even more wonderful miracles. On the very seashore, fresh

---

[19]Greek Anthology, Palatine Anthology, v, 160 (Loeb Classics).
[20]Joseph. *Wars* i, 86, 155; *Ant.*
xiii, 356, 396; xiv, 75.

[21]Mk. 5:1–20; Mt. 8:28–34; Lk.
8:26–39.

crowds collected. A synagogue chief named Jair fell down at his feet, begging: "My little daughter is about to die; come and lay your hands upon her that she may be saved and live."[22]

As Jesus went off with Jair, a great crowd following and jostling against him, there came a woman; twelve years she had been afflicted by a flow of blood, "suffering much from many physicians and having spent all her possessions and being not at all better but rather worse" is the unflattering comment of our author. Standing behind Jesus in the crowd, she touched the fringed border of his garment; at once the fountain of her blood was dried up and she felt in her body that she was healed from her scourge. But Jesus, realizing immediately that the Power had gone out of him—we are in the full realm of magic—demanded: "Who touched my garments?" The disciples were impatient, "You see the crowd jostling against you, and are you asking: 'Who touched me?'" But the woman, fearing and trembling, knowing what had been done for her, fell down to him and told him the whole truth. Jesus reassured her: "Daughter, your faith has cured you; go in peace and be whole from your scourge."[23]

While Jesus was yet speaking to her, news arrived for the synagogue head: "Your daughter is dead! Why trouble the Rabbi any more?" "Do not fear! Only believe!" answered Jesus. Taking Peter, James and John, he enters the house and reprimands the family and neighbors: "Why are you making an uproar and weeping? The child is not dead, rather she is sleeping." Naturally they laughed at him.

Sending them all out and taking only the parents and the three chosen disciples, Jesus grasps the child by the hand and says *"Talitha kumi";* our story teller can authenticate his tale

---

[22]Mk. 5:21-24a; Mt. 9:1, 18 f.; Lk. 8:40-42a.   [23]Mk. 5:24b-34; Mt. 9:20-22; Lk. 8:42b-48.

by quoting the very expression used by the great healer in his native Aramaic, the translator of course knows the meaning: "Young lady, I tell you: Arise!" But Jesus orders emphatically that no one should know of the miracle, a clear hint that all was not so well as our story teller would have us believe.[24] For despite these tales of triumph over disease and even death, we soon read the confession that Herod Antipas was pressing his search for Jesus.[25]

"After these things," says John, referring back to his own doubtless more historical account of these events in and about Capernaum, now lost from his narrative, Jesus went off across the Lake of Galilee. He reached the opposite shore at the northeast corner, a little beyond the exit of the Jordan into the lake and the site of Beth Saida.[26] Here for the moment Jesus was safe, though since the territory belonged to the tetrarch Philip, Antipas' brother, it behooved him to remain as quiet as possible. According to another story, when Jesus was not far from Beth Saida, a blind man was brought to the great healer. Jesus took him outside the village; how the inhabitants of Julias, "Hellenized" a whole generation since they had been given city status, would have raved at that lowly title![27] He spat in the blind man's eye and asked if he saw anything. The reply was that the man saw men as trees walking about. Next Jesus laid hands on his eyes and the man saw everything clearly. He was sent home but was warned not to enter the village.[28]

Jesus had not evaded the crowds by crossing the lake. It was only a walk of an hour or so around the lake from Caper-

---

[24]Mk. 5:35-43; Mt. 9:23-25; Lk. 8:49-56.
[25]Lk. 9:9.
[26]To Beth Saida itself, Lk. 9:10.
[27]Jn. 1:44; Lk. 9:10 correctly call

Beth Saida a city; cf. C. C. McCown, "The Problem of the Site of Beth Saida," *Journal of the Palestine Oriental Society*, X, 1930, 32 ff.
[28]Mk. 8:22-26.

naum to Beth Saida and a great number of people were following on foot to see more signs wrought by Jesus on the
sick. To escape them, Jesus went up into the nearby mountain
and sat there with his disciples. Lifting up his eyes and seeing
how great a crowd was coming toward him, Jesus summoned
Philip, who as a native of Beth Saida[29] ought to know the
neighborhood, and asked: "Where can we buy loaves so that
these may eat?" The answer was: "Five hundred denarii
worth of loaves are not enough for that, even so that each
might take a little." But Andrew, who was also a native of
Beth Saida, reported: "Here is a boy who has five barley
loaves and two little fish as relish; however, what are these
among so many?" Jesus nevertheless gave order: "Make the
people recline." "But there was much grass in the place" ob-
serves John in surprise; it was not too late in the summer for
grass to remain unwithered in a secluded spot in the Jordan
valley, not far from the great Huleh swamp.

Jesus therefore took the loaves and, having given the usual
thanks before meal, he distributed them to those who were
reclining, and so also with the fish, as much as they desired.
When they were fed, he says to his disciples: "Collect the
remaining fragments so that nothing is lost." They therefore
collected them and filled twelve baskets with the fragments
from the twelve barley loaves which remained over from
those who had eaten.[30]

The men, therefore, seeing the signs which he did, said:
"This is in truth the Prophet who is coming into the world."
By his healing miracles, Jesus was proved to be the Messiah
preached by John; if he would not proclaim himself, the en-
thusiastic crowd would seize him and make him king by force.

---

[29] Jn. 1:44.
[30] Jn. 6:1–3, 5, 7–13; Lk. 9:10–
17; Mk. 6:30–44; Mt. 14:13–21;

secondary account, Mk. 8:1–9; Mt.
15:32–38.

Realizing what was in their minds, Jesus withdrew into the mountain alone.[31] He had escaped the threatened crown but the intention would be known. Thereafter Philip would be as suspicious as his brother.

But when it became late, the disciples went down to the sea and entered a boat to return to Capernaum.[32] It was already dark and Jesus had not yet appeared. The sea was rising under the great wind which was blowing. They had rowed but twenty-five or thirty stades, barely three or four miles, when they saw Jesus walking by the sea and drawing near the boat. They were afraid but he says to them: "It is I; do not fear!" They wished to take him into the boat but at once it was at the land to which they were going.[33]

Next day, the crowd which stood on the other shore of the sea realized there was no other small boat except one, and that Jesus had not entered into the boat with his disciples; rather his disciples had gone away alone, though there did come small boats from Tiberias near the place. When therefore the crowd saw that Jesus was not there nor his disciples, they themselves entered into the boats and came to Capernaum, seeking Jesus. Finding him on the other side of the sea, they asked him: "Rabbi, how did *you* come here?"[34]

The question is not answered in our sources, for there is another gap in John's narrative. Next we find Jesus teaching in the Capernaum synagogue.[35] His words, once given by John, have been supplanted by one of the Evangelist's long-winded sermons. We do learn that the Jews muttered about him and asked: "Isn't this fellow Jesus, Joseph's son, whose father and mother we know?"[36] Here only in our sources is Jesus' proper patronymic employed; there is no hint that Joseph was yet living.

We must deeply regret that the editor has not preserved the content of this sermon, for it was to be the last ever preached in a synagogue. In it Jesus probably hinted something of his coming fate, perhaps he also at last made it perfectly clear that he did not consider himself the Messiah announced by John. Three times in our other Lives we are told how Jesus informed his disciples that he would be surrendered up into the hands of men who would kill him. Likewise we are told that the disciples did not understand the saying and were afraid to ask him the meaning.[37]

Whatever had been said in the sermon, it marked a great decline in Jesus' popularity. On hearing it, many of his disciples declared: "Hard is this saying! Who can hear it?" Realizing what his disciples were muttering among themselves, Jesus demanded: "Does this cause you to stumble? There are some of you who do not believe!"[38] Upon this therefore many of his disciples went back home and walked no more with him.

Deeply wounded by their desertion, Jesus turned to the Twelve: "Do *you* also intend to leave?" Simon Peter answered him: "Master, to whom shall we go? We have believed and know that you are the Holy One of God!"[39] Far indeed is this almost despairing cry of Peter from the triumphant recognition of Jesus' messiahship assigned him by the other and later biographers.[40]

---

[36] Jn. 6:41a, 42a.
[37] Earliest account, Mk. 10:32–34; Mt. 20:17–19; Lk. 18:31–34, going up to Jerusalem, and so placed considerably later. Second source, Mk. 8:31; Mt. 16:21; Lk. 9:22. Latest source, Mk. 9:31 f.; Mt. 17:22 f.; Lk. 9:44 f.
[38] Jn. 6:60 f., 64a.
[39] Jn. 6:66–69.
[40] Mk. 8:29; Mt. 16:16; Lk. 9:20.

Peter's reply did not satisfy Jesus: "Did I not choose *you* as the Twelve and one of you is an *Accuser?*" The word in Aramaic was undoubtedly Satan, with a double meaning, an accuser at a trial and the Devil himself. Again and again John calls Judas Iscariot *the* Satan, he can never forgive him for his treachery; here he bursts out: "But he was speaking of Judas, son of Simon, the man of Karioth, for he was to betray him, he, one of the Twelve!"[41]

"After these things," another section of John is lost, "Jesus travelled about in Galilee, for he would not travel about in Judæa, because the Judæans sought to kill him."[42] For the details of these travels, we must turn to less trustworthy sources. Behind their tales of further wondrous miracles, we everywhere recognize a harried, fleeing Prophet.

Upper Galilee through all history has been economically the back country of Tyre and little more. From it came the chief food supply of the great trading metropolis.[43] In his flight after the disastrous sermon at Capernaum, Jesus crossed the Tyrian frontier to the low slopes behind the city and through orchards and gardens overlooking the Mediterranean. He entered a house and did not wish anyone to know it, good indication that he was in fact an exile. But the presence of the wonder worker could not be hid. A woman whose daughter suffered from an unclean spirit fell at his feet and begged that the demon be expelled. One writer calls the woman a Canaanite; Canaan was an ancient name of Phœnicia, and as late as the Hellenistic period Phœnician legends on the coins

---

[41] Jn. 6:70 f.—This very title of Satan is transferred by Mk. 8:33; Mt. 16:23 to Peter, who a few lines before has so triumphantly announced Jesus as Messiah! The answer to this libel is found in Lk. 22:31.

[42] Jn. 7:1.

[43] I Kings 5:9b, 11; Acts 12:20.

of Laodicea-Berytus call it "Mother in Canaan."[44] The other
says that she was a Greek, a Syro-Phœnician by race, a good
illustration of the degree to which these "Greeks" had actually
been Hellenized. Jesus' harsh response: "Let the children first
be fed, for it is not right to take the loaf from the children
and throw it to the puppies," and the woman's deprecating
reply: "True, Master, but even the puppies under the table
eat from the children's crumbs" smacks more of the exclusive
primitive Jewish church than of the kindly teacher; the
apologetic tone in explaining an undesirable miracle in behalf of a Gentile woman is the best evidence that her faith
was indeed rewarded.[45]

Laish, through Dan and Paneas the predecessor of Cæsarea
Philippi, had been a "Sidonian" foundation.[46] From their
modern successor Banias a direct road still connects with
Tyre and with Sidon. It was natural that Jesus should next
retire to Cæsarea's territory, even though under the rule of
Antipas' brother Philip. Here and not at Capernaum Peter's
confession is placed in the later Lives. Six days after, they
date the supreme vision which convinced the disciples that
their Master was indeed the Messiah. They tell how Jesus
took Peter, James, and John into the high mountain, Hermon,
towering above Cæsarea Philippi at the Jordan source. There
the favored three saw Jesus transfigured before them, his
garments gleaming white as no earthly fuller could cleanse
them. Moses and Elijah appeared and talked with their own
Master as an equal. Peter cried out: "Rabbi, it is good for
us to be here; let us make three booths, one for you, one for
Moses, and one for Elijah." A cloud overshadowed them;
to this day, we may climb the Lebanons in summer for the

---

[44]G. F. Hill, *Catalogue of the Greek Coins of Phœnicia*, 1910, I, 52.

[45]Mk. 7:24-30; Mt. 15:21-28.
[46]Jud. 18:7.

view, only to have it obscured suddenly by chilling clouds. From the cloud they heard a voice: "This is my beloved Son. Hear him!" Then without warning they saw only Jesus.[47] That a vision was actually seen on Hermon can scarcely be doubted; that the recollection was colored by later experiences must be equally obvious.

On their return from the Mount, they find that the other disciples have failed in their attempt to cast out from a child a deaf spirit; Jesus succeeds, but we have a broad hint that not all attempted healings were successful.[48] Jesus entered Galilee—but secretly; he did not wish that any man should know it.[49] When Jesus cured the sick, always now he gave order that the healed man should tell no one; as regularly they disobeyed and spread the glad news. Such was the case of the deaf and dumb man into whose ears Jesus put his fingers, spat, and touched the tongue; looking up into heaven and sighing, he said: "Ephphatha," that is "Be opened!"[50]

No longer did Jesus dare travel by land. From a boat in which he might quickly make his escape if need arose, he made brief visits to the various parts of Dalmanutha.[51] One of the hamlets thus visited was Magdala, the "Fort";[52] an hour's walk north along the shore from Tiberias will bring us to Mejdel, its successor, hidden in a nook along the shore. If we are fortunate, we may listen to the music of a marriage dance and recall Mary the Magdalene, from whom Jesus cast out seven evil spirits.[53] Would we know their names, we need only turn to a book which Jesus read, the *Testaments of the*

---

[47]Mk. 9:2–8; Mt. 17:1–8; Lk. 9:28–36.

[48]Mk. 9:14–29; Mt. 17:14–18; Lk. 9:37–43.

[49]Mk. 10:32; Mt. 20:17; Lk. 18:31; from later source, Mk. 9:30.

[50]Mk. 7:32–37; apparent duplicate, Mt. 9:27–31.

[51]Mk. 8:10.

[52]Mt. 15:39.

[53]Lk. 8:2; Mk. 16:9.

Twelve Patriarchs.[54] Another town visited was Chorazin, two miles north-northwest of Capernaum up a side valley, which still preserves considerable ruins of a synagogue.[55]

For the historian, this is the most difficult chapter in the ministry of Jesus to write. Our sources are generally late and overlaid with marvels. But despite the marvels, the evidence is overwhelming that Jesus was in flight and that he was fully conscious of his danger. Of the itinerary of that flight, the stories furnish a rough outline.

---

[54]*Testaments of the Twelve Patriarchs,* Reuben 2 :2.

[55]Lk. 10 :13–15 ; Mt. 11 :21–23. H. Kohl and C. Watzinger, *Antike Synagogen in Galilaea,* 1916, 41 ff. ; J. Ory, *Quarterly Statement, Palestine Exploration Fund,* 1927, 51 f.

CHAPTER VII

HOSTILE HIGH PRIESTS

SUKKOTH, the "Feast of Booths," which we translate by
"Tabernacles," was at hand. It began Tishri 15, which in this
year 29 A.D. was October 13. Jesus' brothers therefore said
to him: "Leave here and go into Judæa, so that your disciples
there may also see the works you are doing. For no one does
anything in secret and himself seeks to have public attention.
If you are really doing these things, make yourself known to
the world." The sneering brothers had not yet given James
to be the revered head of the Jerusalem church when John
wrote: "For even his *brothers* did not believe on him!" Jesus
therefore says to them: "My time has not yet arrived but your
time is always ready; *you* go up to the feast, I cannot go up
to the feast because *my* time has not been finished." Having
said these things, he remained in Galilee.[1]

But when his brothers had gone up to the feast, then he
went also, not openly but in secret. The Judæans—by whom
we are to understand normally the high priestly group and
their attendant scribes and police—therefore were looking for
him at the feast and saying: "Where is he?" There was much
debating about him by the crowd, the pilgrims come to the
feast. Some said: "He is a good man," others: "No! Rather
he is leading astray the mob." However, no one spoke openly
about him in fear of the hierarchy. It was already the middle
of the eight days' feast, about October 17, when Jesus appeared. At once he went up into the Temple, where he began

[1] Jn. 7 :2–6, 8 f.

to teach. The Judæans therefore wondered: "How does this fellow know letters, never having been a student?"[2]

Jerusalem was still in an uproar. Like a good practical Roman administrator, Pilate was more interested in the physical welfare of his subjects than in their souls. To his mind, the Holy City would not lose its sanctity if its close-packed quarters became more sanitary. He therefore decided that an aqueduct should bring water to Jerusalem from the great reservoirs two miles south of Bethlehem now called the "Pools of Solomon." Here from early times a series of tanks, partly cut from the rock of the valley which descends from east of the Hebron road toward the Dead Sea, had collected clear cold water from numerous tiny springs in the limestone strata. Gradually a system of small rock-cut aqueducts had been constructed to carry water into these tanks until the head of the system was fifty miles distant from the city. In all probability, attempts to provide Jerusalem from these pools had been made before Pilate, but they would not meet the requirements of Roman engineers.

Aqueducts still providing the Imperial City with the flowing water of its many famous fountains, aqueducts on the far frontiers of empire, some in use, others gaunt ghosts of former prosperity, magnificently testify to one of the most beneficent effects of Roman rule. To such an improvement, the Jerusalemites could raise no objection. The priests should welcome a change which would substitute pure living water in temple ritual in place of the stale liquid stored in the reservoirs. They should be glad to make their contribution to the cost of the new construction from the Korbana,[3] the "dedicated" temple treasure.

Such a contribution from the priests would appreciably

---

[2]Jn. 7:10-15.   [3]Korban, Mt. 27:6.

lower the tax imposed for the new convenience on the people in general. The selfish priests did not see it that way. *They* were in no need of water. Underneath the whole temple platform lay huge tanks for storage of rain water, thirty-six in all and extending down to sixty feet deep in the rock. The largest, the "Great Sea," had a capacity of two million gallons; its bottom and sides were carefully cemented, channels of intersection, draw offs, passages for inspectors guaranteed that the water would remain pure and cool.

The feast of Tabernacles arrived and with it Pilate's cohort. Galilæan pilgrims also poured in. Sight of the Roman soldiers recalled Pilate's attempt to desecrate the Holy City with his idolatrous standards. The priests had no difficulty in persuading these intense nationalists that use of the Korbana by the procurator for secular purposes was only one more example of Pilate's sacrilegious determination. Crowds surrounded the procurator's tribunal, angrily denouncing the profanation. Pilate had scattered throughout the crowd disguised soldiers. This time he was determined to see the matter through, but in the meanwhile he had thought up a new device which should afford the demonstrators proper punishment without danger of their being considered martyrs. This time the disguised soldiers were strictly prohibited from using their swords; they were to beat up the demonstrators with clubs. At a signal from the tribunal, they went to work with a will; many of the demonstrators died or were seriously injured from the beating, many others were trodden to death under the feet of the fleeing mob.[4]

Again Pilate had blundered seriously. The mob had been dispersed, the prestige of Rome had been restored, but at too high a price. Too many pilgrims had lost their lives; on the

---

[4]Joseph. *Wars* ii, 175 ff.; *Ant.* xviii, 60 ff.

return of their companions to Galilee, they would be bewailed as martyrs to the sacred duty of pilgrimage. In Pilate's eyes, the most unfortunate result for the immediate future was that by this outrage inflicted upon his Galilæan subjects Antipas was thoroughly angered and henceforth was at enmity with the procurator.[5] Unfortunately for Pilate, the sons of Herod, as well as the high priests, had influence in high quarters at Rome. To the end of his reign, Tiberius was always to support Antipas.

Jesus fortunately had been absent from the Holy City when the massacre took place. Unfortunately he arrived while Jerusalem was yet seething with excitement, sorrow, and anger over the incident. It was impossible to escape being drawn into the controversy; already there had been too much discussion about him by the pilgrims.

Eyewitnesses, "certain men present at that very time," informed Jesus of the "Galilæans whose blood Pilate mingled with their sacrifices." If they had expected him to sympathize with them in their anti-Roman attitude, they were badly mistaken: "Do you think that these Galilæans were sinners because they suffered these things? No, I tell you! Rather, if *you* do not repent, you shall all likewise perish!" Apparently about the same time a water tower in connection with the aqueduct had collapsed with serious loss of life. "Or those eighteen upon whom fell the tower in Siloam and killed them, do you think *they* happened to deserve it beyond all the men living in Jerusalem? No, I tell you! Rather, if *you* do not repent, you shall all likewise perish!"[6] Such an answer must have shocked and alienated his auditors; obviously Jesus was no nationalist Messiah, from him they could expect no restoration of the hoped-for kingdom.

---

[5]Lk. 23:12.   [6]Lk. 13:1-5.

During his quiet years in Nazareth, Jesus had read the Wisdom of Ahiqar. One story had made a great impression on his mind. As we remember, Ahiqar had adopted his nephew Nadin and had made him his successor at the royal court; the ungrateful Nadin caused his uncle to be ordered to death, but Ahiqar was saved by a friend more grateful than the adopted son. Restored to power, Ahiqar punished the wicked Nadin by compelling him to listen to parables and wise sayings.

On one of these occasions, "Nadin answered and said to Ahiqar: 'My father Ahiqar, such things be far from you; do to me according to your mercy. For God also forgives the fault of man, and you too forgive me this my folly. And I will tend your horses and feed your pigs, which are in your house' "—Jesus had already used this detail in his story of the prodigal son—" 'and I shall be called wicked, but you, do not plan evil against me.'

"Ahiqar answered and said to him: 'My son, you have been to me like that palm tree which stood by a river,' " the scene is here laid on the Tigris, " 'and cast all its fruit into the river,' " for north of Babylonia the palm does not bear. And when its master arrived to cut it down, it said to him: " 'Leave me alone this year, and I will bear for you carobs." Its master said to it: "You have not been industrious about what is your own, how can you be industrious about what is not your own?" ' "[7]

Palm trees would be inappropriate in upland Palestine where the fig and the olive covered the landscape, but the motif was exactly what was needed to drive home still deeper the moral: "A certain man had a fig-tree planted in his orchard. And he came seeking fruit and did not find any. Then

[7]Ahiqar, Syriac 8:34 f.

said he to the vinedresser: 'Look, it is three years since I
have been coming and seeking fruit on this fig tree, and even
yet I do not find anything; cut it down!' But the vinedresser
answered: 'Master, leave it alone this one more year, until
I dig around it and throw on manure; if it makes fruit for
the future—but if not, you shall cut it down.' "[8] Here Jesus
expresses all his fears for the future.

For the second time after so brief an interval, nationalistic
Jews had forced just now a conflict with Rome. No thinking
man who realized Rome's might could avoid a fear that one
or two more such conflicts would result in Rome losing
patience and bringing about complete destruction. It took no
particularly wise prophet to foresee the fall of Jerusalem long
before the year 70. And the worst of it is that the destruction will be perfectly justified. God's people still dream of an
earthly kingdom. They refuse to accept the Kingdom of the
Heavens. If they do not repent, God simply *must* punish his
people. As John the Baptist has predicted, the tree must be
hewn down. Yet Jesus still hopes against hope that at the very
last moment Israel may bring forth fruits meet for repentance
and thus be saved.

One day, we learn from another narrative, Jesus was passing along the street and met a man who had been blind from
birth. Curiously his disciples inquired: "Rabbi, who sinned,
this man or his parents, that he should be born blind?" Accepting as they did the current belief that physical disability
must be the consequence of sin, the disciples thought that the
problem of responsibility would be in such a case a pretty
question for discussion. "Neither this man nor his parents,"
was the surprising reply; "rather that the works of God might

---

[8]Lk. 13:6–9; from this grew the tale of the cursed fig tree, Mk. 11:12–14, 20 f.; Mt. 21:18–20.

be made manifest in him." Having spoken thus, Jesus spat on the ground, made mud of the spittle, and anointed his eyes with the mud. "Go! Wash in the Pool of Siloam!" was the order.

In imagination we may watch the blind man hurrying along the road which from west of the Temple walls descended the Cheesemaker's Valley under the viaduct leading to the Hasmonæan Palace. It was a fine road, twenty-five to fifty feet wide from curb to curb, and paved by Herod's orders with great blocks of hard whitish limestone. Now and then he would stumble over the manholes, projecting a foot and a half above the pavement, which permitted cleaning of the drain below. Leaving on the right the main road leading on to the southern gate, the blind man felt his way, right hand on the rock of the scarp, down thirty-four monumental steps of alternate broad and narrow tread. Turning left through an opening in a low parapet, he was sheltered by the covered arcade which surrounded the pool, seventy-five by seventy-one feet on the side. In a court to the south, he prepared to take his bath, and then bathed in the water brought from Gihon's spring under the rock of Ophel by Hezekiah's aqueduct.[9]

On his return, the blind man could see. The neighbors therefore and those who had noticed him formerly because he was a beggar said: "Is not this fellow the one who used to sit and beg?" Others said: "This *is* he"; others: "No! Rather he is like him." He himself said: "I am he." They therefore said to him: "How therefore were your eyes opened?" He answered: "The man called Jesus made mud and anointed my eyes and said to me: 'Go to Siloam and wash!' I therefore went and washed and saw again." And they said to him: "Where is he?" He says: "I do not know."

---

[9]F. J. Bliss and A. C. Dickie, *Excavations at Jerusalem,* 1898, 132 ff.

They bring to the high priests, Annas and Caiaphas, him who was once blind, for it was the sabbath when Jesus made the mud and opened his eyes. To strict legalists, this was violation of the holy day. Again therefore they asked him also how he saw again. The answer was the same: "He put mud on my eyes and I washed and I see." Some therefore said: "This fellow is not from God, because he does not keep the sabbath"; others said: "How can a man who is a sinner do such signs?" And there was a division of opinion among them. They say therefore to the blind man again: "What do *you* say about him since it was *your* eyes he opened?" He said: "He is a prophet."

The hierarchy therefore did not believe that he had been blind and saw again until they called the parents of him who had seen again. Of them they demanded: "Is this your son, who, you say, was born blind? How therefore does he see *now?*" His parents therefore answering said: "We do know that this is our son and that he was born blind, but how he sees now or who opened his eyes *we* do not know; ask *him!* He is of age, he can speak about himself." These things his parents said because they feared the hierarchy, for already they had agreed that if any one confessed him Messiah he should be excommunicated from the synagogue. For this reason, his parents said: "He is of age, ask him!"

They called therefore a second time the man who was blind and said to him: "Give glory to God; we know that this fellow is a sinner." He answered therefore: "Whether he is a sinner I do not know. One thing I *do* know is that, having been blind, right now I see!" They said therefore to him: "What did he do to you? How did he open your eyes?" Completely disgusted, the man answered impudently: "Just now I told you and you did not listen; why do you wish to hear it again? Do *you* too intend to become his disciples?" This was rank insubordination to ecclesiastical authority and it made them ridiculous in public; their ruffled feelings could be soothed only by giving him a good calling down: *"You* are that fellow's disciple, but *we* are disciples of Moses. We *know* that God has spoken to Moses, but as for this fellow, we do not know from where he comes."

Still more impudently the man retorted: "Why, this is a surprise! *You* do not know from where he comes, and yet he opened my eyes! *We* know that God does not hear *sinners,* but rather, if any one is God-reverencing and does his will, *him* he hears. From eternal ages it was never heard that any one opened the eyes of one *born* blind; if this man were not from *God,* he could do nothing." The facts were against them and the high priests could only answer: "In sin were you born utterly, and are *you* teaching *us?"* If they could not best him in argument, the high priests did possess ecclesiastical power and they threw him out.[10]

On account of these words, which John has so amusingly reported, there arose a division among the Judæans. Many said: "He has an evil spirit and is crazy! Why do you listen to him?" Others maintained: "These are not the sayings of one possessed by an evil spirit! Can an evil spirit open the eyes of the blind?"[11]

Were not this an account of a miraculous healing, we should have had no hesitation in accepting it as completely authentic. Certainly it is no dead production of a professional writer of formal literature; it has the "feel" of genuine life, even to a somewhat robust humor. To seek an explanation from parallel miracle stories of the middle ages, whose authors admittedly

---

[10]Jn. 9:1–3, 6–34; *cf.* Mt. 12:22;   [11]Jn. 10:19–21.
Lk. 11:14.

could have had this narrative for model, betrays complete misunderstanding of historical method.

Judged by any admissible criterion, the story must be extremely early. The high priests fear that Jesus may be identified with the Messiah, but he is evidently the Coming One of John, not the Christ of the Gentile Church. To the beggar, Jesus is only a prophet, a miracle worker like such a predecessor as Elijah, a man who reverences God. Had the recorder of this tale thought of Jesus as a supernatural being, he would never have repeated the thoroughly irreverent humor of the original.

Science tells us categorically that no man blind from birth ever recovered his sight through a miracle. We moderns accept the dictum. Our sources for Jesus' life however add other tales of his cure of the blind. They repeat other accusations that his cures were performed by the aid of demons. We have Jesus' own reply to these accusations.

One accusation was: "He has Beelzebul." We know, as his accusers did not, that Zebul the Lord (Baal) was an ancient Canaanite divinity whose name we may find on the Phœnician tablets from Ras Shamra, written in the later second millennium before our era in a language strangely close to the Hebrew of our Bible. Another accusation was: "By the demons he casts out the demons." Jesus answered by a "comparison" which illustrates the typical form of argument employed by contemporary Judaism:

How can Satan cast out Satan?

If a kingdom is divided against itself,
    That kingdom is unable to stand;
And if a house is divided against itself,
    That house is unable to stand;

And if Satan rise up against himself and is divided,
    He cannot stand but has come to an end;
And if I by Beelzebul cast out the demons,
    By whom do *your* sons cast them out?
But if I by God's finger cast out demons,
    Then has God's Kingdom come upon you.
No one can enter the house of the strong,
    To plunder his personal possessions,
Unless he first binds the strong,
    And then he will plunder his house.
If the householder they have called Beelzebul,
    By how much more the sons of his house.[12]

But expulsion of the demon is not enough: "When the unclean spirit goes out from the man, it passes through waterless places seeking rest and does not find it. Then it says: 'Into my house from which I came out I will return.' And coming, it finds it empty, swept and adorned. Then it goes and takes along with it seven other spirits more wicked than itself, and entering in, they dwell there. And the last condition of that man is worse than the first."[13] Only when the Spirit of God has taken the place of the evil spirit is the man safe.

Just outside the Gate of the Flock in the northern city wall and before the hill of Beth Zatha lay the Pool of Beth Hesda, the "House of Mercy," which had been excavated in a shallow draw running southeast to the Kidron from the southern slopes of the hill in order to catch the water oozing from the rock. The pool, about a hundred and ten feet a

---

little west of north and south, was double, each half surrounded by porticoes of Corinthian columns, which thus gave
the effect of five porticoes. In them lay a crowd of sick, the
blind, lame, and paralyzed, waiting for the movement of the
water, since it was believed that at certain irregular intervals
an angel descended and stirred the waters; the first to enter
immediately after was healed. This belief was not confined
to Jews: One Roman lady left a votive image of her foot
with the inscription: "Pompeia Lucilia dedicated it"; a second
woman dedicated a female figurine, a third individual an
elaborate shrine, a shell niche over four twisted columns,
between which reared up the snake of his patron, Aesclepias,
god of healing.[14]

When Jesus visited the pool, he noticed one man who had
lain there thirty-eight years in his sickness. Seeing him lying
there and knowing that he had been there so long a time,
Jesus asks him: "Do you wish to be well?" The sick man
answered him: "Master, I have no man, when the water is
stirred, to put me into the pool, but while I am coming another steps down before me." Jesus says to him: "Arise! Lift
up your pallet and walk!" And at once the man became well
and lifted up his pallet and walked.[15]

Again we have an account of a healing miracle. There is
this time again archæological evidence for the site and also
this time epigraphic as well as traditional evidence for further
miracles. There is another story of what happened after the
miracle, and again it is most plausible and lifelike.

Once again it was the sabbath on that day. The Judæans
therefore said to him who was cured: "It is the sabbath and

---

[14]H. Vincent and F. M. Abel, [15]Cf. Mk. 2:11; Mt. 9:6; Lk.
Jérusalem, II, iv, 1926, 669 ff.; 5:24.
685 ff.

it is not right for you to lift up your pallet." He answered them: "He who made me well himself said to me: 'Lift up your pallet and walk!' " They asked him: "Who is the fellow who said to you: 'Lift and walk'?" But he who was healed did not know who he was, for Jesus had slipped off, a crowd being in the place. Afterward Jesus finds him in the temple and says to him: "See, you have become well; sin no more lest a worse thing happen to you."[16] The man went off and told the Judæans that it was Jesus who had made him well. On account of this, the Judæans were persecuting Jesus because he had done it on the sabbath.[17]

But Jesus answered them:[18] "Did not Moses give you the Law? And yet not one of you carries out the Law! Why are you seeking to kill me?" The crowd retorted: "You have an evil spirit! Who is seeking to kill you?" Jesus had already realized that it was only a question of time before the high priests succeeded in finding an excuse to put him out of the way, but he went bravely on: "I did one work and you are all surprised at it. Moses has given you circumcision, and yet on the sabbath you circumcise a man. If a man receives circumcision on the sabbath, so that the Law of Moses may not be broken, are you angered at *me* because *I* made a *whole* man well on the sabbath? Judge not according to appearances, rather judge righteous judgement."

Some therefore of the inhabitants of Jerusalem itself said: "Is not this fellow the man they are seeking to kill? See, he is speaking openly, and they say nothing to him! Do the rulers actually think that *he* is the Messiah?" This was intended for irony since they went on: "Nevertheless, we know this fellow and from where he comes; but when the Messiah

---

[16]*Cf*. Mk. 2:5; Mt. 9:2; Lk. 5:20.   [18]Jn. 5:17a.
[17]Jn. 5:1–16.

comes no one will know from where *he* comes!" They sought therefore to arrest him, and yet no one laid his hand on him— because his hour had not yet come!

In contrast to the Jerusalemites, many of the pilgrims yet believed on him and were saying: "When the Messiah comes, will he do more signs than this man does?" The high priests heard the crowds arguing thus about him and sent police to arrest him. But the crowds continued the debate. Some said: "This man is in truth the Prophet!" Others were saying: "This is the Messiah!" Against them still others urged: "What! Does the Messiah come from *Galilee?* Has not the scripture declared that from the seed of David and from Bethlehem, the village where David lived, comes the Messiah?" John has no answer to this objection; when he wrote, it had not yet been "discovered" that Jesus was in truth of David's seed, that Jesus was actually born in David's Town.[19] A division of opinion therefore arose in the crowd on account of him; some of them wished to arrest him; however, no one laid hand on him.

The police therefore returned to the high priests, who demanded: "Why did you not bring him?" They therefore answered: "Never did man speak thus as this man spoke." The high priests scornfully asked: "Are you too led astray? Has any one of the ruling class believed him? However, this crowd, not knowing the Law, is accursed." This was typical of the higher classes, not only of the high priests but unfortunately equally of the Pharisees; all were contemptuous of the peasants, the "people of the soil."

One of the ruling class, Nicodemus, did pluck up courage

---

[19]This is incontrovertible evidence that John's narrative was written before the "discovery" of the Davidic birth and birthplace as a consequence of the expected second return in A.D. 40.

to protest: "Does our Law condemn a man unless it first has heard from him about himself and knows what he is doing?" Sneeringly his colleagues replied: "Are you too from Galilee? Investigate! You will discover that from *Galilee* arises no prophet!"[20] They conveniently forgot Jonah of Gath Hepher. They conveniently forgot also the commandment: "Thou shalt not kill!"

---

[20]Jn. 7:19–27, 30–32, 40–52.

CHAPTER VIII

CONSOLATION AND WARNING

FUNDAMENTAL in Jesus' teaching was the Kingdom of the Heavens. This Kingdom was ruled by the Father in the Heavens. These troublous days, when the disciples could not but worry about the future, were appropriate for a consolation which should further their knowledge of this kindly Father.

In beautiful, rhythmical language Jesus reassured them: "Do not be anxious for your soul, what you shall eat or what you shall drink, or for your body, what you shall wear. Is not the soul more than the food and the body more than the clothing? Look at the birds of the heavens! They neither sow nor harvest nor gather into granaries, and yet your Heavenly Father feeds them; are you not of more value than they? Are not two sparrows sold for an *as?*" a coin of the least value; "and yet not one of them shall fall to the ground without your Father. But even the hairs of your head are numbered; fear not, therefore, you are worth more than many sparrows!"[1]

"And which of you, by taking care, can add to his stature one cubit? And as for clothing, why do you worry? Observe the flowers of the field, how they grow! They neither toil nor spin; but, I tell you, not even Solomon in all his glory was clothed like one of these. But if the grass of the field, today living, tomorrow thrown into the potter's kiln, God so clothes, will he not much more *you,* little of faith?

---

[1]Mt. 6:25 f.; Lk. 12:22–24, 6 f.

"Do not therefore be anxious, saying: 'What shall we eat?' or 'What shall we drink?' or 'What shall we wear?' For all these the foreign peoples seek. For your Heavenly Father knows that you need all these. But seek first his Kingdom, and all these shall be added to you. Do not therefore be anxious for the morrow, since the morrow will be anxious for her own; sufficient for the day is her evil."[2]

Of all pre-Christian works of piety, the book of Tobit most emphasized the virtue of almsgiving:

Turn not your face from a poor man,
    And God will not turn his face from you;
So long as is ability in your hand to do alms, so do,
    And if riches are removed from you, do alms;
And you shall acquire possession,
    And if you make it do alms
A good treasure is laid up
    Which you acquired against the Day of Wrath,
Because alms delivers from Death,
    And does not allow you to come into Darkness.[3]

Do good, and Evil shall not find you;
    Better is prayer with fasting
And almsgiving with righteousness
    Than riches without righteousness.
Better is it to give alms than gold to lay up,
    Almsgiving delivers from Death and purges away all
      Sin,
Those who do alms shall be fed with Life,
    Those who commit sin are foes to their own life.[4]

---

[2]Mt. 6:27-34; Lk. 12:25-31.   [4]Tobit 12:8-10.
[3]Tobit 4:7-10.

In imitation of Tobit, Ben Sira had said:

> Store up almsgiving in your treasuries,
> And it shall deliver you from all Evil.[5]

Jesus must have had these passages in his mind when he bade the disciples not to worry about the future and hoard for it: "Fear not, little flock, for it is your Father's pleasure to give you the Kingdom.

> Sell your goods and give alms,
> Make for you purses that do not age.
> Treasure not for you treasures on the earth,
> Where moth and mice destroy,
> Where thieves bore through and steal.
> But treasure for you treasures in the heavens,
> Where neither moth nor mice destroy,
> Where thieves bore not through nor steal,
> For where is your treasure, there too is your heart![6]

Asher had said: "The treasure of the inclination is filled with an evil spirit."[7] Jesus saw both sides of the matter: "The good man from the good treasury brings out good things, and the wicked man from the wicked treasury throws out wicked things."[8]

When he gives alms, the good man is only following the example of his Heavenly Father: "Which of you shall have a friend and shall go to him in the middle of the night and say to him: 'My friend, I need three loaves, since my friend has come on a journey to me, and I do not have anything to give him'? And the man inside, answering, shall say: 'Don't

---

[5]Ecclesiasticus 29:12.
[6]Mt. 6:19–21; Lk. 12:32–34; Jas. 5:3.
[7]*Testaments of the Twelve Patriarchs*, Asher 1:7, 9.
[8]Mt. 12:35; Lk. 6:45.

trouble me! Already the door is closed and my children are with me in bed. I can't get up and give it to you!' I tell you, even if he will not get up and give it to him because of his being a friend, yet because of his shamelessness" in keeping on calling, "he will get up and give him whatever he needs."[9]

> Ask and it shall be given you,
>> Seek, and you shall find,
>>> Knock and it shall be opened to you;
>> For every one asking receives,
>>> And the one seeking finds,
>>>> And to the one knocking it is opened.[10]

"Or what man is there from you, of whom his son asks a loaf, who will give him a stone? Or if he asks a fish, will he give him a snake? Or if he asks an egg, will he give him a scorpion? If, therefore, you, evil as you are, know how to give good gifts to your children, by how much more will your Father who is in the Heavens give good gifts to those asking him?"[11]

To illustrate more fully how they must always pray and never grow weary, Jesus followed with this story: "There was a certain judge in a certain city, not fearing God and not feeling shame before man. There was also a certain widow in that city and she kept coming to him, saying: 'Give me justice against my opponent in the law suit.' For a time, he would not; after this, he said to himself: 'Even though I do not fear God or feel shame before man, nevertheless, because this widow keeps on making a nuisance of herself to me, I

---

[9]Lk. 11:5–8.
[10]Lk. 11:9b–10; Mt. 7:7 f.; *cf.* Jas. 1:5; 4:3.

[11]Lk. 11:11–13; Mt. 7:9–11.

will give her justice, lest she keep on coming and in the end wear me out.' "[12]

There is not a little bitterness in the moral. Every one of the bystanders could recall only too well incidents in which unjust decisions had been rendered by unrighteous judges. Seeing that his tale was well received, Jesus went on: "There was a certain rich man who had a steward. This man was accused to him of squandering his possessions. Calling him, he demanded: 'What is this I hear about you? Render the account of your stewardship, because you are to be no longer steward.' The steward said to himself: 'What shall I do since my master is taking away my stewardship? To dig I have no strength. To beg I am ashamed. I have decided what I shall do, so that, when I am deprived of my stewardship, they will receive me into their own homes!'

"And summoning each one of his own master's debtors, he said to the first: 'How much do you owe my master?' He said: 'A hundred *baths* of oil.' The steward said: 'Take your documents of indebtedness and, sitting down, write quickly fifty.' Then to another he said: 'But you, how much do *you* owe?' He replied: 'A hundred *kors* of grain.' He was told: 'Take your documents and write eighty.' And the master commended the steward of unrighteousness because he had acted shrewdly. For the sons of this age are wiser than the children of the light toward their own generation."[13]

Accustomed as were his hearers to parables which made only one single point, they would be startled by this one; could Jesus actually be following the example of the master in commending the dishonest steward? The moral to the story attempted to make this clear: "I tell you to make friends for

---

[12]Lk. 18:2–5.　　　　[13]Lk. 16:1–8.

yourselves from the Mammon of the Unrighteousness so that, when *it* fails, they," the angels, "may receive you into the eternal tabernacles."[14] The obscure saying was intended to make clear that riches in themselves may be unrighteous; properly used for God's service, they may save one's soul. By his shrewdness, the dishonest steward was rewarded by an earthly habitation; by honest foresight, the righteous obtain eternal homes.

Generous almsgiving is the best method of using possessions. But this does not at all imply that men should neglect their daily tasks: "He who is faithful in the least is also faithful in the much, and he who is dishonest in the least is also dishonest in the much. If therefore in the unrighteous Mammon you have not proved faithful, who will trust you with the true? And if in what is another's you have not proved faithful, who will give you your own?"[15] In Ahiqar's parable to Nadin, the master says to the barren palm tree: "You have not been industrious with what was your own, and how will you be industrious with what is not your own?"[16] Jesus has revised the familiar saying to make perfectly clear that he is not advising any neglect of earthly possessions.

But property must not possess the man:

No one can be slave to two masters:
   For either the one he will hate and the other love,
   Or one he will cherish and the other despise;
You cannot be slave to God and Mammon![17]

Once more Jesus feels it necessary to return to the theme and hammer home the need of honest, faithful labor: "For

14Lk. 16:9.
15Lk. 16:10-12.
16Ahiqar, Syriac 8:35.
17Lk. 16:13; Mk. 6:24; Jas. 4:4.

the Kingdom of Heaven is just like a man who was travelling abroad and summoned his own slaves and handed over to them his property. And to one he gave five talents but to another two and to another one, to each according to his capability. And he travelled abroad. But going off at once, the one receiving the five talents traded with them and made five more. In the same fashion, the one having the two made two more. But the one receiving the one, going off, dug in the ground and hid the silver of his master.

"But after a long time, the master of those slaves comes and makes an accounting with them. And coming forward to him, the one receiving the five talents brought five more talents, saying: 'Master, five talents you handed over to me; see, five more talents I have gained!' To him his master says: 'Fine! Good and faithful slave! Over few things you were faithful, over many I shall place you. Enter into the joy of your master.' The one with the two, coming to him, also said: 'Master, two talents you handed over to me; see, two more talents I have gained.' His master says to him: 'Fine! Good and faithful slave! Over few things you were faithful, over many I shall place you. Enter into the joy of your master.'

"The one receiving the one talent, coming forward to him, said: 'Master, realizing that you are a hard man, reaping where you did not sow and gathering from where you did not scatter, I went off and hid your talent in the ground. See, you have your own!' But his master, answering, said to him: 'Wicked slave and lazy! You knew that I reap where I did not sow, and gather where I did not scatter; you ought therefore to have entrusted my silver to the bankers and returning I should have received back my own with interest. Take away therefore from him the talent and give it to him having the five talents. For whoever has, to him it shall be given and added to him, but as for him who has not, it shall be taken from him, even what he has.' "[18]

Once more we have illustrated the fact that each individual parable of Jesus is intended to make one single point. He is not reversing the Mosaic prohibition of interest.[19] He is not approving the harshness of the master. He is only driving home the need of faithful service. But there is also a warning to those who have labored faithfully and have been rewarded:

> To whom much is given,
>   Of him much is required;
> And to whom they entrust much,
>   The more of him they ask.[20]

Peter asked Jesus: "Master, how long shall my brother sin against me and I forgive him? Until seven times?" This was a pertinent question, now that the hierarchy was so vigorously attacking Jesus. To Peter's amazement, he was informed: "I tell you: Not until seven but until seventy times seven!"[21] Of course, this was only a more emphatic way of saying: "Always!" Jesus goes on to explain by another parable:

"For the Kingdom of the Heavens is like a man who wished to cast up accounts with his slaves. And beginning to make an accounting, one was brought to him, a debtor for ten thousand talents. And as he had nothing with which to repay,"—it was an impossible debt—"the master ordered him to be sold with his wife and his children and everything that he possessed, and thus he would be repaid. The slave, therefore, falling down, begged him, saying: 'Master, be patient

---

[18]Mt. 25:14–29; Lk. 19:12–27, a later, apocalyptic form of the story; moral alone, Mk. 4:25; Mt. 13:12; Lk. 8:13.
[19]Exod. 22:25; Lev. 25:36; Deut. 23:19.

[20]Lk. 12:48.
[21]Cf. Ecclesiasticus 28:2–4; Testaments of the Twelve Patriarchs, Gad 6:3 ff.

with me, and everything I will repay you.' Moved with compassion, the master of that slave freed him and forgave him the loan.

"But that slave, going out, found one of his fellow slaves who owed him a thousand denarii. Seizing him, he choked him, saying: 'Pay up if you owe anything!' Falling down, therefore, his fellow slave begged him, saying: 'Have patience with me and I will repay.' But he would not, rather he went off and threw him into prison until he should repay the debt.

"His fellow slaves, therefore, seeing what had happened, were grieved terribly and going, informed their master of all the happenings. Then summoning him, his master says to him: 'Wicked slave! All that loan I forgave you because you begged me; ought *you* not also to have had pity on your fellow slave as I too had pity on you?' And his angered master handed him over to the torturers until he should hand over all that he owed. Thus also my Heavenly Father will do to you if you do not forgive, each his brother from your hearts. For if you forgive men their transgressions, your Heavenly Father will also forgive you; but if you do not forgive men their transgressions, neither will your Father forgive your transgressions."[22] Long before, Jeshua, Sira's son, had taught: "Forgive your neighbor the injury, and all your sins will be forgiven you."[23]

"Make quickly a compromise with the litigant going to law against you" for an unpaid debt, "while you are yet on the road with him going to court, lest he should hand you over to the judge, and the judge to the bailiff, and you be thrown into jail. In truth I tell you: You shall not at all get out from there until you have surrendered up the last *quad-*

---

[22]Mt. 18:21–35; Lk. 17:4, introduction only; Mt. 6:14 f., moral only; *cf.* Mk. 11:25.

[23]Ecclesiasticus 28:2; *Testaments of the Twelve Patriarchs,* Gad 6:3–7.

rans."[24] Be prepared for the Last Judgement, when you shall meet your God, at once prosecutor and judge.

More than two centuries before, Antigonus of Socho, a famous Jewish Father despite his heathen name, had said: "Do not be like slaves who minister to the master for the sake of receiving a bounty, but be like slaves who minister to the master not for the sake of receiving a bounty. And let the fear of Heaven," God himself, "be upon you."[25] Apparently this Jewish sage with the Greek name was opposing the religious innovation according to which the good were rewarded by a Resurrection of the Flesh. Jesus made the well-known saying the basis for a story with a different moral:

"But what one of you, having a slave plowing or keeping the flock, will say to him as he comes in from the field: 'Come forward at once and sit down to eat'? Rather will he not say to him: 'Prepare something I can eat and, girding yourself, wait on me until I eat and drink, and after this eat and drink yourself'? Is he thankful to the slave because he did his commands? Thus also you, when you have done all commanded you, should say: 'We are unprofitable slaves; we have done only what was our duty to do!'"[26]

Jesus was invited to a dinner. Observing how the guests were hunting out the best seats, he recalled the advice of Solomon:

> Glorify not yourself in the king's presence,
> And stand not in the place of great men;
> For better to be told: "Come up here!"
> Than to be lowered in the prince's presence.[27]

---

[24]Mt. 5:25 f.; Lk. 12:58 f., Roman administrative terminology better represented by the Greek. *Quadrans* appears in Hebrew as *Qudrantes,* Jerusalem Talmud, Kiddushim I, 58d; Tosephta, Baba Bathra V, 12; Kiddushim 12a.

[25]Pirqe Aboth, 1:3.

[26]Lk. 17:7–10.

[27]Proverbs 25:6 f.

This was paraphrased for the benefit of the diners: "When you are invited by anyone to marriage feasts, do not recline on the first seat, lest perchance one more honored than you has been invited by him. Then coming, the man who invited both you and him will say to you: 'Give this man the place!' Then you with shame will begin to take the lowest place," the only one left. "Rather, when you are invited, go and sit down in the last place, so that, when the man inviting you comes, he will say to you: 'My friend, go up higher!' Then there will be glory for you before the face of all reclining with you. For everyone exalting himself shall be humbled, and the one humbling himself shall be exalted."[28]

Solomon's advice is for the guest; Jesus adds further advice for the host: "When *you* make a luncheon or a dinner, do not call in your friends or brothers or relatives or rich neighbors, lest perchance they too invite you in return and that makes it compensation for you. Rather, when *you* make a banquet, invite poor, maimed, lame, blind, and you shall be blessed, because they have nothing by which to reward you; for it shall be rewarded you at the resurrection of the righteous."[29]

On hearing this, one of his fellow guests smugly remarked: "Blessed is he who eats bread in the Kingdom of God." This of course implied that the Kingdom was not to come until after the resurrection; such was not in the least the belief of Jesus. Asked when the Kingdom comes, he had replied: "The Kingdom of God does not come through close observation" of the heavens in accordance with the practices of the astrologers; "neither shall they say: 'Lo! Here!' or 'There!' For lo, the Kingdom of God is within you."[30] Unlike most of his

---

[28]Lk. 14:7–11; moral only, Lk. 18:14b; Mt. 23:12.
[29]Lk. 14:12–14.

[30]Lk. 17:20 f., later employed to head unauthentic apocalyptic sayings!

contemporaries, unlike even John the Baptist, Jesus did not think of the Kingdom either as nationalistic or as beginning after the grave: to him the Kingdom was a living, ever-present force in the hearts of its members, one of the greatest of the Master's teachings.

To explain this Kingdom to his self-satisfied fellow guest, Jesus told a story: "A certain man was making a great dinner. And he invited many. At the hour of dinner, he sent out his slave to remind those invited: 'Come, for the dinner is already prepared.' And they began, all as one, to make excuses. The first one said: 'I have bought a field and I have need to go and see it; I beg you, have me excused.' Another said: 'I have bought five yoke of oxen and must go to try them out; I beg you, have me excused.' Still another said: 'I have married a wife; on account of this, I am unable to come.' The slave, returning, reported to his master these things.

"Then the angered master of the house said to his slave: 'Go out hastily into the streets and lanes of the city and bring in the poor and maimed and blind and lame.' The slave said: 'Master, what you ordered has been done, and yet there is room.' The master said to the slave: 'Go out into the roads and hedges and force them to come in so that my house may be filled. For I tell you that not one of those men invited shall taste of my supper.' "[31] His tale needed no further moral.

Crowds still followed him but Jesus was now thoroughly disillusioned. From them he could expect no genuine disciples. To discourage them, he announced: "If any one comes after me, and does not hate his own father and mother and wife and children and brothers and sisters and even his own soul, he cannot be my disciple. For what one of you, wishing to

---

[31]Lk. 14:15–24; Mt. 22:1–10, badly muddled rewriting as apocalyptic.

build a tower, does not first, sitting down, reckon the cost, whether he has enough for completion, that, perchance, having laid a foundation and not being able to complete it, all those seeing him will begin to make sport of him, saying; 'This fellow began to build and was unable to finish'?

"Or what king, going to meet another king in war, will not, sitting down, first take counsel whether he is able with ten thousand to meet in battle the one coming against him with twenty thousand? But if not, while his opponent is far distant, sending an embassy he asks for peace. Thus therefore every one of you who does not renounce all his possessions is not able to be my disciple."[32]

One day, a man called out from the crowd: "Rabbi, order my brother to divide with me the inheritance!" Apparently he was a younger son, not content with his normal third, but demanding the half. Sharply Jesus retorted: "My good fellow, who set up *me* as judge or arbiter over you?" Turning to the crowd, he continued: "Watch and guard yourselves from all covetousness, for man's life is not in any abundance from his possessions."[33]

To illustrate the point came another of the stories: "The ground of a certain rich man bore well. And he debated with himself, saying: 'What shall I do? For I have no place where I can store my fruits. This I will do: I will pull down my storehouses and will build greater, and there I will store all my grain and goods. And I will say to my soul: Soul, you have many things, laid up for many years; take your ease, eat, drink, make merry!'[34] But God said to him: 'Senseless! This night your soul they will demand from you! What have

---

[32]Lk. 14:25 f., 28–33.
[33]Lk. 12:13–15.

[34]*Cf.* Tobit 7:9; Ecclesiasticus 8:15.

you prepared? For whom shall it be?' Thus is he who treasures up riches for himself and not toward God."[35]

Sira's son had long since observed how people thought:

> The rich man labors to gather riches,
>   And when he rests it is to partake of delights.[36]

Actuality was far different. By his obsequiousness the merchant may acquire wealth, but

> One waxes rich through making himself lowly,
>   And this will be the lot of his reward:
> The time he says: "I have found rest,
>   And now will eat from my good things,"
> He knows not what shall be his lot,
>   To others he shall leave it and shall die![37]

Jesus went farther in his teaching: "Whoever seeks to find his life shall lose it, but whoever loses it shall gain it."[38] "For what profits a man to gain the whole world and to forfeit his soul? For what will a man exchange his soul?"[39]

The contrast goes beyond the grave: "A certain man was rich. And he was clothed with purple and byssus, enjoying himself every day sumptuously." As a rich man, he would be a conservative and therefore a Sadducee; he would accordingly take no stock in the new belief, quite unwarranted by anything he could find in the Law of Moses, that the dead were rewarded in any life beyond the grave. "But a certain beggar, Lazar by name," abbreviated from the Biblical Elea-

---

[35]Lk. 12:16–21.
[36]Ecclesiasticus 31:3.
[37]Ecclesiasticus 11:18 f.

[38]Lk. 17:33; 9:24; Mt. 10:39; 16:25; Mk. 8:35; Jn. 12:25.
[39]Mk. 8:36 f.; Mt. 16:26; Lk. 9:25.

zar, "was thrown down at his magnificent gateway." The
term used, *pylon,* brings at once to mind the huge decorated
entrances to Egyptian temples and hints of an origin by the
Nile.

About the time when Jesus was preaching, there was copied
in the current demotic writing of Egypt an ancient tale. It was
attributed to Khamuas, a well-known son of the Pharaoh
Ramses II, who was high priest (*setme*) of the god Ptah of
Memphis. On a time, Setme Khamuas looked down from his
house and beheld two funerals. One was of a rich man; he was
carried out to his grave in the desert necropolis with full pomp
and accompanied by much laudation and wailing. The other
was of a poor man, wrapped only in a mat, and with no
mourners to follow. Setme thought in his heart: "How much
better is the lot of the rich man than of the poor man in
Amenti," the place of the dead. He was terribly perturbed in
his heart when his supremely wise son, Si-Osir, informed
him that his own lot in Amenti would be that of the poor man
and not of the rich.

To convince and console his father, Si-Osir led Setme to
the gate of Te through which they entered Amenti. The high
priest was conducted hall by hall to the seventh, where he
beheld Osiris judging the dead, weighing good deeds against
evil. Close to him, in great honor, stood a man clad in byssus;
Si-Osir informed his father that this was the poor man who
had been carried out from Memphis wrapped only in a mat.
Justified before Osiris, the poor man had been granted the
elaborate funeral outfit of the rich, who, requited for the
excess of his evil deeds, had been punished. Setme had already seen him, though without recognition; he was the man
in the fifth hall the bolt of whose door was fixed in his eye

while he made prayer and great lamentation. Setme returned to earth grieving, for to no mortal could he reveal what he had seen.[40]

The story travelled to Palestine. In Ascalon, not far beyond the Egyptian border, it assumed this form: Two men were students together. One died and no one accompanied his corpse to the grave. The other died, the son of a tax collector, and the whole city formed his cortege. A dream showed their fates reversed. One abode in a garden, under the trees and by the springs; the son of the tax collector lay with his tongue close to the water which he could not reach.[41]

On the lips of Jesus, the tale assumed new meaning: Lazar "was full of ulcers. And he would have been glad to be fed by the droppings from the rich man's table. Even the dogs came and licked his ulcers.

"And it came to pass that the beggar died. And he was carried away by angels to Abraham's bosom. The rich man also died. And he was given formal burial.

"And in Sheol, lifting up his eyes and being in torture continually, he sees Abraham far away and Lazar in his bosom." In the thought of the time, one of the rewards of the righteous was the opportunity to gloat over the sufferings of the no longer fortunate wicked.[42] "And he shouted: 'Father Abraham, pity me! Send Lazar that he may dip his finger tip in water and cool my tongue, for I suffer anguish in this flame!' But Abraham said: 'Child, remember that you received in full your good things in your life and Lazar equally the evil. But now *here* he is comforted and you are in torture. And in addition to all this, between us and you a great chasm

---

[40]F. L. Griffith, *Stories of the High Priests of Memphis*, 1900, 44 ff.

[41]Jerusalem Talmud, Haggiga II, 77d, 38; Sanhedrin VI, 23c, 26.
[42]*Cf.* Enoch 62:11 f.

has been established, so that those wishing to cross from here to you are not able, nor you to cross from here to us.'

"The rich man said: 'I beg you, therefore, father, to send him to my father's house, for I have five brothers, that he may testify to them lest they too come into this place of torture.' But Abraham says: 'They have Moses and the Prophets; let them hear *them!*' But he says: 'No, Father Abraham! If only one should go to them from the dead, they would repent.' But he said to them: 'If they do not listen to Moses and the Prophets, not even if one rises from the dead will they be persuaded.' "[43]

The moral was perfectly clear to the hearers. The poor would rejoice in the promise of a happier life in the world to come. The well-to-do would be offended. As Sadducees, they did not accept the testimony of the Prophets. Had a man appeared with the claim that he was risen from the dead, he would have been denounced as an impostor. At the best, his appearance would have been explained away as a lying vision. As for rewards to the righteous in the after world, such a belief might be condoned as useful in keeping the populace quiet in this one certain life. But such preaching by a wandering prophet might become dangerous; there was one more reason why Jesus should be suppressed.

---

[43]Lk. 16:19–31.

CHAPTER IX

UNRIGHTEOUS SCRIBES

SCRIBE, in every language of every land in the Near East, always bears the primary meaning of "secretary," whether applied to the all powerful Secretary of State or to the humblest member of the official hierarchy. So long as a Jewish "nation" existed in any form, scribe would continue to retain this meaning. Ezra as a "scribe of the Law" and therefore a religious teacher, was the exception. The scribes of Jesus' time were not teachers; the Pharisees were just beginning to realize the possibilities of the teacher's influence.

Contemporary high priests were neither religious teachers nor religious leaders. Supervision of the temple ritual was a minor part of their functions. Their true importance lay in the fact that they were the administrative heads of the Jewish "nation." For this reason alone vassal princes or Roman procurators kept tight in their own hands the right of appointment and dismissal, and frequently exercised this prerogative. As administrative heads, the high priests employed their own staff of scribes. Of these, the great majority attended to the finance and other routine business permitted to the "nation"; relatively few were "lawyers," and their duty was to establish precedents for the courts, themselves a division of the administrative system.

Since all the scribes were dependents of the high priests, it went without saying that they were all members of the Sadducean sect, which to the pious meant that they were without religion. Only after the collapse of the aristocracy through the revolution of 66 A.D. and the destruction of the "nation" four years later, was this scribal hierarchy wiped out and the term scribe applied in the sense of Ezra to the spiritual leaders of the new Pharisaic orthodoxy. It should be obvious that we shall look in vain for the decisions of the Sadducean scribes in the Mishna collected soon after by their bitter opponents, the deeply religious Pharisees.[1]

Not only was this scribal hierarchy irreligious from the viewpoint of the pious, they were hated by the common people and loathed by the intelligent and thoughtful. Josephus the historian cites example after example of the scandalous character of the high priests, their insolence and search for unrighteous gain. As a single instance, when Ishmael, son of Phabi, was made high priest by Agrippa, not long before the great revolt, the high priests and the city leaders were at open war. Each side was assisted by gangsters. Murder had become a political weapon. Nor did the common people escape. The high priests actually went so far as to send their slaves to the peasants' threshing floors and seized the tithes assigned to the local priests, many of whom in consequence died of starvation.[2]

That in these vicious practices the high priests and their hangers on were only following earlier precedents is amply borne out by a popular squib preserved in the Talmud. It is

---

[1] It cannot be too emphatically insisted that all the passages where Pharisees are bracketed with scribes, high priests, Herodians, or other opponents of Jesus, are interpolations. Often they break the sense, sometimes the result is sheer nonsense. In no case is the accusation appropriate to the Pharisees, who, whatever their shortcomings, were not addicted to the special type of sin charged by Jesus against the scribes, in fact, the Pharisees did not have the opportunity! The author of our first Gospel, though himself a Jew, is definitely anti-Semitic; the Pharisees are included in his sweeping though irregularly added condemnation. From him, later copyists appear to have taken the "Pharisees" for the interpolations dropped hit-or-miss here and there.

[2] Joseph. *Ant.* xx, 179 ff.

directed against the principal high priestly families who between them were looting and ruining the nation. Apparently it was composed and sung during the high priesthood of this same Ishmael, son of Phabi; among the other families condemned are those of Boëthus, whose name was often applied by the Jewish Fathers to the Sadducees, of Annas, primarily responsible for Jesus' crucifixion, and of Cantharas, who ruled in apostolic times:

> Woe to me from the house of Baitos!
> Woe from their clubs!
> Woe to me from the house of Hanan!
> Woe from their whispers!
> Woe to me from the house of Qathros!
> Woe from their pens!
> Woe to me from the house of Ishmael!
> Woe from their fists!
> They are high priests and their sons treasurers,
> Their sons-in-law overseers, and their slaves beat
> the people![3]

Decades earlier, Jesus had presented exactly the same picture: "On the throne of Moses sit the scribes"; the original word was *qatedra,* a transliteration of the Greek *kathedra.* The term was used for the throne of Moses himself,[4] for the chair of the wise man[5] as for the "throne" of the Greek philosopher, and for the seats of the members of the Sanhedrin at Alexandria.[6] Such a "throne" of an elder, in basalt and with an Aramaic inscription, has been found in the

---

[3]Babylonian Talmud, Pesahim 57a.

[4]Exodus Rabba 43:5 (Horeb edition).

[5]Lamentations Rabba under verse 2:10.

[6]Jerusalem Talmud, Sukkot 55a; Babylonian Talmud, Sukkot 51b; Tosephta, Sukkot 4:6.

ruins of a synagogue at Chorazin.[7] "All therefore which they bid you, perform and observe. But their *works* do not, for they talk but do not perform.[8] For I tell you: Unless *your* righteousness shall excel that of the scribes, you shall not at all enter into the Kingdom of the "Heavens."[9]

From their fruits you shall know them:

Do they gather grapes from thorns,
    Or from thistles figs?
So every good tree makes good fruits,
    But the rotten tree makes bad fruits.
A good tree is not able to bear bad fruits,
    Nor a rotten tree to make good fruits.
Every tree not making good fruit
    Is cut down and thrown into the fire![10]

Either make the tree good and its fruit good,
    Or make the tree rotten and its fruit rotten,
        For from the fruit the tree is known.
Offspring of vipers,
    How are you able to speak good things,
        Evil as you are!
The good man from his heart's good treasure brings out good,
    And the wicked man from the wicked brings out
        wickedness,
        For from the heart's abundance the mouth speaks.[11]

There can be no question as to which group belong the scribes: "They bind heavy burdens and lay them upon the

---

[7] J. Ory, *Quarterly Statement, Palestine Exploration Fund*, 1927, 51 f.

[8] Mt. 23:2 f.

[9] Mt. 5:20.

[10] Mt. 7:16-19.

[11] Mt. 12:33-35; Lk. 6:43-45; Jas. 3:12; *cf.* Mt. 3:7 f., 10; Lk. 3:7-9. In considerable part, Jesus is quoting John the Baptist.

shoulders of men; but they themselves will not move them with their finger." The burdens are literal; the scribes enforce the taxes. The taxes are heavy but it would be too much to expect a bureaucracy to participate in their payment. Jesus might well have had in mind the opposition of the hierarchy to the use of the temple treasure in lightening the heavy taxation for the new water supply.

Their exactions might appear slightly less intolerable were they not accompanied by ridiculous exhibitions of ostentatious self-righteousness: "All their works they do to be seen by men. For they make broad their amulets." Pious Jews bound on their brow and arms *tephilim*, little boxes containing precious extracts from God's Law, which they wore to show forth their love and reverence; the oversized boxes employed by these scribes were not genuine *tephilim*, in bitter punning they have become nothing but *totephoth*, pagan charms![12] "And they extend the fringes" of their prayer shawls to appear more impressive. "But they love the chief places at the festivals, and the first thrones in the synagogue"; here they would sit with their backs to God's Holy Temple and to the ark which enshrined His own Law in order to face the congregation so that their honorable estate might be recognized. They love "also the salutations in the bazaars and to be called by men 'Rabbi.' "[13]

Some years before the public ministry of Jesus, the "lawyers" among these scribes had compiled a new law code; it was in the sacred language, Hebrew, and was called the Book of Decrees. Naturally it represented the Sadducean ideal of strict and literal interpretation. It was laid before the San-

---

[12] I owe the suggestion to Rabbi George Fox. Years ago I purchased in Jerusalem such an oversized box; according to Rabbi Fox: "It is much the largest I have ever seen."

[13] Mt. 23:4-7; Mk. 12:38 f.; Lk. 20:46; 11:46, 43.

hedrin for discussion; passage was certain, for the hierarchy was in the majority. The Pharisaic minority protested.

One of the laws bore the heading: "These are those who are stoned; those who are burned; those who are slain; and those who are strangled." A Pharisee demanded the basis for their judgement. The Sadducees could only point to the book itself. He retorted: "From where in the Law do you find the proof that this one is guilty of punishment by stoning, this one by burning, this one by slaying, and this one by strangling?" They did not know how to bring a proof from the Law. The wise men, the Pharisees, said to them: "Is it not written: 'According to the Law which they shall teach you'?[14] And this teaches that they should not write any laws in a *book!*" The Pharisees declare that the Law of Moses is the only written law which is authoritative, all expansion or development for legal purposes in a court of law must be oral, and of course from their own mouths. But their protest was ineffective, for they were in the minority.

Other quotations come from this Book of Decrees. The Disciples of Baitos (Boëthus), another name for the Sadducees, used to say: " 'Eye instead of eye; tooth instead of tooth.'[15] If a man knocked out the tooth of his companion, he knocks out that man's tooth; if he blinded the eye of his companion, he shall blind his eye. They shall be equally alike." To the Pharisees, this was barbarous revenge. As an example of slander, the Book of Decrees took the case of the bride falsely accused by her new husband of previous unchastity: " 'And they shall spread the cloth before the elders of the city'[16]; the words are as they are written," they must be taken literally according to the Sadducees. Another decree dealt

---

[14]Deut. 17:11.   [16]Deut. 22:17.
[15]Exod. 21:24; Deut. 19:21.

with the man who refused to carry out the duty of marrying his deceased brother's wife to raise up to him seed: " 'She shall spit in his face.' "[17] The Mosaic prescription is to be literally retained; the Pharisees were satisfied if she spat on the ground before him.

The wise men said to the Sadducees: "Is it not written: 'The Law and the Commandments which I wrote to teach them?'[18] This means: The Law which I wrote and the Commandments to teach them. And it is written in another place: 'And now write for yourselves this song and teach it to the Sons of Israel and put it in their mouths.'[19] 'Teach it to the Sons of Israel' means the scriptures; 'put it in their mouths,' these are the Halakot."

Pharisaic instinct was right, the laws ascribed to Moses were relics of a barbarous age, and must be mitigated to fit the conditions of a more civilized era. The Pharisees, however, were wrong in their exegesis, and it made no impression on the hierarchy, to whose advantage it was that the laws should continue harsh. The Book of Decrees remained in force thirty-six years after Jesus' death. Only in the Great Reform of A.D. 66 were they formally abrogated amid popular rejoicing; the day of their abolition was henceforth kept as a holiday when fasting and mourning were out of place. Throughout the succeeding centuries, the Law of Moses has been interpreted according to the more kindly Pharisaic principles.[20]

---

[17]Deut. 25:9.
[18]Exod. 24:12.
[19]Deut. 31:19.
[20]The Book of Decrees was in all probability deliberately destroyed in 66 A.D. The date of its abrogation is given in the Aramaic "Book of Fasts," compiled at this time, cf. Solomon Zeitlin, *Megillat Taanit*, 1922; Hans Lichtenstein, "Die Fa-

stenrolle," *Hebrew Union College Annual*, VIII–IX, 1931–32, 295 ff. The scattered Talmudical references to explain this passage were early brought together in scholia to this tractate, and are edited by Lichtenstein in the cited article. From this they have been translated by A. T. Olmstead, *Journal of Near Eastern Studies*, I, 1942, 53 f.

No more than his fellow Jews did Jesus dream of abrogating the Law of Moses. In the one preserved fragment of an original Aramaic Gospel, Jesus makes his attitude toward the Law perfectly clear:

> I did not come to take away from the Law of Moses,
> But rather I came to add to the Law of Moses.[21]

As a loyal Jew, he could not deny that the Law had come through Moses from God Himself. He was sympathetic to the Pharisees, and it is quite in the Pharisaic manner that Jesus contrasts his own teaching with that of the Sadducean Book of Decrees. But he himself had been called of God as a prophet; accordingly he possessed the right to make public God's latest messages. He begins with what Moses said to the Israelites, then the too literal Sadducean interpretation, finally his own exposition; while the Pharisees must distort the plain letter of the Law to liberalize the strict scribal decisions, Jesus treats the Law as only the first step in a development which culminates in his own commands, backed only by his prophet's authority. But Jesus is no legist, he is not interested in the law as such; it is therefore no cause for surprise that from the purely moral standpoint his interpretations are even more strict. But it is just in what Jesus *added* to the Law of Moses that we must seek his true greatness.

"You have heard that it was said to those before: 'Do not kill'; then 'Whoever kills is liable to the punishment.' But *I* tell you: Everyone angered at his brother shall be liable to the divine punishment.

"Furthermore: 'Whoever shall say to his brother "Raqqa," ' " a term of abuse and so slanderous, " 'shall be accountable to the Sanhedrin.' " This cannot be the great

---

[21]Babylonian Talmud, Shabbat 116b; *cf.* Mt. 5:17.

national court but the local Sanhedrin, which in later times consisted of thirteen members and was established in every village of over 120 souls.[22] "But whoever shall say 'More' " —meaning Fool—"shall be liable to be thrown into the Gehenna of the Fire."

"If therefore you are offering your gift upon the incense altar"—Jesus is speaking in Jerusalem, perhaps the altar is in sight—"and there you remember that your brother has something against you, leave there your gift before the incense altar and go away; first be reconciled with your brother and then come and offer your gift."[23]

"You have heard that it was said: 'Do not commit adultery.' But I tell you: Everyone looking upon a woman with desire for her has already committed adultery with her in his heart."[24]

"But it was said: 'Whoever would divorce his wife, let him give her a writ of divorce.' But I tell you: Everyone divorcing his wife makes her an adulteress."[25]

Did this mean that divorce was illegal under any possible condition? The case of Herodias and Antipas still was being debated; if Jesus answered in the affirmative, he might become embroiled with the tetrarch. Point-blank he was asked: "Is it lawful for a man to divorce his wife?"

Jesus' reply again invoked scripture: "Have you not read that the Creator from the beginning 'male and female made them'? He said: 'For this reason a man shall leave his father and his mother and shall cling to his wife and they two shall be one flesh.' So then they are no longer two but instead are

---

[22]Joseph. *Ant.* iv, 214 ff.; Mishna, Sanhedrin, i, 4, 6; *cf.* Mt. 10:17; Mk. 13:9.
[23]Mt. 5:21-24.
[24]Mt. 5:27 f.; *cf. Testaments of the Twelve Patriarchs,* Benjamin

8:2: "He who has a pure mind in love does not look upon a woman for fornication."
[25]Mt. 5:31 f.; *cf.* 19:9; Mk. 10:11 f.; Lk. 16:18.

one flesh. What therefore God has joined together let no one separate!"

"Why then," his hearers inquired, "did Moses command to 'give a writ of divorcing' and to divorce?" Answer was not difficult: "Moses for your hardness of heart permitted you to divorce your wives, but from the beginning it was not so!"[26] From the harsh Mosaic Law Jesus appeals to the law of nature promulgated at the very time of creation. Of more immediate importance, he had avoided the trap; unlike John the Baptist, Jesus could not be accused of *maiestas* before Antipas.

Jewish practice allowed such oaths as "By the Temple"; "By the Temple service"; "By Jerusalem"; "By Heaven and earth"; "By the life of your head";[27] not so Jesus. "You have heard that it was said to those before: 'Do not swear falsely,' but 'Pay to the Lord your oath.' But *I* tell you: Do not swear at all, neither by the heaven, because 'it is the throne of God,' nor by the earth, because it is the 'footstool of his feet,' nor toward Jerusalem, because it is 'the city of the great King,' neither shall you swear by your head, because you cannot make one hair white or black. Let your 'Yes' be 'Yes' and your 'No' be 'No.' And whatever is more than these is from the Evil One."[28]

"You have heard that it was said: 'Eye in place of eye' and 'Tooth in place of tooth.'" The Book of Decrees still enforces the Mosaic Law in its most literal form. "But *I* tell you: Do not resist the Evil One. Rather, whoever strikes you on the jaw, turn to him also the other side. Whoever wishes

---

[26]Mt. 19:3–8; Mk. 10:2–9; quoted as an ordinance of the Lord, I Cor. 7:10 f., 25.
[27]Mishna, Nedarim 1:3; Shebuoth 2:9; 4:13; Sanhedrin 3:2; Babylonian Talmud, Taanith 24a; Tosephta, Nedarim, 1:3.
[28]Mt. 5:33–37; Jas. 5:12; *cf.* II Enoch 49:1; Ruth Rabba, under verse 3:18.

to go to law against you and would take your tunic, let him
have also the cloak. And whoever would impress you" on
government business "to go with him one mile, go with him
yet another two. To him who begs from you, give, and from
him who wishes to borrow from you turn not away."[29]

"You have heard that it was said: 'Love your neighbor'
and 'Hate your enemy.' But *I* tell you: Love your enemies,
do good to those hating you, bless those cursing you, pray for
those mistreating you,[30] so that you may become sons of your
Father in the Heavens. For *He* makes his sun rise upon the
wicked and the good, and rains upon the righteous and the
unrighteous. For if you love those loving you, what pay do
you have? Do not even the tax collectors the same? And if
you salute your brothers only, what more do you do? Do not
even the Gentiles the same?"

Every one of his auditors had listened to the recitation of
the Aramaic Targum after each verse of the Law was read
in the synagogue service. They would remember how before
the verse: "Whether it is cow or ewe, you shall not kill both
it and its young on the same day" the interpreter would pre-
fix the explanation: "My people, sons of Israel, as I am
merciful in heaven so shall you be merciful on earth."[31] To
their memories of this gracious saying, through constant
repetition in the synagogue become almost a part of scripture, Jesus appeals when he closes this section of his dis-
course: "*You* therefore be merciful as your Father in the
Heavens is merciful."[32]

"Love your enemies." Almost we are prepared to assert

[29]Mt. 5:38–42; Lk. 6:29 f.   [32]Mt. 5:43–48; Lk. 6:31–36; Jas.
[30]So Lk. 6:27 f.   1:3 f.
[31]Lev. 22:28; Jerusalem Talmud,
Berakot 9c; Megilla 75c.

that this is the finest of Jesus' sayings. But another still finer is to come.

"What is hateful to you do not to another," said Tobit to his son Tobias.[33] The saying is repeated in slightly modified form in a story told by the rabbis. Shammai and Hillel were the two great rival teachers of Pharisaic doctrine in Jesus' boyhood; Shammai was the stricter and less accommodating, Hillel pointed the way to the kindlier Pharisaism of later generations. "A stranger came before Shammai and said to him: 'Make me a proselyte on condition that you teach me the whole Law while I am standing on one foot.' Shammai pushed him away with the measuring rod in his hand. The stranger said the same before Hillel, who made him a proselyte; he said to him: 'What is hateful to you, do not to your comrade. This is the whole Law and the remainder is commentary.' "[34] The story is in Hebrew, only Hillel's saying has retained its original Aramaic form.

The saying of the unknown author of Tobit, slightly revised by the great Pharisaic teacher, deserves all the praise lavished upon it. But when all is said, the fact remains that the command is negative. Jesus made the command positive:

> All that you wish men to do to you,
> So also do *you* to them,
> For *this* is the Law and the Prophets.[35]

Once again Jesus turns to what was so dear to his heart, almsgiving: "Take care that you do not your 'righteousness' before men, to be seen by them; if you do, you have no payment with your Father in the Heavens. When therefore *you*

---

[33]Tobit 4:15.
[34]Babylonian Talmud, Shabbat 31a.

[35]Mt. 7:12; Lk. 6:31.

do alms, do not trumpet it before you, just as the hypocrites do in the synagogues and on the streets, that they may
be glorified by men. In truth I tell you: They have received
their pay. But *you,* in doing alms, do not let your left hand
know what your right is doing, in order that *your* alms may
be in the Secret Place. And your Father, watching in the
Secret Place, will reward you in the open."[36]

"When *you* pray, do not be like the hypocrites. For *they*
love to pray standing in the synagogues and on the corners
of the open squares that they may be seen by men. In truth
I tell you: They have their pay. But when *you* pray, 'enter
into the chamber and shutting the door,' pray to your Father
who is in the Secret Place, and your Father, watching you
from the Secret Place, will reward you in the open. But in
praying, do not talk idle words like the Gentiles, for they
think they will be heard for their wordiness. Be not therefore like them, for your Father knows what you need before
you ask him."[37]

"But when *you* fast, do not become like the hypocrites, sad
of look. For *they* make invisible their faces[38] in order that
they may be seen by men to be fasting. In truth I tell you:
They have received their pay. But *you,* in fasting, anoint
your head and wash your face, in order that you may not be
seen by men to be fasting, but rather by your Father who
is in the Secret Place. And your Father, watching from the
Secret Place, will reward you in the open."[39]

"But why do you notice the speck of dried straw in your
brother's eye, but the beam in your own eye you do not recognize? Or how can you say to your brother: 'Allow me to

---

[36]Mt. 6:1–4; *cf.* Babylonian Talmud, Sotah 9a: God sitting in the
Secret Place will punish openly the
woman sinning in secret.

[37]Mt. 6:5–8.
[38]So *Testaments of the Twelve
Patriarchs,* Zebulon 8:6.
[39]Mt. 6:16–18.

pluck out the speck of dried straw from *your* eye'? And look
at the beam in your *own* eye! Hypocrite! Pluck out first from
your own eye the *beam,* and then, seeing clearly, pluck out
the *speck* from your brother's eye."[40]

Judge not that you be not judged,
   Condemn not, that you be not condemned;
Release, and you shall be released,
   Give, and it shall be given to you:
Good measure, pressed down, shaken together,
   Running over, shall they give into your bosom;
For with what judgement you judge shall you be judged,
   And with what measure you measure shall it be measured
      to you.[41]

No doubt many in the crowd were hangers-on of the hierarchy. To them Jesus now addressed himself directly: "But
woe to you scribes, hypocrites, because you shut the Kingdom
of the Heavens before the face of men. For *you* will not
enter in nor will you permit those trying to enter in to
enter."[42] Jesus is preaching the Kingdom, the hierarchy is
doing its best to discredit his teaching.

In view of the known rapacity of the hierarchy, he was
quite justified in pronouncing the next woe: "Woe to you
scribes, hypocrites, because you eat up widows' houses, even
while in pretense you make long prayers; therefore you shall
receive the greater condemnation."[43] His auditors would
realize that Jesus was prophesying the condemnation of these
sinners to Gehenna's fires.

"Woe to you scribes, hypocrites, because you go about the
sea and the dry land to make one convert. And when he has

---

[40]Mt. 7:3-5.
[41]Lk. 6:37 f.; Mt. 7:1 f.; in part,
Mk. 4:24.
[42]Mt. 23:13; Lk. 11:52.
[43]Mt. 23:14; Mk. 12:40.

become one of you, you make him twice again more a son of the Gehenna than yourselves!"[44] Could Jesus be referring to a notorious incident which had rocked the Jewish community at Rome ten years before? Perhaps he was not, at least it is worth repeating in this connection.

Many highborn Roman women had been converted and openly were recognized as Jewish proselytes. Among them was the lady Fulvia. She became acquainted with four of her new coreligionists. Their leader professed to be "an exegete in the Law of Moses"; actually he had left home in flight from an accusation of a serious crime. In her enthusiasm for her recently adopted religion, Fulvia was easily persuaded to make a generous donation of purple and gold for the Jerusalem Temple.

Fulvia's husband Saturninus became suspicious and complained to Tiberius. By the emperor's orders, an investigation was opened, and it was discovered that the four had retained the gift for their own use. Unfortunately for the Jewish colony at Rome, the discovery followed immediately after discovery of an even worse oriental scandal through which another Saturninus had been wronged still more terribly. The wife of this Saturninus, Paulina, was also a devout proselyte, but of Egyptian Isis; through bribery of the native priests, a Roman lover dressed as the jackal god Anubis had intercourse with the unsuspecting Paulina. She boasted of the god's favor, the lover boasted to her of the deception.

Terrible was the emperor's wrath. The priests were crucified, the temple was razed, the statue of the goddess was hurled into the Tiber. Then the Jewish scandal broke. The whole Jewish community was banished from Rome. Those Jews, four thousand in number, who possessed the lesser

---

[44]Mt. 23:15.

Latin citizenship, were promptly enrolled in the legions and sent into a worse banishment in unhealthy Sardinia. Those who refused to serve under the idolatrous standards because of religious scruples were executed.[45]

Could the recollection of the gold wrongly diverted from its rightful destination have turned Jesus' thoughts to the Temple gold? At any rate, he continued: "Woe to you blind guides, who are saying: 'Whoever shall swear by the Temple, it is nothing; but whoever shall swear by the gold on the Temple, he is bound by his oath.' Fools and blind! For which is the greater, the gold or the Temple which makes holy the gold? And 'whoever shall swear by the incense altar, it is nothing; but whoever shall swear by the gift upon it, he is bound by his oath.' Blind! For which is greater, the gift or the incense altar which makes holy the gift?

"He therefore who swears by the altar, swears by it and by everything upon it. And he who swears by the temple swears by it and by Him who is dwelling within it. And he who is swearing by heaven swears by the throne of God and by Him who is sitting upon it.[46]

"Woe to you scribes, hypocrites, because you tithe the mint and the dill and the cummin, and have left undone the weightier things of the Law, the justice and the pity and the faithfulness. But these you ought to have done and not left the other undone. Blind road guides, straining out the louse (*qalma*) but the camel (*gamla*) swallowing down.[47] Leave them alone! They are blind guides! And if blind guides blind both shall fall into a pit.[48]

"Woe to you scribes, hypocrites, because you cleanse the

---

[45]Joseph. *Ant.* xviii, 65 ff.; Suetonius, *Tiberius* 36.
[46]Mt. 23:16–22.

[47]Mt. 23:23 f.; Lk. 11:42.
[48]Mt. 15:14; Lk. 6:39.

outside of the cup and of the platter, but within they are full of extortion and of excess. Blind! First cleanse the inside of the cup and of the platter, so that the outside may also become clean.[49]

"Woe to you scribes, hypocrites, because you are like whitewashed tombs, which outwardly appear beautiful, but within are full of the bones of dead men and of all uncleanness. Thus also *you* appear to men righteous, but within you are full of hypocrisy and lawlessness.[50]

"Woe to you scribes, hypocrites, because you build the tombs of the prophets and adorn the memorials of the righteous. And you say: 'If *we* had been in the days of our fathers, *we* would not have been partners with them in the blood of the prophets.' So you witness against yourselves, because you *are* the sons of those murdering the prophets. And *you* bring to completion the measure of your fathers. Serpents, offspring of vipers! How can *you* flee from the judgement of the Gehenna?"[51]

These sayings Jesus spoke in the treasury, teaching in the Temple. So bitterly anti-hierarchical were they that we are not surprised that the high-priestly adherents took up therefore stones to throw at him. Jesus must hide himself and slip out of the Temple. John repeatedly expresses his wonder that his Master was not arrested; he can explain only it by saying that Jesus' time had not yet come.[52] Jesus himself lamented: "Jerusalem! Jerusalem! Who kills the prophets and stones those sent her! How oft have I longed to gather your sons, like a bird gathering her brood under her wings—and you would not!"[53]

---

[49] Mt. 23 :25 f.; Lk. 11 :39 f.
[50] Mt. 23 :27 f.; Lk. 11 :44.
[51] Mt. 23 :29–33; Lk. 11 :47 f.

[52] Jn. 8 :20, 59.
[53] Mt. 23 :37; Lk. 13 :34.

What followed Jesus' flight from the Temple we cannot learn from the mutilated extracts from John's narrative. One single episôde is elsewhere preserved. On leaving the city, Jesus descended into the Kidron gorge and climbed up the steep opposite slope past the garden of Gethsemane and the groves which gave their name to the Mount of Olives. Just over the crest, on the saddle before the steep breakdown over barren wastes to the Jordan and Dead Sea, lay Bethany, two miles from Jerusalem. Here the escaping prophet found hospitality with a certain Martha, whose brother Lazar was apparently still in Jerusalem awaiting the end of the feast.

Martha's sister Mary spent all her time sitting at Jesus' feet and listening to his conversation. To Martha, this was pure selfishness; worried about preparations for the coming meal, she demanded: "Master, don't you care whether my sister has left me to do the serving alone? Order her therefore to assist me!" Jesus answered: "Martha, Martha, why are you worried? Mary has chosen the better part which shall not be taken away from her. For few things are necessary for the dinner; even one single course will be enough." Martha must learn that food is relatively unessential; what is truly important is to learn and do the will of God.[54]

How Jesus returned home to Galilee we do not know. We hear next of scribes, come down from Jerusalem, who complain: "Why do *your* disciples not walk according to the traditions of the elders, but instead with defiled hands eat the loaf?" They had followed Jesus from Jerusalem only to make trouble; the question was not honest. Jesus counterattacks: *"You* reject the command of *God* to keep the traditions of *men,"* for there was indeed no scriptural basis for the custom of washing ceremonially before meals. There was

---

[54]Lk. 10:38–42; *cf.* Jn. 11:1.

in truth a much worse example of how they had followed the precedents of men in flat disobedience to the direct commands of God.

Certain shrewd Jews had made with the official scribes a deal by which they might defraud their own parents and avoid the necessity of affording them financial support by the device of a legal fiction, dedication of their property to the Temple. "Moses said: 'Honor your father and your mother' and 'He who speaks evil of father or mother, let him die the death.' But *you* say: 'If a man shall say to his father or his mother: "Korban [dedicated] is what should have been owed you by me" '—you no longer permit him to do anything for his father or for his mother, making of no account the word of God by your tradition which you handed down. And many similar things you do." Returning to the original charge, Jesus concluded: "Nothing outside the man, entering into him, is able to defile him; rather, what is going out from the man is what defiles the man."[55]

---

[55]Mt. 15:1-6, 11; Mk. 7:1, 5, 8-13, 15; quoted, Rom. 14:14.

CHAPTER X

RESPITE

EARLY in December, Jesus set his face toward Jerusalem. He was leaving Galilee for the last time, never again would he behold his native country. In addition to the Twelve, he was accompanied by a number of women whom he had healed of disease or from whom he had expelled evil spirits; among them was Mary of Magdala, from whom he had driven out seven demons, Johanna, wife of Herod Antipas' steward, and Susanna. In gratitude for their cure, they provided from their own means the simple food required by the Master and his disciples.[1]

From this time onward, the women were in constant attendance on Jesus. They stood at the cross, they watched the entombment, they were witnesses to his resurrection.[2] Mary, Jesus' mother, was also with them, for she too was at the cross.[3] The disciples were not entirely dependent on the women for their living expenses, since Judas Iscariot, as treasurer of the little company, carried a box into which the pious cast their alms.[4]

With anxious hearts, the pilgrims slipped away from dangerous Galilee and descended to the Great Plain, intending to follow the direct path along the spine of the ridge to the Holy City. They had just crossed the frontier between Galilee and Samaria and were entering one of the hamlets on the plain when there met them ten lepers, who stood afar off and

---

[1]Lk. 8 :2 f.; Mk. 16 :9 f.
[2]Mk. 15 :40 f.; 16 :1; Mt. 27 :47, 55 f.; 28 :1; Lk. 23 :49, 55; 24 :10.
[3]Jn. 19 :25.
[4]Jn. 12 :6.

lifted up their voices, calling out: "Jesus! Master! Pity us!" As soon as they heard the order: "Show yourselves to the priests," they hurried off and were cleansed on the way. One of them, seeing that he was healed, turned back, with a loud voice glorifying God. He was a Samaritan; Jesus asked in surprise: "Were there not ten cleansed? Where are the nine? Were none to be found returning to give glory to God except this alien?" The man was encouraged: "Arise and go! Your faith has saved you!"[5] There must be an element of truth in the narrative. It cannot have been all invented, it is in such complete contrast to what followed.

On his way, Jesus had sent forward before his face messengers to make ready for him in a larger village. When he entered this Samaritan village, he was refused lodging because his face was going up to Jerusalem. Topography and village temperament alike suggest this was En Gannim, "Fount of Gardens," in its pretty little nook at the southeast corner of the Great Plain, and dominating the entrance to the main north-south road through Samaria. A score of years later, the inhabitants of Ginæ, by the murder of a Galilæan pilgrim, were to start a civil war which resulted in Jewish extermination of numerous Samaritan villages.[6] Their successors, in the modern Jenin, have become notorious for their anti-foreign excesses. No wonder those "Sons of Thunder," James and John, angrily demanded permission to inflict proper punishment: "Master, do you wish us to command fire to come down from heaven and consume them?" Jesus rebuked them: "You do not realize of what kind of spirit you are! For I did not come to destroy men's lives but to save them."[7]

---

[5]Lk. 17:11–19; later form, Mk. 1:40–45; Mt. 8:2–4; Lk. 5:12–14.

[6]Joseph. *Wars* ii, 232; iii, 48; *Ant.* xx, 118.
[7]Lk. 9:51–56.

On this last journey to Jerusalem, Jesus definitely discouraged converts. To one who said: "Rabbi, I will follow you wherever you go," he answered: "For foxes there are holes and for birds of the heavens nests, but for a son of man there is no place where he may lay his head." To his command: "Follow me!" another replied: "Master, allow me first to go and bury my father." Bluntly Jesus answered him: "Follow me! Leave the dead to bury their own dead, but you go and make known the Kingdom of God." To a third who promised: "I will follow you, Master, but first permit me to bid farewell to those in my house," Jesus announced: "Who puts hand to plow and looks back is not fit for the Kingdom of God."[8]

Another time, as Jesus was going out into the road, a young man came running up and knelt before him, asking: "Good Rabbi, what shall I do to inherit the life of the coming Age?" Jesus objected: "Why do you call me good? None is good except one, God! You know the commandments: 'Do not kill! Do not commit adultery! Do not steal! Do not witness falsely! Do not defraud! Honor your father and your mother!'" Proudly the young man answered: "Rabbi, all these things have I guarded from my youth." Jesus, looking at him, loved him and said: "One thing you lack; go, sell whatever you have, and give to the poor. You shall have treasure in heaven. Come, follow me!" But the young man's countenance fell at the saying, and he went off sorrowful, for he had great possessions.[9]

Jesus commented to his disciples: "Children, how difficult is it for those having riches to enter into the Kingdom of God! It is easier for a camel to pass through the eye of a

---

[8]Lk. 9:57-62; Mt. 8:18-22.   [9]Mk. 10:17-22; Mt. 19:16-22; Lk. 18:18-23.

needle than for a rich man to enter into the Kingdom of God." Surprised, they inquired: "Who, then, can be saved?" Jesus replied: "With men, impossible, but not with God; for all things are possible with God!"[10]

The Holy City was reached at Hanukka, the Feast of Lights, celebrated by the Jerusalemites in commemoration of the rededication of the Temple by Judah the Maccabee on December 24, 165 B.C. It was winter, for Hanukka began Chislev 25, in this year 29 A.D., December 21. Jesus was walking about in Solomon's Colonnade, along the east side of the Temple, overlooking the Kidron Gorge and with a fine view up the Mount of Olives. In remembrance of this visit, his disciples later were to make it their own place of preaching.[11]

The Judæans, representatives of the hierarchy, surrounded him and demanded: "How long will you keep in suspense our minds? If you are the Messiah, tell us plainly!" Their attitude was so hostile that Jesus could only repeat: "I told you and you did not believe; the works which I am doing testify for me." This reply deliberately sidestepped the direct question, but what more could Jesus say? It did make perfectly clear that Jesus considered himself a prophet sent by God; it might be twisted to mean that he claimed to be the Messiah.

This was the sense in which his opponents pretended to take it. Once again the Judæans took up stones to stone him. Jesus protested: "Many gracious works have I shown you; on account of which of these works àre you going to stone me?" Back they shouted: "For a gracious work we are not going to stone you"—they could safely admit he had performed wonders—"but for blasphemy!" Stoning was the legal

---

[10]Mk. 10:23-27; Mt. 19:23-26;   [11]Acts 3:11.
Lk. 18:24-27.

punishment for blasphemy, but the charge must be legally proved and before the proper legal authorities. Had Jesus been killed at this moment, it would have been an outrageous example of lynch law without the slightest pretense of legality. To have claimed that it was a formal execution for the religious crime of blasphemy would only have made matters worse. Whatever the expectations of the pilgrims, many of whom would still support him, Jesus himself had never openly announced himself as the Messiah, and the charge would be difficult to prove. There was real danger of exciting pilgrim riots in retaliation.

Much more serious, blasphemy was not a crime according to Roman law. The Sanhedrin had been deprived of the right of capital punishment. Roman troops were watching the city during the feast and would be prompt to execute the authors of a disturbance. The mob cooled down as they realized the danger of the situation.

There was one alternative for the high priests. They did have the right to arrest the disturber. Once in prison, the pilgrims might forget him; after they had returned home and the troops once more were in barracks at Cæsarea, Jesus would quietly disappear.

They sought therefore to arrest him, but Jesus escaped from their hand. Down the dreary road to Jericho and the Dead Sea he hurried with his disciples and crossed the river to the Circuit of Jordan, the deserted region just north of the Dead Sea, where John was at the first baptizing. Here he might hope to escape both the high priests and Antipas.

There Jesus remained two or three months. Of this period of withdrawal, we know practically nothing. Our only information is to the effect that many were coming to him and saying: "John did indeed no sign, but everything which John

said about this man was true." Already the Baptist was coming to be regarded by the disciples as the Forerunner, his
prediction of the Coming One was being applied to Jesus.
And many believed on him there.[12]

On a previous visit to Jerusalem, Jesus had become acquainted with a family in Bethany and had been received into
their home.[13] Now in Trans-Jordan, he received word from
the sisters Mary and Martha: "Master, see, he whom you
love is ill." After the news had been received that Lazar was
sick, Jesus remained in the place where he was two days more.
There was reason for his hesitation, Bethany was barely two
miles from Jerusalem and the high priests.

Then after this he says to his disciples: "Let us go into
Judæa again." Thoroughly alarmed by his proposal, his disciples say to him: "Rabbi, right now the Judæans are seeking to stone you, and are you going there *again?*" His only
reply was: "Lazar our friend has fallen asleep; however, I
am going to awaken him." His disciples therefore said:
"Master, if he is sleeping, he will be made well." But, as
John points out, Jesus had been talking of his death while
they thought he was talking about the rest of sleep. Then
therefore Jesus spoke to them plainly: "Lazar is dead, and I
am glad for your sakes that I was not there; however, let us
go to him." Thomas therefore said to his fellow disciples:
"Let *us* go too and die with him!" We cannot doubt that
Thomas was sure that in going to Bethany Jesus was deliberately meeting his doom.

On their way, they would pass through Jericho. Sitting by
the road just outside the city was Bar Timæus, a blind beggar. Hearing that Jesus of Nazareth was coming, he cried
out: "Jesus, pity me!" The bystanders ordered him to be

---

[12]Jn. 10:22-24, 31-33a, 39-42.   [13]Lk. 10:38-42.

quiet, but he kept on shouting. Jesus stopped and commanded that he be brought forward; then the bystanders encouraged him: "Cheer up! Rise! He is calling you!" Throwing aside his garments, Bar Timæus jumped up and approached Jesus, who asked him: "What do you wish that I should do for you?" The blind man answered: "Rabbuni, to receive my sight." Jesus told him: "Go, your faith has cured you." We are told that he received his sight and followed Jesus on the road.[14]

As Jesus was traversing Jericho itself, a man called Zakkai (Zacchæus), the head tax collector and certainly well-to-do since he probably received also for transmission the income from the precious balsam grove, wished to see Jesus. Because he was short of stature he was unable to see over the crowd. Knowing that Jesus must follow the direct road to Jerusalem, he ran ahead and climbed a sycamore tree. When Jesus came to the place, he looked up and said: "Zakkai, hurry, come down, for today I must remain at your house." Zakkai hastily climbed down and welcomed him joyfully.

All who saw it muttered: "With a *sinner* he has gone to stay!" But Zakkai, standing, announced: "See, Master, the half of my property I am giving to the poor; if I have wrongfully extorted anything from anyone"—as a tax collector this was more than possible—"I am restoring fourfold." Jesus commended him: "This day has salvation come to this house, since he too is a son of Abraham."[15]

This might be the time and place when other tax collectors asked Peter if his Rabbi did not pay the half shekel, the annual tax to support the Temple. When Peter approached Jesus with the question, he was asked: "What do you think, Simon?

---

[14]Mk. 10:46–52; Mt. 20:29–34;   [15]Lk. 19:1–9.
Lk. 18:35–43.

Do the kings of the earth," the Roman emperors, "take tax
or census from their sons or from the foreigners?" There
could be only one answer: Everyone knew that Italy was free
from tribute; citizens wherever they lived paid only the five
per cent inheritance tax. The crushing burden lay on the provincials. Peter naturally replied: "From foreigners." "Well
then," said Jesus, "the sons are free men." However, the
story goes on, so that Jesus would not be a cause for stum-
bling, Peter was bidden to fish in the lake; he would catch
a fish and the shekel found in its mouth would pay for them
both.[16]

Payment of the Temple half shekel was due in the month
Adar, which began this year February 23. During this part
of the year 30 A.D. Jesus was not at Capernaum, where the
episode in its present miraculous form is located. There would
be no difficulty if it actually took place at Jericho and at this
time; if so, the journey to Bethany was at the end of February or the beginning of March.

Jesus now began the steep climb along the Jerusalem road
on his way to Bethany. The plain, alternately stifling hot
and then swept by bitter winds from icy Hermon, was left
behind. At this season, the perspiration started by the sharp
grades would be chilled suddenly by fresh blasts. The disciples had further cause for shivering; they were terribly
afraid, but they kept loyally on. The crowds which followed
with them were happy and excited; *they* were persuaded
that the Kingdom of the Heavens was immediately to appear![17]

With so large a company, there was no danger of brigands;
tales of less fortunate travellers would be told when they
paused for rest at the inn half way up the ascent. Jesus

---

[16]Mt. 17:24-27.   [17]Lk. 19:11, 28.

arrived at Bethany and found that Lazar had been four days in the tomb. Since the village was but fifteen stades, not quite two miles from the Holy City, many of the Judæans, —here used for Jerusalemites—had come to Mary and Martha to comfort them for their brother. Martha, therefore, when she heard: "Jesus is coming," went out to meet him, but Mary sat in the house.

Martha said to Jesus: "Master, if you had been here, my brother would not have died; however, I know that whatever you ask of God, God will give you." To this hint that she was hoping for a miracle, Jesus answered: "Your brother will arise." Still hesitating to believe that Jesus actually meant what his words might imply, Martha said: "I know that he will arise in the resurrection on the last day." Then she hurried off to call her sister Mary in secret and to announce: "The Master is here and is calling for you." Rising up quickly, Mary went to meet him, though Jesus had not yet entered the village, but was instead in the place where Martha had met him. The Judæans therefore who were with her in the house and were comforting her, seeing that Mary arose quickly and went out, followed her, thinking that she had gone to the tomb to wail there. Mary, therefore, when she had come where Jesus was, seeing him, fell at his feet, saying to him: "Master, if you had been here, my brother would not have died."

Jesus, when he saw her wailing and the Judæans coming with her wailing, moaned in spirit and troubled himself and said: "Where have you buried him?" They say to him: "Come and see." But Jesus wept; the Judæans therefore said: "See how he loved him!" And some of them said: "Could not *he,* who opened the eyes of the blind, have brought it about that this man also should not die?" Jesus, therefore, again moaning to himself, comes to the tomb; now it was a cave and a stone was laid upon it.

Jesus says: "Take away the stone!" The sister of the dead man, Martha, says to him: "Master, already he smells, for it is the fourth day." They therefore raised the stone. But Jesus lifted his eyes upward and said: "Father, I thank you because you heard me." And saying these things, with a loud voice he shouted: "Lazar, come out!" And the dead man came out, his feet and hands bound with bandages and his visage covered about with a napkin. Jesus says to them: "Unbind him and let him go home." Many therefore of the Judæans who came to Mary and had observed what Jesus did believed on him.[18]

Such is the story originally told by John and with all the circumstantial detail of the convinced eyewitness. It is utterly alien in form to the literary miracle tale. As with so many accounts found in our best sources, the historian can only repeat it, without seeking for psychological or other explanations.

Some of the bystanders were undoubtedly convinced that they had witnessed a miracle. Many others, however, of the Judæans, as clearly were not, and they went off to the high priests and informed them what Jesus had done. To these hardened unbelievers, of course, the report was only further proof that Jesus was an impostor. But many did believe the report and that was highly dangerous. The high priests convened the Sanhedrin and said: "What are *we* doing? For this fellow is doing many signs. If we let him go on, everybody will come to believe on him and the Romans will come and take away both our Holy Place and our nationality." This was sound practical common sense. Temple and nation

---

[18]Jn. 11:1, 3, 6–8, 11b–14, 15b–24, 28–39, 41, 43–45.

had been destroyed before, in the next generation both would be destroyed forever, and the menace was plainly to be recognized. Already the threat of incipient revolt must have reached the procurator's ears.

Presumably it was Anas who had opened the discussion; it was his son-in-law Caiaphas, the high priest in that very year in contrast to the ex-high priest, who chided them: "You know nothing at all! Do you not realize that it is expedient for you that one man should die in behalf of the people and the whole nation should not be destroyed?" Again we must admit that this was hard cold common sense; what did the life of a Galilæan artizan count when by his death, even though he was innocent, he might save the whole Jewish people? From that day therefore they plotted how to kill him.[19]

Jesus, therefore, no longer travelled about openly among the Judæans. He must seek a place of concealment. Bethany, though so close to Jerusalem, was already on the verge of the desert. He need walk along this desert edge only a few miles north, parallel to and but a few miles east of the great north-and-south road along the plateau crest, to where a sudden drop of a thousand feet brought him down to the hidden valley where nestled Ephraim. Its only approach, in our own day held by force against unwelcome intrusion, was an execrable trail. Here Jesus was safe. Almost as important, Jesus and his disciples were comfortable. A fine spring just above the village offered pure water for drinking and irrigated the whole valley. There would be plenty of simple food; perhaps the onions were already popular. Numerous caves gave cheap shelter. Even in late winter the air would be balmy, for the sheltered valley, looking to the east, lay but 1400 feet above

[19]Jn. 11:46–50, 53.

the sea. The place bore the name of the great tribe of Ephraim, megalithic remains testified to those far-off days. Perhaps from his Bible reading, Jesus remembered how David's wicked son Absalom killed his brother Amnon at a sheepshearing in Baal-hazor near Ephraim. Here Jesus tarried with his disciples.[20]

---

[20]Jn. 11:54; II Sam. 13:23 ff. Modern Samieh, east of Kefr Malik. W. F. Albright, *Annual of the American Schools of Oriental Research,* IV, 1924, 127 ff.; *Journal of the Palestine Oriental Society,* III, 1923, 36 ff.

CHAPTER XI

PLOTS

PASSOVER was at hand and many went up to Jerusalem from the countryside before the feast to purify themselves. They sought therefore Jesus and were saying to one another as they were standing in the Temple: "What do you think? That he will *not* come to the Feast?" The high priests had given orders that if anyone knew where he was, he should make it known so that they could arrest him.[1]

Jesus, therefore, six days before the Passover,[2] came to Bethany, where was Lazar, whom he had raised from the dead; this was Saturday, April 1, of the year of our Lord 30. They made for him a dinner there—Sabbath ended at sunset—and Martha once more served,[3] but Lazar was one of those who reclined at meal with him. Mary therefore took a pound of pistic nard ointment, very expensive, and anointed the feet of Jesus and wiped with her hair his feet,[4] and the house was filled with the fragrance of the ointment. One of his disciples, therefore, Judas, the man from Karioth, who was to betray him, says: "Why was not this ointment sold for three hundred denarii, and given to the poor?" With unexpected venom, the usually objective John breaks out: "But he said this, not because he cared for the poor, but rather because he was a thief; and having the money box, he lifted from it what was thrown in!" Jesus rebuked his false disciple: "Let her alone to keep it for the day of my

---

[1] Jn. 11 :55–57.
[2] Jn. 12 :1.
[3] *Cf.* Lk. 10 :40.
[4] *Cf.* Lk. 7 :37 ff.

burial; for the poor you have always with you, but me you
do not have always!" The shadow of his fate already hung
heavy above Jesus.[5]

A great crowd of the Jerusalemites, learning that Jesus
was in Bethany, came out to visit the place, not on account
of Jesus alone, but rather that they might also see Lazar,
whom he had raised from the dead. But the high priests
plotted how they might likewise kill Lazar, because on account of him many of the Judæans were going off and believ-
ing in Jesus.[6]

Next day, Sunday, April 2, a great crowd which had come
to the feast, hearing that Jesus was approaching Jerusalem,
took branches of the palm trees and set out to meet him.
He was greeted by shouts of "Hoshana,"—God saves,—
"Blessed is he who is coming in the Name of the Lord!"
That they meant the Baptist's Coming One was made evident by the further shout: "The King of Israel!"

Jesus would have none of this demonstration. Having
found a young ass, he seated himself upon it in token of
humility. The crowds which had followed him from Bethany
responded to the pilgrim shouts by telling how they themselves had witnessed Jesus calling Lazar from the tomb
and raising him from the dead. Still more people trailed
along because they had heard of the signs which he had done
and were hoping to behold more.[7]

The picture is perfectly clear. Only the pilgrims, so many
from Galilee, were hailing Jesus as the national Messiah.
The crowd which had followed him from Bethany recog-

---

[5]Jn. 12:1–8; much later version,
Mk. 14:3–9; Mt. 26:6–13, which is
placed in the house of Simon the
Leper by confusion with the Simon
of the quite different story Lk.
7:36–47.

[6]Jn. 12:9–11.

[7]Jn. 12:12–14a, 17f.; cf. the much
less plausible account, Mk. 11:1–10;
Mt. 21:1–9; Lk. 19:29–38.

nized him as a prophet and great wonderworker but nothing more. As he entered Jerusalem, the whole city was
excited and asked: "Who is this?" The crowds replied: "This
is the Prophet, Jesus, from Nazareth of Galilee."[8] The
pilgrims, with their wild salutations to the coming King of
Israel, were no longer in evidence.

Such a demonstration thoroughly alarmed the members
of the hierarchy. Among themselves, they were saying to
one another: "Do you observe that you are accomplishing
nothing? The whole world has gone after him!"[9] There
was reason for their alarm. It had become only too clear
that they were bitter opponents of Jesus; should the pilgrims
declare him king, the high priests would be the first to be
killed. Of course the revolt would be put down, a Galilæan
mob could not face Roman troops, but for the hierarchy it
might be too late. Fortunately for them, Jesus refused to take
advantage of his opportunity. Jesus entered the Temple,
visited each corner as a simple pilgrim, and at evening returned to Bethany with the Twelve.[10]

Jesus had carefully avoided any action which might hasten
his death. But he was doomed; the shouts of the pilgrims
had sealed his fate. No longer were the crowds discussing
as a more or less hypothetical question whether he *might*
be the hoped-for Messiah, he had openly been hailed as the
King of Israel! Whether Jesus considered himself a pre-
tender to the Jewish throne was no longer material; he had
been so proclaimed and under Roman administrators suspicion of revolt was as fatal as the reality. Jesus' cleansing
of the Temple at the Preceding Passover had implanted the
seeds of such a suspicion in Pilate's mind; he would be con-

[8]Mt. 21:10 f.   [10]Mk. 11:11.
[9]Jn. 12:19.

vinced now that those notorious rioters, the Galilæans, would seize the first opportunity to put their plans into execution. Open revolt might easily break out, if the situation were not skilfully handled.

What was Jesus to do? When again he visited Jerusalem, certain Greek-speaking pilgrims approached Philip and requested: "Sir, we wish to see Jesus." Philip had been an inhabitant of Julias-Beth Saida, a bilingual city, and therefore was able to understand them. Taking with him another bilingual disciple, his fellow citizen Andrew, Philip came to Jesus and was prepared to act as interpreter. Jesus however went off and hid himself from them![11]

One of these days, he was strolling in the Temple. Representatives of the hierarchy demanded: "By what authority do you do these things? Or who gave you authorization to do these things?" That was one issue which Jesus did *not* wish to debate with those who did possess the authority to challenge his right to teach; cleverly the issue was avoided: "I will ask you one word and you answer me, and I will tell you by what authority I do these things. The baptism of John, from heaven was it or from men? Answer me!" The counter question worked. The representatives of the hierarchy were in a quandary: "If we say: 'From heaven,' he will say: 'Why therefore did you not believe him?' But if instead we say: 'From men' "—they feared the huge crowds of Passover pilgrims who were eagerly listening and who without exception had believed John a prophet. They could only respond: "We do not know." With full approval of the crowds, Jesus could answer: "Nor do *I* tell *you* by what authority *I* do these things."[12]

---

[11]Jn. 12:20–22, 36b.

[12]Mk. 11:27–33; Mt. 21:23–27; Lk. 20:1–8.

In point of fact, the hierarchy had *not* accepted the divine mission of the Baptist. To drive home this realization and to alienate from them still further his auditors, Jesus resorted to the anecdote: "What do *you* think? A man had two children. Coming to the first, he said: 'Child, go today and work in the vineyard.' But he, answering, said: 'I will not!' But afterward, repenting, he went off to it. Then coming to the second, the father spoke likewise. But he, answering, said: 'I will, Sir,' and he did not go. Which of the two did the will of his father?" His hearers, of course, answered: "The first."

Then Jesus turned on the officials: "The tax collectors and the harlots shall go before *you* into the Kingdom of God. For John came to you on the road of righteousness and you did not believe him; but the tax collectors and the harlots did believe him. But *you,* seeing this, did *you* repent afterward to believe him?"[13]

Such a denunciation could only infuriate the more the official class. But Jesus' shrewd counter question had destroyed the last chance of arresting him on the charge of illegal teaching, of resistance to the civil authority. Perhaps he could be more deeply embroiled with the Roman government. By his entrance into the Holy City accompanied by a shouting crowd, convinced that he was about to restore the Kingdom to Israel, he must have already drawn the attention of Pilate; surrounded by approving crowds, he might be goaded into admissions which could be construed as opposition to Roman authority.

There appeared certain Herodians, doubtless from his native Galilee, who had followed their leader Antipas on his pilgrimage to the feast.[14] Obsequiously, as befitted courtiers,

---

[13]Mt. 21:28–32.   [14]*Cf.* Lk. 23:7.

they began: "Rabbi, we know that you are honest and do not
have undue regard for any one; for you do not consider the
face of man, rather in truth you teach the road of God."
After this none too subtle invitation to speak his mind without fear or favor of man, the trap was sprung: "Is it lawful
to give census [tribute] to Cæsar or not? Shall we give or
not give?" No doubt the Galilæan pilgrims, whose fathers
and elder brothers, perhaps also they themselves, had taken
part in the wild insurrection against the first imposition of
the census twenty-four years before, were hoping that Jesus
would give a negative answer and then at once proclaim
Jewish independence.

It was a clever trap and could not fail. If Jesus replied
in the negative, he was subject to immediate arrest for
maiestas, treason against the person of the emperor; if in
the affirmative, he would lose his revolutionary following,
the crowds might turn against him. Jesus was not deceived
by their oily hypocrisy. Indignantly he demanded: "Why
are you trying to entrap me? Bring me a denarius that I may
examine it!" A denarius was brought and Jesus inquired:
"Whose is this image and legend?" There could be only one
answer: "Cæsar's." Then he made his pronouncement:
"What is Cæsar's return to Cæsar and what is God's to
God!"[15]

Again Jesus had escaped the trap. He had proved himself
a good subject, ready to pay the tribute assessed by the emperor. He had announced the doctrine of separation of church
and state; every Roman administrator would approve, at least
when Roman religion as the religion of the state and of the
emperor was not concerned, and most particularly in the case
of the Jews, who did so often confuse the two. When the

---

[15] Mk. 12:13–17; Mt. 22:15–22; Lk. 20:20–26.

time came, Pilate could be persuaded that Jesus was a simple preacher of righteousness, without political aspirations. The pilgrims, however, were at last completely disillusioned. Jesus could not possibly be the Messiah for whom they had longed, and we hear no more of them. Their disappearance might have freed Jesus from the suspicion of revolt; it also freed the hierarchy from the fear of mob action if they arrested him. Jesus at last was at the mercy of his personal enemies.

They were not yet quite ready for the final stroke. In fact, the next attack was much less serious. From the standpoint of "philosophy," as Josephus would have put it, the outstanding difference between the hierarchy and the majority of the population was that the former as Sadducees did not accept the comparatively new doctrine of the resurrection of the body which consoled the masses. Learned men of this persuasion sought to discredit Jesus by an example of their tricky reasoning. They were at least as good dialecticians as their Pharisaic opponents, and they put a question which they were sure would stump an unlearned Galilæan villager:

"Rabbi, Moses wrote for us: 'If the brother of anyone dies and leaves behind a wife and leaves no child, his brother should take the woman and raise up seed to his brother.' There were seven brothers. And the first took a wife and dying left no seed. And the second took her and died, not leaving behind seed, and the third. In the same manner also the seven did not leave seed." This was a problem which had troubled the judges, as we learn from the Book of Decrees.[16] "Last of all the woman died. In the resurrection, whose wife shall the woman be? For the seven had her as wife."

---

[16]Cf. p. 184.

Jesus knew the Book of Decrees. He was as well acquainted with Moses' Law as they. Like them, he could employ Jewish dialectic: "Is it not on account of this that you go astray, not knowing the scriptures or the Power of God? For when they arise from the dead, they neither marry nor are given in marriage, rather they are like angels in heaven. But concerning the dead, that they *are* raised," Jesus turns from the quibble to meet the real issue, "have you not read in the Book of Moses, in the Section of the Bush, how God spoke to him, saying: 'I, the God of Abraham and the God of Isaac and the God of Jacob?' He is not the God of dead men but rather of living. Greatly you go astray."[17]

So vigorous a refutation of the Sadducees naturally pleased the Pharisees. Seeing that Jesus had answered them well, one of the scribes, evidently of the Pharisaic party, asked: "What is the commandment first of all?" Jesus quoted: "First is: 'Hear, Israel, the Lord is our God, the Lord is one. And you shall love the Lord your God from all your heart and from all your soul, and from all your mind, and from all your strength.'"

Dan had taught: "You shall love the Lord with all your life and one another with a true heart."[18] Jesus went far beyond this: "Second is this: 'Love your neighbor as *yourself.*' Greater than these is no other commandment."

The scribe commended him: "Well have you said in truth, Rabbi, that he is one, and there is no other except him. And to love him from the whole heart and from the whole understanding and from the whole strength and to love the neighbor as oneself is much greater than all whole burnt offerings and sacrifices," discredited as they had been by the hands of an

---

[17] Mk. 12:18–27; Mt. 22:23–33; Lk. 20:27–38.

[18] *Testaments of the Twelve Patriarchs,* Dan 5:3.

unworthy high priesthood. Pharisaism at its best could have
been represented by no finer exponent. "You are not far from
the Kingdom of God" expressed Jesus' full appreciation.[19]

"Who *is* my neighbor?" inquired a bystander. Within the
last month or so, Jesus himself had toiled up the desolate
road from Jericho to Jerusalem. The robber tales which be-
guiled the journey would be still vivid in his memory. Upon
them he drew for one of the best beloved of his parables:

"A certain man happened to be going down from Jerusalem
to Jericho. And he fell among robbers," who have always
infested this desert road whenever administration has weakened. In addition to taking all his money, the robbers "also
stripped him and beat him up and went off." Within our own
memory, foreigners have been robbed by the Jehalin tribe
along the Dead Sea shore, stripped of every shred of clothing,
and left to wander stark naked under the blazing sun and
over the sharp rocks of the gorges back to civilization.

"But by chance a certain priest was going down by that
road," returning to his home in Jericho when his term of
service in the Temple was completed. "And seeing him, he
went by on the other side," he feared contamination from
a possible dead body. "Likewise a Levite, happening on the
place and seeing him, went by on the other side." These are
representatives of the hierarchy, but the pious Pharisees, we
observe, are not mentioned.

"But a certain Samaritan, journeying along, came to him;
and seeing him, he was moved to compassion. And coming
up to him, he bound up his wounds, pouring on oil and wine.
And placing him on his own beast, he brought him to an inn
and cared for him." Thirty-odd years ago, the traveller might
visit its successor, marked as such by the deep well which

---

[19] Mk. 12:28–34a; Mt. 22:34–40; Lk. 10:25–28.

alone on the barren road afforded water. In it he might purchase post cards or native clothing and relics. During the interval, government has again broken down, robbers have again infested the road; today we behold new ruins.

"Next morning, the Samaritan took out two denarii and gave them to the innkeeper, saying: 'Take care of him, and whatever more you spend, on my return I will give you.' Who of these three seems to you to have been neighbor to him who fell among robbers?" Refusing to employ the hated term Samaritan, his questioner replied: "He who showed pity on him." Sternly Jesus bade him: "You go and act like him!"[20]

Love for one's neighbor was indeed prescribed by the Mosaic Law, but the context strictly limited the love to an Israelite.[21] Even with this limitation, the priest and the Levite had disobeyed the Law. In his scriptures, the Samaritan read exactly the same Mosaic Law, including the same limitation to Israelites which he with perfect logic could identify with his own people. But *he* went beyond the Law's letter to its spirit and accepted the obligation of a universal brotherhood.

Under any circumstance, we should hail this as one of the very finest of Jesus' teachings. When we realize that the parable was told a bare two or three days before the crucifixion, when we realize that Jesus was perfectly aware of the horrible death so soon to be faced, the beauty of Jesus' character becomes irresistible.

In his parable of the Good Samaritan, Jesus had not introduced the Pharisees. Just before he had indeed commended one of them. They were, to be sure, pious, but theirs was no more the highest type of piety than was that of the elder brother in the story of the Prodigal Son. "Two men went up to the Temple to pray, one a Pharisee, the other a tax col-

---

[20]Lk. 10:29b–37.   [21]Lev. 19:18.

lector. The Pharisee, standing upright, prayed these things to himself: 'God, I thank you that I am not as the rest of men, extortioners, unjust, adulterers, or even as this tax collector,'" who most certainly might be supposed an extortioner. "'I fast twice in the week,'" even more than was demanded, "'I tithe all, whatever I obtain.' But the tax collector, standing far away, would not even lift up his eyes to heaven, but instead kept beating his breast, saying: 'God, have pity on me, the sinner!'" The Pharisee was not praying to be heard of men, he spoke to himself in a whisper, but he was conscious of his self-righteousness; the tax collector thought only of his sinfulness and of his need of mercy. "I tell you, *he* shall go down to his house justified instead of the other."[22]

No further attempt was made to entrap Jesus with questions.[23] For the next day or two, he was permitted to continue teaching in the Temple and healing the sick.[24] At night he went out to Bethany and lodged there.[25] The hierarchy was still seeking the exact means to destroy him but as yet in vain, the crowds remained enthralled by his teaching.[26]

Two days before Passover, Wednesday, April 5, the high-priestly leaders held a consultation to determine what measures should be taken to seize Jesus. It was agreed that it must be by craft and not during the feast, lest perchance there should be a disturbance among the people. After the pilgrims had returned home, there would be no danger of resistance from the mob; after the feast, Pilate and his troops would retire to Cæsarea, authority in the Holy City would then revert to high-priestly hands, and Jesus could be put quietly out of the way.

---

[22]Lk. 18 :10–14a.
[23]Mk. 12 :34b.
[24]Mt. 21 :14–16.

[25]Mt. 21 :17.
[26]Lk. 19 :47 f.

The decision was wise. It was suddenly reversed when one of the Twelve, Judas Iscariot, appeared with an offer to betray Jesus. Gladly the high priests accepted the offer and promised the traitor that he would be well paid. Henceforth Judas was seeking how he might most conveniently betray his Master.[27]

One last idyllic picture brightens the prevailing gloom. Sitting opposite the Temple treasury, Jesus was watching the crowds throwing into the treasury their offerings of bronze coins. Many of the well-to-do threw in handfuls of the small change. One poor widow threw in two *lepta,* coins so small that they are explained as worth one *quadrans,* a Roman copper coin of the slightest value. Jesus explained to his disciples how great actually was this sacrifice: "This poor widow threw in more than all the others, for they threw in from their surplus, but she out of her want threw in all she possessed, her whole living."[28]

It was now Thursday, April 6, the day before Passover began.[29] Jesus brought together the Twelve for what he realized would be their last common meal. Ignorant of the new menace from one of their own number, the disciples were still hoping that the Kingdom would be proclaimed openly on the great day of the feast. They began to dispute among themselves as to which should be the greatest![30] The sons of Zebedee, James and John, went so far as to ask that they might sit, one on his right and the other on his left when he came into his glory.[31] The remaining ten were highly indignant at the presumption; Jesus rebuked them: "The kings

---

[27]Mk. 14:1 f., 10 f.; Lk. 22:1-6; Mt. 26:1-5, 14-16, another source.

[28]Mk. 12:41-44; Lk. 21:1-4.

[29]See Appendix for note on Gospel chronology.

[30]Lk. 22:24.

[31]Mk. 10:35-37; Mt. 20:20 f., where the blame for the request is transferred to the mother.

of the nations hold sovereignty over them and those having authority over them are called Benefactors"; thousands of papyri and inscriptions prove the constant if hollow use of Euergetes (Benefactor) in titles. "But *you* should not be thus; rather, let the greater among you become as the younger, and he who is in the place of leadership as the one serving. For who is greater, the one reclining or the one serving? Is not he who is reclining? But *I* am among you as the one serving."[32]

Jesus wished to be remembered, not in the pride of leadership, but as humble. He would give his disciples an example. After supper was over, Jesus rises and lays aside his outer garment, the *tallith*. And taking a linen towel, he girded himself. Then he pours water into the ewer and begins to wash the disciples' feet and to wipe them with the linen towel by which he was girded. When he came to Simon Peter, that impetuous disciple protested: "Master, are *you* washing *my* feet?" "What I am doing you do not just now understand, but you will realize it afterward," was the answer. Again Peter objected: "You shall not wash *my* feet to the end of time!" Jesus replied: "If I shall not wash you, you have no share with me." Suddenly veering, Peter then says: "Master, not my feet only but also the hands and the head." Still Peter did not understand; "he who has been cleansed has need only that the feet be washed, otherwise he is entirely pure. And *you* are pure, but yet not all." At this point, John bursts out: "For he knew who would betray him! On account of this he said: 'Not all are pure.'"

When therefore he had washed their feet and had resumed his outer garment and had reclined again, Jesus said to them:

---

[32]Lk. 22:25-27; less correctly, Mt. 23:11; Mk. 9:35, moral only. Mk. 10:42-44; Mt. 20:25-27; *cf.*

"Do you not understand what I have done for you? You call me 'The Rabbi' and 'The Master'; you say well, for so I am. If therefore *I,* the Master and the Rabbi, have washed *your* feet, *you* too ought to wash one another's feet. For I have given you an example, that as I have done for you, you also should do." This was to be Jesus' very last teaching, a lesson in true humility.[33] His example was followed literally; near the end of his own life, Paul bears witness that the ceremony of foot washing was still regularly celebrated.[34]

After he had said this, Jesus went on to explain his statement that not all were pure. Troubled in spirit, he announced: "In very truth I tell you that one of you will betray me!" The startled disciples therefore looked at one another, wondering of whom he spoke. One of the disciples was reclining on the bosom of Jesus, at his right, he whom Jesus loved; thus modestly John identifies himself as an eyewitness. Simon Peter therefore, some distance away, beckons to him to discover who the traitor might be. Reclining thus on Jesus' breast, John asks: "Master, who is it?" Jesus therefore answered: "He is the one for whom I dip the choice morsel and give to him." Dipping therefore the choice morsel, he took it and gave it to Judas, Simon's son, the man from Karioth; thus solemnly John reveals the terrible secret. Again he bursts out: "And after the choice morsel, then Satan entered into him!"[35]

Jesus therefore says to him: "What you are doing, do more quickly!" The tension of waiting was becoming intolerable; knowing that he was doomed, Jesus could only hope that it

---

[33]Jn. 13:1a, 2b, 4–6, 8–15. Assuming that this was the Paschal Meal, the Synoptists, Mk. 14:12–17, 22–25; Mt. 26:17–19, 26–29; Lk. 22:7–20, describe the Last Supper in terms of the Passover ritual, while the ceremony is that of the developed Eucharist.

[34]I Tim. 5:10.

[35]*Cf.* Lk. 22:3.

would all be quickly over. But no one of those reclining with him realized why their Master had thus spoken to Judas. Some thought, because Judas was in charge of the money box, that Jesus meant: "Buy what you need for the Feast," since the Paschal Meal was to be eaten on the following night; others believed that Judas had been instructed to give something to the poor. Having thus brazenly received the choice morsel, Judas hurried off at once on his mission of betrayal. And it was night.[36]

Having said this, Jesus went out from the city with his disciples. They crossed the dry bed of the Kidron gorge and entered a garden named Gethsemane, the "Oil Press." It lay on the slope of the Mount of Olives, approximately where today we may visit the rival Latin and Russian shrines. But Judas too—the traitor—knew the place, for often Jesus visited there with his disciples.[37]

Leaving them with the warning: "Pray that you do not enter into testing," Jesus went away from them a stone's throw. He knelt down and prayed: "Father, if you so wish, remove this cup from me; nevertheless, let not my wish but rather yours come to pass." On his return, he found the disciples sleeping from very grief. He roused them: "Why are you sleeping? Arise and pray that you do not enter into testing."[38] Even in the face of death, Jesus thought first of his disciples. Their faith would be subjected to the most cruel of tests. Did Jesus foresee that they would fail the test?

---

[36]Jn. 13:21–30; cf. Lk. 22:21–23; later account, Mk. 14:18–21; Mt. 26:21–25.

[37]Jn. 18:1 f.; Mk. 14:26, 32; Mt. 26:30, 36; Lk. 22:39.
[38]Lk. 22:40–42, 45 f.; Jn. 18:11; cf. Mk. 14:32–42; Mt. 26:36–46.

CHAPTER XII

EXECUTION

WHILE Jesus was still talking in Gethsemane with his disciples, torches and lights appeared. In their gleam could be seen weapons and armed men. They formed a detachment from the Second Italian Cohort, which Pilate as usual had brought up from Cæsarea to garrison Jerusalem during the Passover, and were accompanied by the regular Temple police. The entire force was under the command of a military tribune; just possibly his name may have been either Lucius Maesius Rufus or Gaius Paccius Firmus, military tribunes of the Cohors Secunda Italica commemorated by Latin inscriptions.[1]

Jesus went out therefore and asked: "Whom are you seeking?" They answered: "Jesus the Nazoræan." The reply was: "I am he." Judas—the traitor!—was standing by them, for he had carried out his wicked promise and was acting as guide. When therefore Jesus said to them: "I am he," the men fell back; the superstitious soldiery had heard that Jesus was a wonderworker; they feared that his arrest might turn out to be dangerous business. Again he demanded: "Whom are you seeking?" Again they answered: "Jesus the Nazoræan." "I told you that I am he," Jesus insisted, "if therefore you are seeking *me,* allow these others to depart." The request might have been granted but for an untoward incident.

---

[1]*Corpus Inscriptionum Latinarum* XI, 6117; VI, 3528.

In anticipation of the coming declaration of Jewish independence, two of the disciples had brought swords to that last
supper.[2] Pitifully inadequate as two swords would appear to
resist the Roman legionaries, the disciples had no doubt they
would possess miraculous powers. One of the disciples was
Simon Peter. Convinced that the miracle would yet take
place, Peter drew his sword and cut off the right ear of a
slave of the high priest—the name of that slave was Malchus.
To Peter's surprise and despair, Jesus reprimanded him: "Put
,back the sword into the scabbard! The cup which my Father
has given me, shall I not drink it?"[3]

. The military tribune placed Jesus under formal arrest and
ordered him bound.[4] The disciples fled in terror.[5] Among the
bystanders was a young man who followed Jesus for some
distance. Years later, when he came to write his own Life of
Jesus, Mark still recalled vividly how the soldiers attempted
to arrest him and how he, abandoning to them the linen cloth
he had hastily thrown about him, escaped naked.[6]

Bound and shackled, Jesus was first conducted to the residence of Annas. No longer was Annas the legal high priest,
but he still retained the title by courtesy and he was still the
power behind the throne. He was father-in-law of Caiaphas,
actual high priest in that eventful year. Caiaphas, John recalls, was the one who advised the Judæans that it was expedient for one man to die in behalf of the people.[7]

Not all the disciples had continued in flight. Jesus was followed by Simon Peter and another disciple. That disciple
was known to the high priest, Annas, and went in with Jesus
into the high priest's courtyard. John is thus identifying him-

---

2Lk. 22:38.
3Jn. 18:3–8, 10 f.; Mk. 14:45–49;
Mt. 26:47–56; Lk. 22:47–53.
4Jn. 18:12.

5Mk. 14:50; Mt. 26:56b.
6Mk. 14:51 f.
7Jn. 18:13 f.; cf. Mk. 14:53; Mt.
26:57; Lk. 22:54.

self as an eyewitness and explaining how he came to be so fortunate. Peter stood by the door outside; after the episode in the garden, he had reason to be cautious.

The other disciple, known to the high priest, went out therefore, spoke to the porteress, and brought in Peter. The slave girl who was acting as porteress says therefore to Peter: "Are you not also one of this fellow's disciples?" It was the natural assumption. She knew that Peter's friend was a follower of Jesus; under the circumstances it was no more than passing the time of day. But while John was safe, thanks to his acquaintance with Annas, not so Peter, who had just committed mayhem on the high priest's slave. At best, this was a punishable crime, at worst Peter might be accused of resistance to Roman authority. Poor Peter was thoroughly frightened and mumbled: "I'm not!" It was cold around midnight in elevated Jerusalem on this April 6, and the slaves and police had made a charcoal fire and were standing around the brazier and warming themselves. Rashly Peter took his place with them.[8]

There was no formal trial before Annas. As an ex-high priest he possessed only courtesy, not legal standing. A formal trial demanded the presence of the Sanhedrin, which could not legally meet at night. Even if it did meet, the Sanhedrin no longer possessed the right of capital punishment. But Annas was the recognized "boss" of the city and to him Jesus was brought for an informal and highly irregular preliminary examination.[9]

The high priest therefore inquired of Jesus about his dis-

---

[8] Jn. 18:15–18; Mk. 14:54; Mt. 26:58; Lk. 22:54 f.

[9] There is accordingly little point in citing the provisions regarding the Sanhedrin as reformulated after the Pharisaic triumph. They were then purely theoretic. Fortunately, they do prove at least that Mark and Matthew are in error when they speak of a night meeting of the Sanhedrin.

ciples and about his teachings. Jesus replied: "I spoke openly to the world; always have I taught in synagogue or in the Temple, where all the Jews gathered, and in secret have I spoken nothing.[10] Why do you ask *me?* Ask those who heard what I spoke to them; see, these know what I said." The retort was undoubtedly justified, but it was not tactful. The question had not been answered and there need be no reason for surprise that one of the bystanding police slapped Jesus, saying: "Thus do you answer the high priest?"[11] Jesus responded: "If I have spoken wrongly, testify *legally* about the wrong, but if well, why do you beat me?" The assault was a mistake. It gave the impression that the defendant was being deprived of his rights, it brought out sharply the illegality of the whole examination. The hearing was brought to a sudden end and Jesus, once more bound, was hustled off to Caiaphas, the present high priest, who did have the legal right of preliminary examination.[12]

But Simon Peter was still standing and warming himself at the fire. In its light, the police and household slaves examined him more closely. They accordingly demanded of him: "Are not you, also," in addition to John, "one of his disciples?" Again Peter denied and mumbled: "I'm not!" One of the high priest's slaves, a relative of the one whose ear Peter had cut off, persisted: "Did not *I* see you in the garden with him?" By this time all Peter's rash courage had evaporated. Fearing that at any moment he might be arrested for mayhem and for resistance to the government, he therefore denied again emphatically. Immediately a cock crowed.[13]

---

[10]*Cf.* Mk. 14:49; Mt. 26:55; Lk. 22:53.

[11]Compare the similar order of the high priest Ananias to slap Paul on the mouth, Acts 23:2.

[12]Jn. 18:19–24.

[13]Jn. 18:25–27; Mk. 14:66–72; Mt. 26:69–75; Lk. 22:56–62; prediction of denial, Mk. 14:27–31; Mt. 26:31–35.

What took place at the preliminary investigation before
Caiaphas we do not know. Evidently John was not permitted
to listen. Later accounts, involving an illegal night trial before the Sanhedrin, are on their face impossible.[14] The result
of the examination we learn only from what followed: Jesus'
case was presented to Pilate.

From the official residence of the high priest on the southwest hill, Jesus was conducted along the side of Herod's
gardens and palace and straight north across the city to the
Gate of Benjamin. Passing through and turning right, his
escort led him along the street which now filled the deep fosse
once needed to protect the outer face of the second city wall.
Thanks to Herod, the broad street resembled one of the
famous Roman roads at its best. On cement beds had been
laid without mortar huge blocks of the finest local limestone,
a yard or more in size and a foot thick, alternately square and
rectangular; so tightly were they fitted that even now they
have not been dislocated. Like the Roman roads, they were
intended to be used by wheeled vehicles and their blocks were
chiselled with lines at right angles to the curbs in order to
prevent the horses from slipping; despite this precaution, the
blocks are well polished by use.

A hundred yards, and the street was closed by the Tower
of Antonia, through virtue of Pilate's residence for the moment functioning as the Praetorium[15] or official headquarters
of Roman administration in Palestine. To either side rose a
tower seventy-five feet high, set on the native rock which had
been rendered impossible of escalade by a covering of polished stone slabs, and entered by rock-cut stairs from the

---

[14]Mk. 14:55–65, formal condemnation; Mt. 26:59–68, implicit condemnation; Lk. 22:54, 63–65, early
morning trial, no reference to condemnation.

[15]Jn. 18:28, 33; 19:9; Mk. 15:16;
Mt. 27:27.

outside. Between them, the street entered the courtyard through a double gate under round archways.

At this point, the high priests stopped. Did they go farther and enter the Prætorium, they would become polluted and thus unable to eat the approaching Paschal Meal. Pilate must therefore come out to meet them.

It was still very early. The dawn was cold. Pilate had passed an uneasy night keeping down the disorders incident to the Passover season. Irritated, we may be sure, by the untimely summons which interrupted a sorely needed repose, irritated also by the refusal of those stubborn Jewish high priests to defile themselves by entering *his* palace, though well enough they knew what it meant to his discomfort, the shivering Pilate was in no gracious mood. "What accusation are you bringing against this fellow?" he snapped out. The insolent reply: "If this fellow had not been a criminal we should not be turning him over to you," did nothing to soothe the procurator's ruffled feelings. "Take him *yourselves,*" Pilate retorted, "and punish him according to *your* law." This did not at all please the high priests. Their legal competence had been recently confined to punishment of misdemeanors or excommunication of those found guilty of breaches in the religious Law. Capital punishment had been specifically taken from them, but this was what they were implicitly demanding when they answered: "It is not allowed *us* to put any one to death."[16]

By this time, the high priests had learned that they must change their tactics. Pilate had made it perfectly clear that he would not be browbeaten by their bluster. They must present a charge which would terrify the procurator: "We found this fellow leading astray our people, forbidding to

---

[16]Jn. 18:28–31.

give tribute to Cæsar and saying that he himself was Messiah King."[17] This was a downright lie. Many of his auditors could testify that they had heard Jesus preaching: "What is Cæsar's return to Cæsar and what is God's to God."[18] The pilgrims had indeed hailed him as "King of Israel,"[19] but Jesus had refused to accept the title. The charge, however, was sufficiently grave to attract Pilate's attention.

Pilate therefore retired into the Prætorium and summoned Jesus. That the accused would thereby become polluted troubled the high priests not a whit; he would not be alive, they hoped, to eat the Paschal Meal. Past the sentries at the gate and under the watchful eyes of soldiers stationed on rock platforms to right and to left, Jesus was haled into the courtyard. The road continued, marked by the same chiselled lines to prevent the animals from slipping, but to either side the chisel marks were absent as the courtyard expanded to form the Lithostratos or Pavement. This was the proper Greek name; in memory of the rise on which the tower Hananeel had once stood, the natives retained the older Gabbatha, the "Hill."[20] The Pavement proper covered only the northwest corner of the courtyard.

Probably the torches still guttered from the iron brackets whose holes in the blocks may yet be detected. Curious spectators would peer from the arcaded galleries about the four sides of the Pavement. In the growing light, the low channels to carry off the rain water and openings through which were drawn up the fluid from the great double pool of Struthion[21] which extended diagonally beneath the Pavement would be seen. The heavy mass of cut stone which covered the pool

---

[17]Lk. 23 :2.
[18]Mk. 12 :17; Mt. 22 :21; Lk. 20 :25.

[19]Jn. 12 :13.
[20]Jn. 19 :13.
[21]Joseph. *Wars* v, 467.

could not entirely silence the clang of the escort's mailed tread as the sound rumbled back from the empty spaces beneath the fine rounded arches supporting the dividing line between the two halves of the pool.

Jesus was examined by Pilate at his comfort in his residence, the southeast tower, which from the height of a hundred and five feet afforded an unequalled view of both city and Temple.[22] The procurator looked at the accused and felt a doubt; this simple fellow did not have the appearance of a dangerous rebel. Scornfully he demanded: "Are *you* the King of the Jews?"[23] Jesus shrewdly countered: "Of yourself do you say this or did others tell you about me?" With yet deeper contempt, Pilate replied: "Am *I* a Jew? Your *own* people and the high priests handed you over to me. What did you *do?*"

Jesus explained: *"My* Kingdom is not of this world. Were my Kingdom from this world, my attendants would be struggling so that I should not be handed over to the Judæans. But now my Kingdom is not from here." He could not have indicated more clearly that *his* Kingdom was of the Spirit, that he made no claim to be the Messiah whom the Jews, as Pilate only too well knew, expected to restore an independent Jewish kingdom on earth. Pilate could not restrain his sarcasm: "What, *you* a king?" Quietly Jesus answered: *"You* say that I am king; for this I have come into the world, to witness to the truth." Pilate was a hard-bitten Roman official. At many a trial over which he had presided, he had seen the strict letter of the law triumph over simple justice. Born to the upper class, his education had given him some

---

[22]Joseph. *Wars* v, 238 ff.; H. Vincent, "L'Antonia et le Prétoire," *Revue Biblique,* XLII, 1933, 83 ff.; *Le Lithostratos d'après des Fouilles recentes,* 1933.
    [23]*Cf.* Lk. 23:3; Mk. 15:2; Mt. 27:11.

acquaintance with Greek dialectics and a smattering of contemporary philosophy, its learned quibblings, its generally
sceptical and negative attitude. No wonder he asked ironically:
"What *is* truth?"

Nevertheless, Pilate had been persuaded that Jesus was
nothing but a religious fanatic, that he was preaching no
nationalistic uprising which could be a danger to the Roman
government. By now he was satisfied that the high priests,
for devious reasons of their own, were determined to send
an innocent man to his death. Pilate did not like Jews, least
of all the high priestly crowd, as the ten years of his pro-
curatorship amply showed, and for this reason if for no
other he would make up his mind to block their designs.

But there was a much more pressing reason for his reluctance to accede to their demands. Pilate was a procurator,
a governor of the second rank, but of an imperial province
and so directly responsible to the emperor. Tiberius had far
excelled Augustus in his stern adherence to duty, he had
repeatedly and in direct contrast to his predecessor shown
his determination to protect the native population of his
empire against grafting officials and overzealous tax collectors. Senatorial governors, at his insistence, had been condemned again and again for extortion by a reluctant senate;
too cowardly to protest during his lifetime, after his death
the senators revenged themselves by blackening his memory.
Imperial legates had been sharply rebuked and cashiered.
When, for instance, a prefect of Egypt presented to him
more than the assessed tribute, the wrath of Tiberius was
loosed: "I want my sheep sheared, not skinned!" Next year,
the papyri show a new prefect. Six years later, Pilate himself
was to be removed; as an honest man and as an official

responsible to a stern master, the procurator had no desire
to be a party to a miscarriage of justice.

Pilate therefore went out to the Judæans and announced:
"I find in him no *crime*."[24] A crime, not, as we should say,
a misdemeanor, must be *proved* before even a humble provincial could be sentenced in cold blood to death. The accusers
of Jesus insisted: "He is stirring up the people, teaching
through all Judæa and beginning from Galilee up to here."
Pilate caught them up; was the fellow a Galilæan? The harried procurator, unwilling to condemn an innocent man, but
beginning to fear that he could not save him, was delighted
to learn that the accused was a subject of a vassal tetrarch;
most fortunately Herod Antipas, for political if not for
purely religious reasons, actually was present at the great
feast. He had been terribly angered at Pilate when the procurator had massacred his Galilæan subjects at the preceding
feast of Tabernacles;[25] here was the golden opportunity for
Pilate to make his peace by an act of courtesy. By so doing,
he would also wash his hands[26] of the whole unpleasant
problem, particularly as the accused was one of those Galilæans who were always making trouble for Rome.

Much as Antipas appreciated the courtesy, it was a ticklish
task which had been handed him. Jesus was indeed his own
subject, but right now he was in Jerusalem, for the moment
official headquarters of the procurator; no wise vassal prince
violated Rome's jurisdiction. After a brief examination,
Jesus was sent back with the word that nothing against the
accused could be found. But Pilate's main objective had been

---

[24]Jn. 18:33–37a, 38. According to
Mk. 15:3–5; Mt. 27:12–14, Jesus
made no reply at all to the accusations and questionings! In Lk. 23:4,
Pilate's denial of crime is watered

down to "fault," which is meaning-
less in the mouth of a Roman official.
[25]Lk. 13:1; *cf.* p. 149.
[26]Taken literally, Mt. 27:19, 24b.

attained; "Herod and Pilate became friends that very day, for before they were at enmity."[27]

Once more Pilate faced the high priests. "You have brought me this fellow as one who was leading astray the people; having examined him before you, I have found in this fellow no crime as regards what you have accused him. Neither has Herod, for he sent him back to us. Nothing worthy of death has been done by him. I will therefore scourge him and release him."[28] Scourging was indeed the Roman equivalent of our third degree, but it was also Roman practice to seize trouble makers, as happened later to Paul and Silas,[29] scourge them as warning, and let them go, assured that the trouble makers would not again risk arrest. Such was the punishment which Pilate proposed for Jesus.

Then Pilate had another inspiration. He had noted the enthusiasm shown by the pilgrim crowds for Jesus and to them he turned: "You have a custom that I should release to you someone at the Passover; do you wish therefore that I should release to you the King of the Jews?" He was hoping that they would shout an affirmative. But he had miscalculated their temper. However much they had been impressed by his teaching and signs, Jesus had alienated them by his tacit admission that tribute should be paid to Cæsar. They belonged to the patriotic party rather than to that of the pious; Pilate's sneering title "King of the Jews," applied to one who had refused their offered throne, roused their antipathy. In Pilate's custody was a notable rebel, who had taken part in a recent insurrection within the city and who in consequence had been

[27]Lk. 23:5–12; Jesus' refusal to answer, the accusations of the high priests, and the mockery by Herod, are not part of Luke's source but have been inserted from the source of Mark and Matthew. *Cf.* also Acts 4:27.
[28]Lk. 23:13–16.
[29]Acts 16:22 f.

imprisoned on the charge of murder. From the Roman viewpoint, Barabbas was indeed a robber, but to the people he was
a hero, and they therefore shouted: "Not this fellow but instead Barabbas!"[30] It is notable that only here does John
even imply that the crowd made demands on Pilate.

Then, therefore, Pilate took Jesus and scourged him. The
scourging should not be misunderstood. In reality, it was
intended as an act of mercy. By inflicting the lesser punishment, Pilate still was hoping to satisfy Jesus' enemies and
thus save his life.[31] The brutal Roman soldiery, plaiting a
crown of thorns, placed it upon his head, threw about him a
purple robe, and called out in mock reverence: *Ave, Rex
Iudæorum,* "Hail, King of the Jews!" Pilate, losing his none
too patient temper, had deliberately insulted the high priests
by asking the crowd if they wished to liberate the King of
the Jews; the Roman soldiers were only imitating their commander, and their mockery was not so much at the expense
of the innocent victim as that of the hierarchy.[32]

Determined to the last to save Jesus if possible, Pilate came
out once more and said to them: "See, I am bringing him
out to you, so that you may realize that I find in him no *crime*
at all." Jesus therefore came out, still wearing the crown of
thorns and the purple robe; pointing to him, Pilate dramatically bade them: "Look at the poor fellow!"[33] Today the
pilgrim is told that Jesus stood at the Ecce Homo arch which
crosses the Street of our Lady Mary. The arch was not erected
until a little more than a century later. As so often, the sacred
structure has been found in a later building. But tradition

---

[30] Jn. 18:39 f.; Lk. 23:17-19, 25a; Mk. 15:6-9, 15a; Mt. 27:15-17, 20 f., 26a; Acts 3:14.

[31] Note especially Peter's speech, "when Pilate had given the decision that he should be released," Acts 3:13.

[32] Jn. 19:1-3; Mk. 15:16-19; Mt. 27:27-30. In Lk. 23:11a the mock-ery is transferred to Herod.

[33] Jn. 19:4 f.

has remembered the actual spot; if from the west we look up toward the arch, we are standing exactly over the double gate to Antonia.

If the procurator had hoped that the sight of the bleeding, humiliated victim would awaken pity, he had underestimated the fury of the accusers. When the high priests and their attendant police—we cannot but observe how carefully John excludes the crowd from the blame—saw Jesus, they repeated the shout: "Crucify! Crucify!" Disgustedly Pilate answered: "Take him *yourselves* and crucify, for *I* do not find in him a crime." This of course they could not do, they did not possess the legal authority. They had failed to prove their charge that Jesus was a potential rebel; they could only fall back on the earlier accusation: "We have a Law and according to that Law he ought to die." Such an argument had no validity under Roman law and Pilate continued to urge dismissal of the case.[34]

Suddenly the Judæans began to shout: "If you release this fellow, you are no friend of Cæsar's! Everyone who makes himself king speaks against Cæsar!" At long last the high priests had discovered how to force Pilate's hand. Violation of Jewish law meant nothing under Roman, but now a definite crime was charged. Jesus was accused of *maiestas,* treason against the person of the emperor. Although not yet extended to the tragically ludicrous degree it was to assume under Caligula, the law against *maiestas* was enforced strictly by Tiberius. Only the year before, 29 A.D., a mere hint of *maiestas* had brought about the banishment of the elder Agrippina, next year, 31 A.D., after the fall of Sejanus, it was to produce still more terrible results.[35]

---

[34] Jn. 19:6–7a, 12a; Mk. 15:12–14; Mt. 27:22 f.; Lk. 23:20–23.
[35] For the law of treason under

Tiberius, cf. F. B. Marsh, *The Reign of Tiberius,* 1931, 289 ff., cf. 185.

Accusation of *maiestas* left Pilate no alternative. Jesus must be condemned or the procurator's numerous enemies would be only too glad to report his failure to the always suspicious Tiberius. Hearing these words, therefore, Pilate brought out Jesus and formally took his place on the tribunal which had been set up on the Pavement. Judgement at once followed. Under the modern street which leads to the Gate of our Lady Mary, a gentle nun from the basilica of the Ladies of Sion will conduct us reverently over this very Pavement.

It was the Preparation, the usual word for Friday; this time it was preparation, not for the sabbath only but also, as John tells us, for the Passover. The hour was about the sixth, not far from noon. Beset by constant worry in the effort to keep the peace during the most dangerous week of the year, the procurator had been compelled to waste six precious hours, interrupted only by the futile effort to persuade Antipas to take over the case, on the trial of an obscure Galilæan villager. By this time, Pilate had completely lost his temper.

By the very fact that he had finally surrendered Jesus to the demands of the high priests, Pilate had freed himself from their further pressure. Without danger of reprisal, he could insult them to his heart's content. "Behold your king!" he mocked them. "Away! Away! Crucify him!" they yelled back. "Shall I crucify your *king?*" was the biting reply. Smugly the high priests—it is not to be overlooked that the crowd was silent—assured him: "*We* have no king but Cæsar." Remembering the already too long list of Jewish revolts, Pilate must have smiled cynically. Then therefore Pilate handed Jesus over to be crucified.[36]

---

[36]Jn. 19:12b–16; Mt. 27:31; Mk. 15:20; Lk. 23:25b.

Bearing for himself the cross,[37] Jesus was led out to the so-called "Place of the Skull," Golgotha. To this day we may follow the sad trail, roughly that of the modern Via Dolorosa.[38] From the Pavement we follow back the line of the paved road in the fosse of the north city wall along the Street of our Lady Mary. At the Chapel of the Spasm, we descend sharply into the depression, which is all that is now left of the "Mortar." There is no trace at this point of the Gate of Benjamin, its place has been taken by the Damascus Gate to the northwest and higher up the valley. But if we turn a bit southeast down the road from the Damascus Gate, we are safely within the old gate; if then we turn west we are close to the inner line of the second wall; if once more we turn south to follow the main north-south street of the modern city to the Alexander Hospice, we are equally close to the wall after it swings south.

At the Alexander Hospice, an aged Russian nun bids us welcome. We pass hastily under an arch built for the emperor Hadrian and over the pavement of his Market Place, for ahead of us lie the massive blocks which Herod erected along the second east-west stretch of the second city wall. Nowhere in Jerusalem can we better examine these remarkable blocks, identified by their size, a yard high and up to a yard and a half long, by their careful smooth dressing, and by their drafted edges. They were used elsewhere by Herod, for the Temple wall, for the great enclosure around the "Tomb of Abraham" at Hebron, and for the "High Place of Abraham" amid the vineyards north of that city, but they should

---

[37]Jn. 19:17 is very emphatic. John appears to be denying the tradition from Alexander and Rufus that their father, Simon of Cyrene, bore the cross, accepted by Mk. 15:21;

Mt. 27:32; Lk. 23:26. Such a substitution, of course, was contrary to Roman procedure.
[38]Cf. H. Vincent and F. M. Abel, Jérusalem, II, 610 ff.

not be called "Herodian"; we recognize Augustan building in
the far more impressive enclosure at Baalbek, erected before
a proper temple was considered needful, and in the monumental temple of Bel at Palmyra.

Unfortunately, we may not look for the gate out from
which Jesus passed in the gate now shown in the Russian
building; it was cut in the remains of the city wall to form
a side entrance to Constantine's Church of the Resurrection.
The city wall has been traced to the north under the Coptic
building, but the gates here are the central entrance of Constantine and the corresponding side entrance to the north.
Still farther north and still unbared must be the gate through
which Jesus passed.[39]

The presence of this great fragment of Herod's wall is
proof absolute that the site of the Church of the Holy Sepulcher lay in the time of Jesus outside the city wall. In the
northwest corner of the Hospice, we are then "outside the
Gate," where Jesus suffered.[40] Our progress is stopped by
modern building, though in the days of Constantine we should
have been already within the Church of the Resurrection. We
must therefore detour around outside in the street and to
the entrance of the present Church of the Holy Sepulcher.
Just within the entrance, we turn right and ascend a steep
stairway some fifteen feet up to the summit of Golgotha. We
are now only eighty yards from the stretch of north-south
wall, but after the wall turns west at the angle its projected
line is barely half a dozen yards south of the traditional hill.

Surrounded by crowds of devout pilgrims, who thrust a
stick into a hole to touch the sacred rock, the only spot where
the original stone is open to inspection, it takes a strong
effort of the imagination to think away the altars and lamps,

---

[39]Vincent-Abel, *Jérusalem,* II, 40 ff.   [40]Heb. 13:12.

the paintings, candles and incense. It is difficult to picture the appearance before the church was built, before the floor was levelled and the rock trimmed down to a cube, when Golgotha was only a rough knoll, close under the wall and sloping down to a garden.

Here they crucified Jesus and with him two others, one on one side and one on the other. Pilate wrote also a good Latin *titulus*[41] and placed it upon the cross; it was written: "Jesus, the Nazoræan, the King of the Jews." This *titulus* therefore many of the Jerusalemites read because the place where Jesus was crucified was close to the gate. And it was written in Hebrew, Roman, and Greek; few of the passers-by would fail to understand, for the three world languages were all represented. The high priests therefore protested to Pilate: "Do not write: 'The King of the Jews,' but instead that *he* said: 'I am King of the Jews.'" Pilate had strongly resented the trick by which he had been compelled to sacrifice an innocent man; now by his grim joke he had his revenge: "What I have written I have written."[42]

The soldiers—they formed the usual *quaternion* or squad of four—when they crucified Jesus, took his outer garments and divided them into four piles, for each soldier one. But the cloak was without seam, woven from the top throughout. They therefore said to one another: "Let us not tear it, but instead throw dice for it, whose it shall be." The soldiers therefore divided these things.[43]

John was an acquaintance of Annas and had been admitted to the preliminary hearing. The same "pull" would have allowed him to stand safely by the cross when the other

---

[41]*Cf.* Suetonius, *Caligula*, 32, 2.   [43]Jn. 19:23, 24a, c; Mk. 15:24;
[42]Jn. 19:16–22; Mk. 15:22, 25–   Mt. 27:35; Lk. 23:34b.
32; Mt. 27:33, 36–44; Lk. 23:27, 32–
34a, 35, 37–43.

disciples were cowering in terror or were in flight. Standing also by the cross of Jesus were his mother, his mother's "sister" Mary, wife of Clopas, and Mary the Magdalene.[44] Jesus, therefore, seeing his mother and the disciple whom he loved standing by, says to his mother: "Woman, see your son." Then he says to his disciple: "See your mother." And from that hour the disciple took her to his own house.[45] This touching little episode must surely come from John himself; he only would have thought the tale worth telling.

Mercifully John and his successors have spared us the grewsome details. Crucifixion of rebels, often by the tens of thousands, was no uncommon practice among the Romans, perhaps the worst blot on the character of a people never famous for tenderness of heart. Mass executions on such a scale are simply too horrible for our minds to realize, even in these days of totalitarian war. Reduced to the agony of a single individual, it is still too ghastly to contemplate, but at least it is more comprehensible. Indecent exposure, the taunts of the populace, the suffering from hunger and thirst, from insects and the blazing sun, the searing torture of the nails, the all too slow draining away of the strength, everything combined to make dying one long inexpressible horror.

In one respect, Jesus was fortunate. He no longer enjoyed the tough resistance of youth. His strength was that of the

---

[44]According to Mk. 15:40, they were Mary the Magdalene, Mary the mother of James the Little, and Salome. Mt. 27:56 omits the title of James and for Salome substitutes the mother of the sons of Zebedee. Lk. 23:27, 49, does not give the names. In the resurrection story, where according to Jn. 20:1; cf. [Mk.] 16:9, Mary the Magdalene alone saw the open tomb, Mk. 16:1 adds Mary the mother of James and Salome, Mt. 28:1, the other Mary, Lk. 24:10, Johanna and Mary the mother of James. Neither here nor in Jn. 6:42 does John give the name of Jesus' mother. Our other sources and the unanimous tradition of antiquity name her Mary and there is no reason to doubt their testimony. That she should have had a sister also called Mary is most improbable; the most natural explanation is that "sister" is to be understood as cousin.

[45]Jn. 19:25-27.

village artizan, not of the peasant. His temperament was
high-strung, not dull; his suffering would be more intense
but more quickly over. For months he had known that he
must die; it would be a relief to have peace. Last night, he
had been allowed no sleep. For the last twelve hours he had
been badgered by constant questioning.

Jesus was exhausted when he was nailed to the cross. His
death could be only a matter of two or three hours. Recog-
nizing that his end was approaching, he moaned: "I am so
thirsty." It would not do for the criminal to die too soon,
before he had amused the bystanders by his prolonged torture. It was not for pity that a soldier filled a sponge from a
skin they had brought with their own ration of sour wine,
and, placing the sponge on a spear, raised it to Jesus' mouth.[46]

When first he had been told that his life was in danger,
Jesus had replied: "I am casting out evil spirits and performing cures today and tomorrow and on the third day I have
finished."[47] Today and tomorrow had passed; as Jesus had
foreseen, the third day had come, the Prophet was indeed
perishing in Jerusalem. Recollection of that first moment of
shocked realization and of how he had answered returned to
Jesus in his last conscious moments. As he took the sour
wine, he faintly murmured: "Finished." Bowing his head,
Jesus gave up the spirit.[48]

At this very hour, the Paschal Lamb was being slaughtered
for the Paschal Meal. His disciples never forgot the symbol-
ism. To Paul, the sacrifice of Jesus was of overwhelming
importance: *"Our* Passover is sacrificed, Christ; therefore
let *us* keep the Feast." To the unknown author of the Letter
to the Hebrews, Moses was the prototype of the Christ: "By

---

[46]Cf. Mk. 15:23, 36; Mt. 27:34,
48; Lk. 23:36.
[47]Lk. 13:32.

[48]Jn. 19:28a, c–30; Mk. 15:23, 33–
40; Mt. 27:34, 45–56; Lk. 23:44–49;
I Tim. 6:13.

faith he made the Passover and the outpouring of the blood."[49]

There is an epilogue. It was April 7, in the year 30 of our era. This year, Friday was not merely the Preparation of the Sabbath, great was the day of *that* sabbath, for when the fifteenth of Nisan, the beginning of the Feast of the Unleavened Loaves, coincided with the sabbath, the day was even more than usual one of joyful celebration.[50] The Judæans therefore requested Pilate that the legs of the criminals be broken and that their bodies should be taken away; the added suffering to be endured by the criminals was in their sight as nothing in comparison to the danger of polluting an especially holy day. The soldiers therefore came and broke the legs of the first and of the other who was crucified with Jesus. We must hope that the soldiers finally put them out of their agony. But coming to Jesus, when they saw that he was already dead, they did not break his legs. One of the soldiers, however, touched his side with a javelin; John heard that out of the wound came blood and water.[51]

The tragedy was ended. Jesus had endured atrocious suffering and was dead because he had excited the bitter hatred of the unprincipled high-priestly gang. Not a voice can be raised in their defense. Josephus has repeatedly and rightly blackened their reputation. Jewish Fathers of a later generation remembered their names only to curse their rapacity and greed.

Mark and Luke but more especially Matthew have bracketed with them the good Pharisees and even the whole people. Matthew, like his Master himself a Jew, goes so far as to make the whole people invoke upon themselves and upon their

---

[49] I Cor. 5:7; Heb. 11:28.
[50] Although our available Jewish evidence comes first from a much later date, the evidence of John is decisive for a much earlier usage.
[51] Jn. 19:31–34.

innocent children the curse of his blood.[52] To those who count Jews among their closest friends, it is a relief to know that John the Apostle, writing less than ten years after the tragedy,[53] puts the blame squarely where it belongs, on the shoulders of those irreligious high priests, Annas and Caiaphas.

This is also the testimony of Josephus: "But there happened at this time Jesus, a wise man; he brought over to himself both many Jews and many Greeks. And Pilate, *urged by the first men among us,* condemned him to the cross. Even until now the tribe of the Christians, named from him, has not ceased."[54]

But, after these things, Joseph of Arimathæa, a disciple of Jesus but in secret through his fear of the hierarchy, asked Pilate to take away the body of Jesus. Perhaps the procurator felt pity and blame and granted the only restitution possible, proper burial for the poor mangled corpse; perhaps he had in mind only further irritation of the high priests. Joseph came therefore and took away the corpse. But Nicodemus came also, he who visited Jesus by night at the first; he was bringing a mixture of myrrh and aloes, about a hundred pounds. They therefore took the body of Jesus and wound it with linen bandages, with the spices, as is the custom to bury. But there was in the place where he was crucified a garden, and in the garden a new tomb in which no one as yet had been

---

[52]Mt. 27:25. But note how Lk. 24:20 confines the guilt to the "high priests and rulers." Paul blames the "rulers of this present age" for the crucifixion, I Cor. 2:8.

[53]Cf. p. 159 n. 19.

[54]Joseph. *Ant.* xviii, 63 f. As it has come down to us, this passage has suffered from Christian interpolations; fortunately, the interpolations are so glaringly Christian in their theology and so badly interrupt the sense they are easily excised, leaving what is quoted above. That Josephus did have an account of Jesus is indicated by Tacitus, *Annals* xv, 44, "The author of this name, Christus, had been brought to punishment in the reign of Tiberius by the procurator Pontius Pilate"; elsewhere, except for one anti-Semitic extract, Tacitus can be proved to have used, not always accurately, only Josephus for his narrative of Jewish affairs.

placed. There, on account of the Preparation and because the tomb was near, they buried Jesus.[55]

Jerusalem in its growth reached out over the garden and hid the tomb under its new buildings. A dozen years later, when Agrippa was king, the line of wall was extended to the north to include the new suburb, and the tomb was no longer "outside the gate." Forty years after the crucifixion, Jerusalem was sacked by the Romans.

Thereafter, the site was occupied only by the camp of the Tenth Legion Fretensis. When Hadrian determined to re-found the city as a colony, Ælia Capitolina from his own gentilic name, the legionary camp determined the form. Over the ruins which now covered the tomb, the emperor built his temple to the Capitoline Triad. Minerva soon became Aphrodite and Aphrodite was worshipped as Syrian Astarte, whose licentious rites profaned in Christian eyes the holy spot.

But the memory of the true site was never lost. When the empire became Christian, the site was excavated with pious care and a tomb was found, forty yards northwest of Golgotha's hill top. Whether the tomb now revered in the Church of the Holy Sepulcher is the actual spot where Jesus' body once lay, we cannot prove; no living man has seen the tomb, it is encased in a modern shrine. Within the church and but a short distance to the west is the so-called Tomb of Joseph of Arimathæa, where we may examine at our leisure a typical *loculus* tomb of the period, a horizontal shaft in the rock into which the body was pushed. Before it are typical "bone boxes" sunk in the rock in which were placed the dismembered bones in secondary burial, a practice abandoned by the Jews within a century or two after Jesus' burial. Similar rock tombs may be visited in the Coptic monastery two hun-

---

[55] Jn. 19:38–42; Mk. 15:42–47; Mt. 27:57–61; Lk. 23:50–56a.

dred feet northeast of the traditional tomb. It is even possible that the actual tomb was destroyed when the floor of the
Church of the Resurrection was levelled. Of one thing the
pilgrim may rest assured, in the Church of the Holy Sepulcher he is close to the site of the actual tomb.

Jesus had lived until near fifty as a humble joiner in a tiny
out-of-the-way hamlet. For little over a single year—475 days
to be exact—he had proclaimed the good news of God's
Kingdom. He had made a few converts, for the most part
from the lower middle class. By his preaching, he had involved himself with the highest ecclesiastic authorities. They
had forced Pilate unwillingly to order his execution by the
cross, the most painful and most disgraceful of deaths.
Henceforth his memory was branded; he had died as a criminal and as a rebel against the all-powerful Roman empire.

Less than three centuries later, this very Roman empire
revered Jesus as its Lord and Master. The once despised
cross soared in the sky above magnificent churches dedicated
to his worship. How did this miracle come to pass?

CHAPTER XIII

THE RISEN MESSIAH

JESUS, accepted by his followers as the long-waited Messiah, was dead, a criminal executed by Roman orders, condemned to the horrible sufferings and public ignominy of the cross. Only a few devoted women and personal friends had witnessed his tragic end. One of his favorite disciples had denied his very acquaintance, the other disciples had fled. The little group of converts he had collected in his lifetime cowered at Jerusalem in an upper room, "mourning and weeping," "their doors shut in fear of the Jews," who had contrived the judicial murder of their Master and might now be expected to attack his followers. They had "hoped that he was the one to redeem Israel," but they had been bitterly disappointed and were utterly discouraged.[1]

On the first day of the week, Sunday, April 9, in this same year 30 of our era, Mary the Magdalene, from whom Jesus had cast out seven evil spirits, came to the tomb. Though it was yet dark, she could see that the round stone which closed the entrance had been rolled away. She ran therefore to Peter and the other disciple whom Jesus loved and says to them: "They have taken away the Master from the tomb and I do not know where they have placed him." Alarmed by the startling news, Peter therefore and the other disciple rushed out and started for the tomb.

Even when describing this solemn moment, John cannot refrain from telling how, as they were running together, he as the younger naturally ran faster than Peter, and how,

---

[1][Mk.] 16:10; Jn. 20:19; Lk. 24:21.

coming first to the tomb, he looked in and saw laid out the bandages but did not enter, courteously awaiting the arrival of his older companion. Following him, Simon Peter also came; entering the tomb, he observed the linen bandages laid out and the napkin which had been on his head, not laid out with the linen bandages, but instead folded in one place to the side. Then the other disciple who came first to the tomb also entered and saw. The disciples therefore went off to their abodes. This is the story of the empty tomb—told by an undoubted eyewitness—full of life, and lacking any detail to which the sceptic might take justifiable objection.[2]

Mary, however, was standing by the tomb outside, weeping. As therefore she looked into the tomb, she sees two angels in white, sitting one at the head and one at the feet, where the body of Jesus had lain. They said to her: "Woman, why are you weeping?" She says to them: "They have taken away my Master and I do not know where they have placed him." Saying this, she turned and observed Jesus standing and did not know that it was Jesus. He says to her: "Why are you weeping? Whom are you seeking?" She, thinking that it was the keeper of the garden, says to him: "Sir, if you have stolen him, tell me where you have placed him, and I will take him away." Jesus says to her: "Mariam!" and she answers with the Aramaic title of deep respect: "Rabbuni!" Mary the Magdalene comes, reporting to the disciples that she had seen the Master.[3]

---

[2]Jn. 20:1–8a, 10; *cf.* Lk. 24:12; the stories of Mk. 16:1–8; Mt. 28:1, 5–8; Lk. 24:1–10, 22–24, are clearly not eyewitness accounts; they are considerably later and have suffered literary "improvement."

[3]Jn. 20:11–16, 18a; that there were other claimants to the honor of having first beheld the risen Lord is implied by the emphasis of [Mk.] 16:9, a fragment or epitome of the Twelve Source, "He appeared *first* to Mary the Magdalene."

This likewise is the testimony of a convinced eyewitness; if modern scholars do not accept the vision as objective reality, the blame should be laid on the psychologist and not on the historian. The sceptics were anticipated by the disciples themselves: "When they had heard that he was alive and had been seen by her, they did not believe," for "these things appeared in their sight as idle talk, and they disbelieved them."[4] But other appearances followed.

Two of Jesus' disciples, who had already heard of the empty tomb, were on their way to Emmaus when a stranger caught up and walked along with them. He noticed their sadness and inquired the reason; did he not know how the high priests had contrived a shameful death for that mighty prophet, Jesus of Nazareth? Pressed to spend the night with them at Emmaus, he sat down to meal, blessed the bread, broke it, and gave to them; their eyes were opened, they knew him, and he vanished from their sight. Hastily they returned to Jerusalem and reported to the gathered Eleven.[5] According to current belief, men could be deceived by a phantom;[6] "neither believed they them."[7]

While it was late on that first day of the week, and the doors where the disciples were assembled had been closed in fear of the Jews, Jesus came and stood in the midst and said to them: "Peace to you!" And saying this he showed them his hands and his side. The disciples therefore rejoiced, seeing the Master.[8] Here again speaks the convinced witness, though the modern psychologist would explain it as an example of "mob psychology." "And he upbraided them for

---

4[Mk.] 16:11;.Lk. 24:11.
5Lk. 24:13–33, 35.
6Lk. 24:37, 39.

7[Mk.] 16:12 f.
8Jn. 20:19 f.; [Mk.] 16:14; Lk. 24:36a, 37–39, 41–43.

their unbelief and hardness of heart because they had not believed those who had seen him after he had risen."[9] Thomas had been too frightened even to meet with the other ten, and when he was told: "We have seen the Master," he refused to believe. When they met again eight days later, he was present and this time was convinced.[10]

Others might now hope to behold the risen Master. Additional appearances are recorded, to another Mary, who may be Jesus' own mother, to Salome and Johanna,[11] and to his formerly sneering brother James.[12] There was a mass appearance to five hundred at once.[13] All these appearances had been in or near Jerusalem; there is also one recorded to the Eleven in Galilee, to the mount where Jesus appointed them; when they saw him they worshipped, but again there is the ominous: "But some doubted."[14]

Now that the repeated appearances had freed the disciples from all doubt as to the actual resurrection of their Master, the story of the open tomb had lost its significance. It might have been quickly forgotten, had it not been already set down in writing and had not the Jews already met the report by the claim that the disciples had come by night and stolen the body. It appeared sufficient refutation to present the counter claim that the high priests had demanded from Pilate a guard of soldiers to prevent this very occurrence, that the guard had sealed the tomb, that an angel had descended and rolled away the stone while the watchers lay like dead men, and that when they recovered they informed the high priests, who bribed them to spread the slander of the stolen corpse.

---

[9][Mk.] 16:14.
[10]Jn. 20:24-28.
[11]Mk. 16:1; Mt. 28:1; Lk. 24:10.
[12]I Cor. 15:7.

[13]I Cor. 15:6.
[14]Mt. 28:16 f.; cf. Mk. 14:28; 16:7; Mt. 26:32; 28:7; perhaps also Jn. 21:1-14.

But the slander would not down and the story must be preserved to meet it.[15]

Such is the outline of the resurrection appearances as we can reconstruct from our sources the earliest accounts. Our picture may not be quite exact, but it cannot be far wrong. These stories must have originated within a few days after the discovery of the empty tomb, and have been written down within the first few years after the organization of the primitive church. Otherwise it is quite impossible to understand the survival of the empty tomb story so unnecessary to confirm their own faith after the full acceptance of the resurrection, or the still more amazing survival of those constant doubts of the disciples themselves, for to invent them only a few years later would have been a public scandal.

Of one thing we may be sure: the appearances cannot be reckoned as mere literary devices. Not only do they betray their primitive character, they do not hesitate to relate to their discredit the doubts of their church leaders, written down and circulated while those leaders were yet living and able if they wished to refute them. Some twenty-seven years after, Paul could appeal to the witness of more than five hundred men who saw Jesus at one time, "of whom the greater part remain until now, though some have fallen asleep."[16] As quoted by his companion Luke, Paul could appeal to the men "who came up with him from Galilee to Jerusalem, who are *now* witnesses to the people" that they saw Jesus after the crucifixion.[17] A chronicler who wrote while Peter was certainly alive makes his hero say to Cornelius: "Him God raised up on the third day, and gave him

---

[15]Mt. 27:62–66; 28:2–4, 11–15; Justin Martyr. *Dial. contra Tryphon*, 108; *Tertullian de Spec.* 30.

[16]I Cor. 15:6.
[17]Acts 13:30 f.

to be manifest, not to all the people, but to witnesses who had already been chosen beforehand by God, to us, who ate and drank with him after he arose from the dead."[18]

Only a genuine psychological experience common to all the leaders of the church can explain these stories, which find an even more explicit explanation in the appearance to Paul, only five years later, and yet as to one born out of due season.[19] Such appearances are absolutely demanded to explain the sudden shift in the feeling of the disciples, one day mourning and weeping, in fear, disillusioned, the next going forth joyfully to danger and death, and always preaching as the one absolute dogma of the new faith the belief in the resurrection.

The appearances continued for a brief time,[20] and then ceased. *We* may postulate reasons of psychology for the cessation; the disciples had another explanation: Jesus had ascended to heaven.[21] From this belief[22] followed inevitably the conclusion: Jesus was Messiah, he would return to save his own.

The simple faith of this earliest church is presented in the speeches of Peter; delivered originally in Aramaic, they have come down to us only in Greek translation and adaptation, but they were written down early and their very character proves their essential authenticity. Jesus the Nazoræan had been a "man proved to be from God by powers and wonders and signs." He had been crucified and slain by the hands of lawless men, the Romans, but only because he had been "surrendered up through the predetermined counsel and foreknowledge of God." God raised him up, as they themselves

---

18Acts 10:40 f.; *cf.* 1:2 f.
19I Cor. 15:8.
20Forty days, Acts 1:3.
21Lk. 24:50 f.; Acts 1:2-12.

22Acts 1:22; 2:33; 3:19-21; Ephes. 1:20; I Tim. 3:16; Heb. 1:3; 10:12; Barnabas 15, 9.

could witness, and made him Messiah. What the Messiah must suffer had been predicted by the prophets, and all had been fulfilled. Jesus was now exalted at the right hand of God. They must repent and be baptized in the name of Jesus Messiah into the blotting out of sins. When they repent, there will come for them "seasons of respite from the face of the Lord." Then he will send "the Messiah Jesus appointed for you, whom heaven must receive until times of restoration of all things" prophesied by the prophets.[23]

The last thought in the minds of the disciples would have been that they were founding a new religion. No more was this world-shaking fact realized by their fellow Jews. To all, the Nazoræans, so called from the home of their founder, formed simply one more sect. To the end of their existence, old-fashioned Jews called them Minim, "sectarians." They were neither so numerous as the Pharisees nor so influential among the peasants contemptuously dubbed "folk of the soil." Yet their Master's teaching was closely akin to Pharisaism; his disciples' report of the resurrection gave welcome confirmation against the hateful Sadducees of the fundamental Pharisaic tenet, life after death. In times of emergency the weight of Pharisaic authority was thrown in favor of toleration; in the words of Gamaliel, "Leave these men alone! If this counsel is from *men,* it will be overthrown; but if it is from *God,* you will not be able to overthrow them."[24]

To others, the Nazoræans were members of a minor sect, of no more significance than the Essenes. More closely they resembled those temporary groups which had formed around some preacher of rebellion or had collected to hear read some

---

[23]Acts 2:14b–36, 38 f.; 3:13–26;   [24]Acts 5:38 f.; *cf.* 23:6–9.
4:8b–12; 5:29–32.

new-found prophecy that God Himself would soon intervene
to save His people Israel. Jesus, their leader, had been crucified
as a rebel; for a time, his disciples would wait his return,
then the whole movement would follow its predecessors into
oblivion. When the high priests arrested Peter and John for a
casual breach of the peace, they were astonished to find that
they were former disciples of Jesus and that they were
preaching his resurrection! Even though these disciples
blamed Annas and Caiaphas for the judicial murder of their
Master, so sure were the high priests of their position that
Peter and John were merely threatened and warned to keep
quiet, then they were released.[25]

High-priestly hopes seemed destined quickly to be fulfilled.
For nearly a decade nothing serious happened. Under the
leadership of Peter and John, the Nazoræans remained quietly
in Jersualem, awaiting the coming of the Messiah. Since he
would return so soon, there was no need of looking to the
future. Converts sold their possessions and the brethren lived
an easy if frugal life in common from the proceeds. There
was no need of formal organization, even a separate synagogue cost too much for their scanty funds. An upper chamber, a simple "place of prayer," sufficed for the prayer and
songs of thanksgiving, the breaking of bread together. More
elaborate ritual they found in the Temple service, for they
even more scrupulously followed the minutest details of the
Mosaic Law, never dreaming that any one could call them
unorthodox. Firebrands like Stephen, Philip, and Paul stirred
up a little trouble but soon disappeared, followed by a sigh
of relief, and again the Nazoræans had peace.[26]

One thing alone kept them from stagnation. So vivid was

---

[25]Acts 4:1–22; later account, Acts   [26]Acts 9:31.
5:17–41.

the impression left by Jesus on his disciples that they could not forget his personality in the glory of the awaited Messiah. They could not confine their preaching to his tragic death, his glorious resurrection, his approaching second appearance; they must describe his gracious life on earth and his still more gracious sayings. Such was the appeal of Jesus, even thus transmitted secondhand, that slowly but steadily the number of converts increased.[27]

Suddenly and without warning, this somnolent little group of Nazoræans was jolted into wild excitement. Like their fellow Jews without exception, they were horrified to learn that the mad Caligula had given order that his colossal statue must be erected in the very Temple itself. Surely this was the Abomination of Desolation standing in the Holy Place which the prophet Daniel had foretold. The two legions brought up by the legate Petronius threatened the extinction of all Hebrews; now the Messiah must come on the clouds with his angels to the aid of his sorely distressed people.[28]

A hitherto unknown apocalypse made its appearance; it claimed to give the very words which Jesus had confided to his most trusted disciples in anticipation of this very crisis. While other Jews, from King Agrippa to the lowliest peasant, did their best to placate the insane emperor and his legate, warning that they would never permit the desecration, even at the risk of their lives, the Nazoræans made their preparations to greet their Master. When shortly after the crucifixion, John had published his Memoirs, he had mentioned without comment the belief of some that Jesus was the

---

[27]Increase from 120 after the Ascension to 3,000 after Pentecost, Acts 1:15; 2:41, must be exaggerated.
[28]Philo, *de legat.* 197 ff.; Joseph.

Ant. xviii, 261; *Wars* ii, 197; Tacitus, *Histories,* v 9, *Annals,* xii, 54; Megillat Taanit, Shebat 22; Scholia; Tosephta, Sotah, 13, 16.

Messiah and the objection of others: "Does the Messiah come from Galilee? Has not the scripture declared that from the seed of David and from Bethlehem, the village where David lived comes the Messiah?"[29] During the last decade, as the Messianic character of Jesus was increasingly emphasized, this serious objection must be met. It was discovered that Jesus *was* a descendant of David; the first genealogy brought the line only through a less important son, Nathan, the later through king Solomon.[30] Each genealogy was accompanied by an appropriate birth story, both agreeing that Jesus *was* born in Bethlehem, though differing in all other details.[31]

The dynastic principle thus established, it was obvious that until Jesus returned he should be represented by his nearest of kin, his eldest surviving brother James.[32] During Jesus' lifetime, James had joined with his brothers in their sneers, they had attempted to have this brother declared insane and imprisoned. Jesus had publicly repudiated them: "A Prophet is not unhonored—except in his own fatherland and among his own relatives and *in his own house.*"[33] James had indeed been converted by the vision of his risen brother,[34] but in the membership list of the earliest community he is lumped with his brothers at the end of the list; unlike the apostles he is not mentioned by name. When a substitute for Judas Iscariot was sought, he was not even suggested as qualified. Not once in the records of the first eight years is James mentioned; once he appears as next in importance to Peter, then Peter and John have disappeared and thereafter James is unquestioned head of the church.[35]

---

[29]Jn. 7:41 f. This is the clearest proof that John's narrative must be very early.

[30]Lk. 3:23b–38; Mt. 1:1–17.

[31]Lk. 1:26–56; 2:1–39; Mt. 1:18–2:23.

[32]Gal. 1:19; Mk. 6:3; Mt. 13:55.

[33]Jn. 7:3–5; Mk. 3:31–35; Mt. 12:46–50; Lk. 8:19–21; Mk. 6:4.

[34]I Cor. 15:7.

[35]Gal. 1:19; 2:9 ff.; Acts 12:17; 15:13; 21:18; Joseph. *Ant.* xx, 200.

James' election deprived Peter and John of their original
leadership. Did Peter the impetuous and John, a "Son of
Thunder,"[36] accept the demotion without protest? John had
composed his Memoirs before the Davidic birth and birthplace of Jesus had come to be accepted; is it an accident that
John goes out of his way to quote the sneering remarks of
the brothers when Jesus refused to go up to Jerusalem in
their company? Is there malice in the aside: "Even his *brothers* did not believe in him"? At any rate, John disappears
from our records after James became the head of the church.

One of our Gospel sources appears to have been composed
about this time. There is an evident attempt to set Peter in
first place. This is particularly conspicuous when we hear
how Jesus asked his disciples: "Who do *you* say that I am?"
and it is Peter who answers: "You are the Messiah!"[37] One
form of the story continues: "And Jesus, answering, said to
him: 'Happy are you, Simon, son of Jonah, for flesh and
blood have not revealed it to you, but my Father who is in
Heaven. And also I tell you: *You* are Rock in name, and
upon *this* Rock I will build my church, and the Gates of
Sheol[38] shall not prevail against it. I will give *you* the keys
of the Kingdom of Heaven, and whatever *you* shall bind on
earth shall be bound in heaven, and whatever *you* shall loose
on earth shall be loosed in heaven.' "[39] In the excitement of
the expected immediate coming, with Peter and James disput-
ing the honor of leading the little flock to welcome the Master,
we can understand the heat of the debate. The reply to this
claim is found a few lines farther on in our present Gospels:
Jesus predicted his coming sufferings and now Peter re-

[36] Mk. 3:17.
[37] Mk. 8:29; Lk. 9:20; Mt. 16:16.
[38] Jerusalem, E. Meyer, *Ursprung,*
I, 112.

[39] Mt. 16:17–19; in weakened form
applied to all the disciples, Mt.
18:18; Jn. 20:23.

buked him; in turn Jesus rebuked Peter: "Get behind me, Satan! For you are not considering the affairs of God but the affairs of men."[40]

Keyed up to the highest expectancy, hourly awaiting the Messiah's arrival and the establishment of the Kingdom in which they all would find high place, suddenly there came the news that Caligula had been assassinated. The Abomination of Desolation was not to be erected, the sign of the end had failed, the second appearance was to be delayed to an increasingly indefinite future.

This realization must have come to the Jerusalem community as a shock, as great as the crucifixion itself. It was the second terrific disappointment the disciples had suffered. Not a few of the faithful must have relapsed out of sheer emotional reaction, "the love of the many became cold."[41] Nevertheless, the shock did not destroy the church or even the belief in the second appearance. But the end of the easy communism had been reached. The ten long years of waiting had strained to the uttermost their resources; henceforth the mother church was officially "poor," and must be supported by the offerings of the faithful outside Judæa. Although formally recognized as the fountainhead of authority, it had lost all vitality. Perhaps after all, quiet, temporizing James was now the best head of a quiescent church.

Thereafter Nazoræan Judaism had no significant inner development. We know only its external history, its struggle to retain its authority against "false apostles," its attempts to enforce Mosaic practices upon recalcitrant non-Jewish converts. In these struggles, the Nazoræan were brought to an unwelcome attention by Jewish and Roman authorities and

---

[40]Mk. 8.33; Mt. 16:23; counter reply, Lk. 22:31 f.   [41]Mt. 24:12.

people alike. Much as they suffered, the bonds of race and religion remained tight; under the leadership of James, their Jewish character was emphasized.

Their fading dreams of a Jewish nationalistic Messiah remained undisturbed by these struggles until there came the third great shock, the assassination of James (62 A.D.) by that vicious son of Annas, Ananus II. Public sympathy was all on the side of "James the Just" and the murderer was quickly punished by deposition from his high rank. But sympathy won no new converts and the ill-starred attempt of his successors once more to enforce Judaic practices on non-Jewish converts snapped the last ties which had survived the death of James.

During these last years, the whole country had been plagued by constant rebellions against Roman authority, by self-styled prophets and Messiahs whose words dimmed the memory of Jesus' sayings. When these uprisings culminated in the Great Revolt (66 A.D.), there was a new crop of these deluded preachers, supported by new outbursts of apocalyptic writings. To the Nazoræans, all this once more presaged the end; in their own apocalypse, they read once more the advice to flee from Judæa to the mountains.[42] They escaped across Jordan to Pella, and thus deliberately broke the bond with the Holy City, four years before Jerusalem fell (70 A.D.).[43]

By so doing, they had deeply offended the nationalists, who, when they returned to temporary control in Bar Kokhba's revolt against Hadrian, slaughtered them unmercifully; the Rabbis complacently remarked: "The zealots are falling upon him."[44] No longer were they called the Nazoræans, they were

---

[42]Mk. 13:14; Mt. 24:16; Lk. 21:21.
[43]Euseb. *Church History*, iii, 5, 3.

[44]Justin Martyr, *Apology*, i, 31. Mishna, Sanhedrin, 9:6.

only Minim, the sectaries; an oath by Jesus was a curse by
the Sorcerer. Although they lived in close touch with the
orthodox, there were slight differences in practice to identify
them. Marriage with their daughters was forbidden; such
marriages were considered by some as the modern equivalent
of passing the seed through the fire to Moloch.

Their Bibles, the Aramaic Targums, were discredited, and
that was not difficult; they contained much that was not in
the original Hebrew, their translations were rarely close. New
and more exact translations were prepared to take their place,
the Targum assigned to Onkelos or the work which later became the Peshitta for the Aramaic-speaking Christians of
Mesopotamia.

The Nazoræan sacred books, written in their peasant
Aramaic soon after the death of the Master, were in constant danger of destruction. The generation of Jewish scholars
which survived the disappearance of Jerusalem debated their
status. Rabbi Johanan, Zakkai's son, who restored Judaism
after the catastrophe, refused to accept these heretic writings
among the books whose sacredness defiled the hands.[45]

What books were to be saved from a fire on a sabbath? Did
the number include these sectarian books because they contained the Divine Name? Rabbi Jose, the Galilæan, who could
invoke personal knowledge of the still functioning temple in
the later discussions, might be cited for an apparently milder
attitude: "On a week day," but not on a sabbath, "he cuts out
the Divine Names and hides and burns the rest." According
to Rabbi Ishmael, redeemed from captivity after the sack of
Jerusalem, "As to the books of the sectaries, who are throwing enmity, envy, and competition between Israel and their
Father in Heaven, certainly their books and their Divine

---

[45]Mishna, Yadaim 4:6; Tosephta, Yadaim 2:13.

Names should be destroyed." Rabbi Tarpon, who as a boy had attended service in the Temple, became so angered when he discussed the fate of these books that he invoked the rabbinical curse, "May I bury my children! If they come into *my* hands, I shall burn them *and* their Divine Names!"[46] All this before the end of our first century!

A tiny minority amid a larger but after 70 A.D. world-hated minority, the sectaries were exposed to constant propaganda, insult, and in time of revolt to actual massacre. Their sacred books were mutilated, hidden, and burned. Messiahs had come and gone and none had succeeded in throwing off the foreign yoke. Jews became wearied of this constant appearance of new Messiahs with their companion writings. As general interest died out, more and more the question must have pressed the sectaries: "Why should *we* continue to believe in Messiah Jesus?"

When ultimately the sect flickered out, there would be little reason to preserve their literary relics, least of all in a synagogue Geniza, where worn-out books were stored, and every inducement to burn them to ashes. Under such unfavorable circumstances, it is almost a major miracle that we have one single fragment of a Gospel source preserved in its original Aramaic form:

"I did not come to take away from the Law of Moses,
"But rather I came to add to the Law of Moses."[47]

---

[46]Jerusalem Talmud, Shabbat 15c; Babylonian Talmud, Shabbat 116b; Tosephta Shabbat 13:5.

[47]Shabbat 116b; *cf.* Mt. 5:17.

CHAPTER XIV

THE CHRIST TRIUMPHANT

SO far as the Jews were concerned, Jesus had failed utterly. He had been rejected, though by no means forgotten, by his own people. That he became a world influence was due to other Jews, of wider insight than the Jerusalem Nazoræans.

Among the converts Peter made at Pentecost were pilgrims from both Roman and Parthian empires. All were Jews by religion though some were Gentile proselytes.[1] They settled down in Jerusalem side by side with the disciples and local converts to await the coming of the promised Messiah, but not always in harmony. A charge of unfair distribution of common funds brought against the apostles by the Hellenists, the Greek-speaking Jews, was quieted by the appointment of a board of seven, all with Greek names, and one a proselyte from Antioch.[2]

To their financial duties was added that of preaching, and in this Stephen excelled. Like his fellow deacons, Stephen came from the wider world, and by no means saw eye to eye with the apostles. He was arrested and brought before the Sanhedrin; witnesses testified that he had said: "This Jesus the Nazoræan will destroy this Holy Place and will change the customs which Moses handed down to us." The charge was more than confirmed by Stephen's reply before the high priest.

---

[1]Acts 2:9–11.   [2]Acts 6:1–6.

After a somewhat Midrashic résumé of biblical history, designed to win the attention of his audience and based on his own Greek Bible, Stephen began his argument with Moses, who killed the Egyptian. "But he supposed that his brothers realized that God through his hand was giving them deliverance"—the last word might also mean salvation, the expression was deliberately ambiguous—"but they did not realize" and so reproached him that he must flee his own people. He was ordered by an angel to return to Egypt and save his own people, "this Moses whom," like Jesus, "they denied, saying: 'Who set *you* up as ruler and judge?' him God sent as ruler and redeemer by the hand of the angel."

"This is the Moses who said to the sons of Israel: 'A Prophet will God raise up to you from among your brethren like me.'" Even then they would not listen. Although "David, who found favor with God, asked permission 'to find a tent dwelling for the House of Jacob,' it was only Solomon who actually built him a house. Nevertheless, the Most High does not dwell in what is handmade, as says the Prophet: 'The heaven is my throne and the earth the footstool of my feet; what sort of a house will you build me, says the Lord, or what is the place of my rest? Did not my hand make all these?'" This was an even more savage attack on the Temple than the testimony of the witnesses had indicated.

Attack on the temple was followed by an equally savage attack on the Sanhedrin itself: "'Stiff-necked and uncircumcised in heart and ears,' always do you 'resist the Holy Spirit; like your fathers' are you also. Which of the prophets did not your fathers persecute? They also killed those who proclaimed before the coming of the Just," a title of Jesus found only in the early speeches and later transferred to his brother James, "of whom you now have become betrayers

and murderers, you who received the Law as ordinances of
angels and kept it not!"[3]

We are not surprised that the Sanhedrin, itself without
legal power of capital punishment, permitted an illegal lynch-
ing; what does astonish us is the wide breach already manifest between the attitude of the Hellenists and that of the
"Hebrew" disciples. Most significant of all, the setting down
in writing soon after of Stephen's martyrology and the careful preservation of his last speech prove that there were
others who agreed with Stephen that the coming of Jesus
had abrogated both Temple and Law.

That Stephen did not stand alone in his revolutionary
beliefs is further proved by the persecution which followed.
In it Saul of Tarsus took a conspicuous part.[4] Always the
guilt lay heavily on his soul. Yet Paul actually could insist
that he was "unknown by face to the churches in *Judaea,*"
that he had on his first trip to Jerusalem met only Cephas
and James, "and no other of the apostles did I see"; "before
God I lie not!"[5] The apostles remained unmolested in Jerusalem.[6] There could be no clearer evidence that the persecution was directed solely against the Hellenists; the original
Nazoræans, by their complete submission to all legalistic prescriptions, had kept their skirts clear.

Already it must have been perfectly obvious that there
was no hope of progress from within the Jerusalem community, which appeared perfectly content to remain a minor
Jewish sect. Far different was the attitude of the Hellenists,
now scattered abroad and everywhere preaching the Word.
First they took refuge in the countryside of Judæa and

---

[3]Acts 6 :8–7 :53.   [5]Gal. 1 :18–22.
[4]Acts 8 :3; 22 :4, 19 f.; 26 :10 f.;   [6]Acts 8 :1.
Gal. 1 :13 ; Philip. 3 :6.

Samaria. Of their activities we have details only about Philip the Evangelist, who made converts in Sebaste, the most Hellenized city of Samaria, baptized the Ethiopian eunuch, preached the good news from Azotos northward, founded no doubt the first churches at Joppa and Lydda,[7] and settled down permanently in Cæsarea, the capital of Palestine and a still more Hellenized city.[8]

The refugees were still farther scattered, to Phœnicia, to Cyprus, and to Antioch. At first they spoke the Word only to Jews, but in Antioch certain Hellenists from Cyprus and Cyrene preached the Lord Jesus also to pagan Greeks. So numerous were the converts that the attention of the populace was attracted; by it the converts were named Christians, a *Latin* term implying that they were followers of one Christ.[9]

The break between Hellenists and "Hebrews" had come. "Jesus Messiah" at best had no meaning for pagans, at worst the suggestion of a national Jewish king was repellent. The "good news of the Lord Jesus," on the contrary, could be made very attractive. When the Antioch proletariat named the converts Christians, the future of a new *religion* was forecast. To pagans and to Gentile converts alike, Christos was never a mere translation of the Jewish title Messiah; whether Christos or Chrestos or in its fuller form Jesus Christos, it was a name, *the* Name into which converts were baptized and by whose mystic power miracles were performed. It was a personal name, not of a Jewish prophet, but of a God who not long since had descended on earth like other deities, who like them had suffered and died, but by his own resurrection and by his continuing wonders had shown himself more powerful than his rivals.

---

[7]Acts 9:32, 36.
[8]Acts 8:1, 4–40; 21:8.

[9]Acts 11:19–21, 26.

As yet, all these implications cannot have been fully realized but their tendency must have been sensed. A Son of God who was also the Lord himself must have been as repugnant to Nazoræans as to their more orthodox Jewish brethren. That the breach between the two branches of Jesus' followers did not become complete earlier was due largely to Paul.

Himself a Hellenist from Cilician Tarsus, he had been converted by the faith and constancy not of the disciples but of the Hellenists. As he always insisted, and rightly, he had not been taught by Jerusalem. Perhaps he does overemphasize his direct inspiration from on high, he had learned the rudiments of the new faith in Damascus, to which refugee Hellenists already had escaped.[10] Before his first visit to the Jerusalem church, there had come to Paul the conviction that he too was chosen to be a missionary to the Gentiles.[11] His cool reception by the Jerusalem church, which feared that his bold preaching might stir up a fresh persecution and after only fifteen days took the first excuse to bundle him off home, did not increase his affection for the mother church, whose sigh of relief at his departure is reflected in Luke's "the church *therefore* had peace."[12] By strong pressure from the mother church, Paul had been exiled to the Gentile field, where it seems he spent his time founding new Cilician churches.[13]

From Tarsus, Paul was brought to Antioch by Barnabas.[14] Henceforth the story of the church, as we know it, is almost exclusively the story of Paul. He never forgot that he was, in a peculiar sense, the apostle to the Gentiles, and on occa-

[10]Acts 9:1 f.; *cf.* I Cor. 15:3.
[11]Acts 9:15; 22:15, 21; 26:17 f.
[12]Acts 9:26-31.
[13]Acts 15:41; *cf.* 15:23.
[14]Acts 11:25 f.

sion he could fight vigorously for his apostolic rights. Always he defended his Gentile converts, and attempts of Jerusalem to Judaize them were met with flaming indignation. His cause triumphed at the Apostolic Council (43 A.D.), which by Apostolic Decree granted full toleration of religious practice to Gentile Christians, though constant vigilance was required to prevent encroachments by irreconcilables.

All this is fully recognized; what is not so well realized is Paul's firm determination to prevent a schism within the infant church. When the issue of eating with uncircumcised Christians was raised at Antioch, Paul boldly carried the case to Jerusalem, whose authority he would gladly recognize—if only it gave the right decision. Fortunately he found in James an equally practical politician. Paul's guarded explanation of how he "laid before them the Gospel preached among the Gentiles, but individually to those of influence,"[15] hints of those behind-the-scene negotiations which preceded the plenary session. He brought with him from the rich Antioch community a generous contribution for the brethren dwelling in Judæa. That it played some part in the compromise is made sufficiently clear by Paul; when James, Cephas, and John, the reputed pillars of the church, gave him the right hands of fellowship after defining their respective spheres of missionary activity, there was one proviso: "Only that we should remember the poor," in other words, aid in the support of the mother church.[16]

Paul continues: "This very thing I made a great effort to accomplish." He was telling the truth; in this as in other details of the compromise, Paul was honestly trying to carry out his promises, as he understood them, to the best of his ability. His letters are filled with begging requests for Jeru-

---

[15]Gal. 2:2.   [16]Acts 11:29 f.; Gal. 2:10.

salem. At great inconvenience and even danger to himself, he went up to the Holy City with the offerings of the faithful. Thus personal relations between the two leaders were kept up and by this personal acquaintance, if not friendship, threatening schism was averted. The compromise was to the advantage of all: Paul enjoyed the prestige connected with the apostles and with Jerusalem; financial support kept the mother church alive and gave it a reverent following. The arrest which brought cessation of Paul's active preaching and ultimately led to his death was caused by the apostle's too willing acceptance of another compromise suggested by James in the vain hope of conciliating the irreconcilables.[17]

Furthermore, there were tendencies within this new Gentile church which Paul could not approve. There was reluctance to continue support of the distant mother church, which all the skilful money-raising technique of Paul's letters[18] could not always overcome. When he was not protesting the attempts of Judaizers, Paul was insisting that he himself was a Jew, that to the Jews were the promises, that the Gentile Christians must become spiritual sons of Abraham. The martyrdom of James, followed so soon by that of Paul, broke the personal bond, and the schism widened.

Paul was not the only Jewish missionary to the Gentiles. We have mention by name of Peter, Apollos, Aquila and Priscilla, Barnabas and Mark. Others may be sought among the friends greeted by Paul. Unknown Jews founded the churches in Rome and elsewhere, unknown Jews translated and adapted the original Aramaic Gospels into Greek or wrote letters to the Gentile faithful.

By the second generation, the breach between the Nazo-

---

[17]Acts 21 :20 ff.   [18]II Cor. 8 f. is a model.

ræans and the Christians had become impassable. While the
Nazoræan sect gradually disintegrated, the Christian religion
went on from triumph to conquest. "The blood of the martyrs was the seed of the church," but the martyrs were now
all Gentile. With the conversion of Gentiles higher in the
social scale, Christianity became respectable. Converts of
greater learning turned the new religion into almost a Greek
philosophy. More and more Christianity became westernized.
All vital thought within the empire to an ever greater degree
was deflected into Christian ways. The towering intellects of
the age were all supporters of that faith. Constantine the
Great brought the Roman world to worship the Christ and
through the great Council promulgated that Nicene Creed
which has henceforth determined the orthodox view of the
Son of God.

Far indeed was the Christ of orthodox theology from the
Carpenter of Nazareth. In these latter days we have again
sought to recover the Jesus of history. In our search, we may
not resort to the facile emotionalism of romance. For us is
the harder path of rigid and painstaking historical research.
Our resources are scanty, four small pamphlets, one in large
part repeating the other, and too often including events and
sayings which we cannot accept as historical.

On the basis of such inadequate source material, how can
the honest historian hope properly to assess the character of
Jesus? He has experienced the difficulty of understanding
the great personages of history, even though aided by masses
of extant written information, often including their correspondence and sometimes their memoirs, even though they
lived under conditions approaching those of our own day.
He knows that he does not fully understand his contem-

poraries, the most intimate friends. There are times he sus-
pects he does not know that complex entity, himself. Nevertheless, his final task cannot be shirked: the estimate of Jesus'
character must be attempted with such material as may be
available. By good fortune, the quantity is more considerable,
the quality is much better, than is too often assumed.

Jesus was a Jew, living in the early first century of our
era, and he can be understood to the full only in terms of
his time and race. His intellectual background was that of the
Jewish lower middle class. This background we may reconstruct roughly from more or less contemporary Jewish writings, though we should be on our guard lest we assign to the
artizan of Nazareth ideas more appropriate to Jerusalem
rabbis. Still greater would be the mistake to believe that
Jesus was influenced seriously by Greek thought, if only in
the highly diluted form discoverable in the somewhat Hellenized oriental cities around him.

To him, the Bible was *the* Book, though read for the most
part in the expanded Targum version. It was in the Law
of his God that he meditated day and night. It was Bible
language which formed his style and colored his thought
and its expression. Reminiscences from other and later books
which have happened to survive prove that his reading was
not exclusively biblical, but there is no reason to suspect
that their influence was particularly significant. The constant
expression of surprise at his knowledge and the flat statement
that he had never been a student indicate that Jesus had not
learned the oral law in a rabbinical school. His parables have
a freshness which prove that they were derived from direct
observation of daily life. A deeper, though more subtle influence came from the synagogue service and the stately cere-

monial of the temple feasts. But his preaching, which makes
special appeal to us of today, could have arisen only from
his own reflections, based on his reading of the scriptures.

Many of his contemporaries, his disciples included, looked
forward tensely to the redemption of Israel; by this they
meant primarily an independent life under a national Messiah. Jesus scarcely could have avoided reading or at least
hearing the wild apocalyptic hopes attributed to Enoch, and
in the little Galilæan hamlet often must have listened to the
debates as to when the Messiah would arrive, but *he* was
never deceived by the mirage. His followers long remembered, though the metaphorical meaning was now forgotten,
how once their Master had been shown "all the kingdoms
of the universe and their glory," his to possess if he declared
himself Messiah, and recognized the temptation for what it
was, the lying vision of the Accuser himself.

In his own consciousness, as to the majority of his
auditors, Jesus was a Prophet, one who announced God's
will to sinful man. Like his mighty predecessors, he preached
righteousness, and his utterances might be stern. The popular modern concept of the "Social Gospel" would, however,
have been simply unintelligible. Righteousness comprised all
that man owed to God; apart from God there was no occasion for separate mention of man's duty to fellow-man.

If we would truly understand Jesus, we must not stop
with his ethical preaching. There is no hint that Jesus ever
considered himself anything but a loyal Jew. He obeyed the
ritualistic prescriptions of daily life. He attended synagogue
service until the doors were closed in his face. Again and
again he risked his life to attend the great festivals at Jeru-

salem. He won spiritual sustenance from the temple ritual while doing his ordered duty. He met his death appropriately at the Passover feast.

Too often we exalt Jesus' teaching only to depreciate that of the rabbis. We wrong the Pharisees and we fail to do justice to Jesus himself, for of all the sects he was most in sympathy with Pharisaic doctrine. Their piety was not simple ritualism, they took joy in observing the most minute prescriptions of the Mosaic Law. To realize their moral superiority, we need only contrast their sayings with the best produced by the post-Augustan revival, the frigid letters of Seneca or the pompous, querulous correspondence of Apollonius. The true attitude of Jesus is shown in that one fragment preserved by his opponents in the original Aramaic:

"I did not come to take away from the Law of Moses,
But rather I came to add to the Law of Moses."

The true greatness of Jesus is to be sought in what he *added* to the Pharisaic Law. Even the finest of their leaders never quite succeeded in freeing themselves entirely from the shackles of legalism, never fully recognized that forms as such have absolutely no value, and that it is only the motive behind the action which brings the full reward of true righteousness. Pharisees had humanized the Law which the Sadducees literally enforced, yet they loved that Law as joyfully as they did their God; they lived a blameless life and they did their duty to their neighbor. What then did they lack? Jesus answered a fine representative of Pharisaism: "You are not far from the Kingdom of Heaven." The negative form of the approval in itself gives the criticism. Pharisaic righteousness was too largely negative in character. Even in its negative form, Hillel's Golden Rule marked a wonderful advance; Jesus, however, was positive: "You must *love* the Lord your God *and* your neighbor as yourself."

Love was the outstanding feature of Jesus' life as it was of his teaching. He went about doing good; so have others, and they have not always been loved. He gave himself, and there were times when he could feel the vital life force pouring out from him. His kindliness won the affection of his hearers, and those best judges of true character, the children, clustered about him. No man could have so impressed himself on his disciples as to survive so shameful a death had he not given and received an intense love. Even today, in far distant lands and under far different environment, despite the handicap of an alien language and a foreign race, the attractiveness of Jesus is strongly felt.

His life is still an inspiration, yet more so his heroic death. Few as are his surviving utterances, they appeal to us today as never before. The Mosaic Law preached love of neighbor, but the neighbor was an Israelite; by one of his most beautiful parables, Jesus proved that the neighbor might be even that most hated and despised of men, a Samaritan. The negative Golden Rule of Hillel was made positive and was extended to all humanity. Jesus' teaching was approved by his life; in complete disregard of worldly reputation, he regularly associated with the tax collector and the sinner, the Samaritan and the fallen woman.

His God is not the stern paternal despot, granting reward for service but more intent on vengeance; he is the loving Father in Heaven, who sends his rain on righteous and unrighteous alike. Formal prayer is unnecessary, the Heavenly Father knows what is needed and will give above what is expected. His Kingdom is no earthly monarchy, its coming marked by signs and portents; "the Kingdom of God is within you," and to enter one must become as a little child.

An early biographer sought to heighten the dramatic effect of the passion story by placing in Jesus' mouth the pitiful lament of the Psalmist: "Eloi, Eloi, lama sabachthani," interpreted as: "My God, My God, why have you forsaken me?"[19] He secured thus the desired human touch, but he did not do justice to his Master. In the midst of the frightful agony, Jesus retained that same confidence in the loving Father which had enabled him calmly to await the inevitable Prophet's doom. Far more truly dramatic was his last word from the cross: "Finished."[20] He had completed the Prophet's work assigned him; the fate of that work might be safely left in the hands of a wise and loving Father.

---

[19]Ps. 22:1; Mk. 15:34; Mt. 27:46.   [20]Jn. 19:30.

ACKNOWLEDGEMENTS

This book has enjoyed the inestimable advantage of composition within the walls of the Oriental Institute of the University of Chicago. There year after year my students have minutely investigated with me in connection with our Seminar in Oriental History the background of New Testament times. Two of these years were devoted to the intertestamental literature, two more to the New Testament itself.

To all these former students I owe a debt of deepest gratitude. Some, now my colleagues, I must mention by name. Professor Raymond A. Bowman has made available to me his unique card dictionary of early Aramaic and has helpfully criticized my attempts to recover the original form of Jesus' sayings. Establishment of the exact chronology for Jesus' life has been made possible by Dr. Waldo H. Dubberstein, who has patiently collected and interpreted the scattered data on Babylonian calendar and chronology and by Dr. Richard A. Parker, who has laboriously calculated the tables through which the dates of the Babylonian months may be turned into our own Julian calendar with rarely the error of a day. Dr. Neilson C. Debevoise has answered my frequent questions on the history, culture, and archæology of the deeper Near East. Dr. George R. Hughes has rechecked for me the demotic original of the Egyptian Lazarus story. Dr. Donald E. McCown, recently inducted into the United States Army, has discussed with me every problem from inception to final manuscript. Professor George G. Cameron has scanned the proof with an editorial eye and has made many valued suggestions.

With my colleague, Professor William A. Irwin, and my former colleague, Professor William C. Graham, now of United College, University of Manitoba, I have enjoyed many fruitful discussions on the Old Testament background. Dr. Samuel I. Feigin has generously opened for me his vast store of Talmudic erudition; some of the most important discoveries which have utilized Jewish sources have grown from one of his casual remarks.

Professor James A. Montgomery of the University of Pennsylvania has been a constant source of encouragement; from him I have learned much, especially as regards Aramaic. Rabbi George Fox of South Shore Temple, Chicago, from his practical experience has evolved several brilliant suggestions. Professor Chester C. McCown of the Pacific School of Religion, and Professor Frederick C. Grant of Union Theological Seminary, New York, have read my original manuscript from the viewpoint of the professional New Testament scholar. A former student, Professor Sherman E. Johnson of the Episcopal Theological School, has from the beginning of my special New Testament studies proved a more than sympathetic critic.

These pages were first written as chapters in a history of the later Near East from Cyrus to Muhammad. That they appear as a separate book is in large part due to the Oberlin Graduate School of Theology, whose faculty generously invited me to hold the Haskell Lectureship for the year 1940–41. The lectures, "Historian and New Testament," were delivered in November, 1940; perhaps fortunately, they could not be printed in their more or less controversial form. So great, however, was the interest of the students, extended to the general public by magazine abstracts and newspaper articles, that it was decided to adapt the studies on Jesus to a wider audience by reverting to the original form. To Dean Thomas W. Graham, Professor C. T. Craig, Professor Francis W. Buckler, and Professor Herbert G. May, especial thanks are due.

This list of acknowledgements would not be complete without grateful remembrance of my instructors at Cornell University. Dr. A. C. White, assistant librarian, year after year read with me Greek Testament, Apocrypha, and Church Father; that he was more interested in Greek moods and tenses than in critical theories I now count a blessing. Professor Henry A. Sill introduced me, by method and then in person, to his own teacher Eduard Meyer, the master of contemporary historians of antiquity. Professor George Lincoln Burr taught me the "Science and Art of History"; his incisive analysis of the defects of contemporary New Testament scholarship first awakened a determination some day to present the New Testament through an historian's eyes.

But it was Professor Nathaniel Schmidt who was my chief mentor. As student and then as assistant, I received from him the broadest of training in Oriental History. He taught me Hebrew and the cognate languages, and introduced me to the intertestamental literature. From him I learned the significance of the "Aramaic Gospel" and he gave me the tools to carry on the investigation. With him I tramped the highways and byways of Palestine. With him I also discussed his forthcoming *Prophet of Nazareth*. Best of all, he exemplified in his own teaching the quotation so often on his lips: "Never to swear by the word of the master."

APPENDIX

A Note on Gospel Chronology

Our sources are agreed that the Last Supper was celebrated on Thursday and that Jesus was crucified on Friday. According to our first three Gospels, Mk. 14:12; Mt. 26:17; Lk. 22:7, the Last Supper took place on the First Day of Unleavened Bread, when they sacrificed the Passover; they therefore describe the Last Supper as the Paschal Meal. Their account has generally been followed by scholars. John, however, describes only an ordinary meal; according to him, Jn. 13:1; *cf.* 18:28; 19:31, the Passover *followed* the crucifixion. That he is correct is fully proved by Jewish authority, Jesus was "hanged" on the *eve* of Passover, Babylonian Talmud, Sanhedrin 43a (uncensored edition).

If further proof is needed, it may be found in the new tables published in 1942 by two of my former students, Dr. Waldo H. Dubberstein and Dr. Richard A. Parker, *Babylonian Chronology, 625 B.C.–46 A.D.* By the use of much hitherto unutilized material from Babylonian tablets, the entire system of nineteen-year cycles, according to which the seven extra months were intercalated to bring the lunar and solar years into agreement, has been worked out. Once this system was established, there remained only long months of laborious calculation from already published astronomical tables; the tables now published give the first day of each Babylonian month for each of these more than six hundred years in terms of the Julian calendar, and they are exact within the day! This almost miraculous precision guarantees their continued use as the foundation for all future chronological studies in the field of ancient history. While yet in manuscript form, they have repeatedly been employed by members of the Oriental Institute staff, *e.g.,* A. T. Olmstead, "Cuneiform Texts and Hellenistic Chronology," *Classical Phi-*

lology, XXXII, 1937, 1 ff.; "Babylonian Astronomy, Historical Sketch," *American Journal of Semitic Languages,* LV, 1938, 113 ff.

Since during this entire period the Jews as well as other peoples of Western Asia employed the Babylonian calendar, all biblical dates between 625 B.C. and 46 A.D., when an extra intercalated month was added by a Parthian king, can be ascertained with equal precision. By one simple addition to our procedure, we can also obtain the date of the crucifixion. All our sources, we have seen, are agreed that the crucifixion took place on Friday. Accepting this as proved, we have only to discover a year within the possible ministry of Jesus on which Passover took place just before or just after a Friday. To make the test is a matter of but a few moments. From our tables we take the date of Nisan 14, Passover, for each of the possible years. From easily accessible perpetual calendars, it is but an instant to determine on which day of the week it fell. Only one year, the year 30 A.D., meets the test; the crucifixion took place therefore on April 7. This conclusion is furthermore corroborated in the most extraordinary manner; more than two centuries ago, great scholars calculated the Easter Cycle, by which the date of our Easter is to this day fixed. To fill up the blank spaces in their tables, they calculated the Easter Cycle back to the beginning of the Christian Era. In these ancient tables, we may still read their date of Easter Sunday for the year 30 A.D. and it is April 9!

By these laborious, roundabout, but rigidly scientific methods, we have determined the exact date of the crucifixion. Few indeed are the dates in Greek and Roman history before Julius Cæsar's reforms which can pretend to anything like the same precision. John has been proved correct, Matthew, Mark, and Luke are proved wrong. We have perfect right to accept as correct the other dates obtainable from John; again it is only a moment to ascertain the date of a given feast in the Jewish calendar, another moment to turn from our tables the Jewish date into one in our Julian calendar. Luke's date for the beginning of the Baptist's preaching is not only confirmed but made far more precise. There remains only the relatively easy task of fitting the minor details into the exactly determined framework; the details may be read in my article, "The Chronology of Jesus' Life," published in the *Anglican Theological Review, XXIV,* 1942, 1 ff.

Since I wrote this article, Dr. Feigin has drawn my attention to the two Geniza lists of Haftarot according to the Triennial Cycle just published by Jacob Mann, *The Bible as Read and Preached in the Old Synagogue,* I, 1940. As we discover on pp. 569, 573, *cf.* 481, the passage read by Jesus before his Nazareth sermon, Lk. 4:18 f., is assigned to the 62nd Seder. This means that the passage was read on the 62nd Sabbath of the Triennial Cycle, which began on the first Sabbath after the feast of Sukkoth or Tabernacles ended, naturally in the previous year. As Sukkoth ended in the year 27 A.D. on October 13th, simple calculation proves that the 62nd Seder was read on December 18, 28 A.D.

This proves that Luke's account of the rejection at Nazareth is correct and correctly placed, that Matthew and Mark are wrong. We have further confirmation of Luke's date for the beginning of John's preaching. The date of Jesus' baptism must be within a few days of December 1, 28 A.D. We can even give the exact length of Jesus' ministry—475 days.

BIBLIOGRAPHICAL NOTES

SOURCES

Authentic source material for the life and teachings of Jesus is to be found only in our four canonical Gospels, traditionally assigned to Matthew, Mark, Luke, and John. A few casual references in other books of the New Testament afford additional proof for certain events and sayings, but contribute nothing new. Apocryphal Gospels and similar writing are historically worthless. One brief reference to Jesus by Josephus in his *Antiquities,* xviii, 63 f., is proved authentic by a back reference to "Jesus, the so-called Christ," as brother of James in xx, 200, but it has been heavily interpolated by a Christian editor. From the original account of Josephus is derived the casual reference to "Christus, punished by the procurator Pontius Pilate," Tacitus, *Annals,* xv, 44. Suetonius, *Claudius,* xxv, 4, apparently thought that "Chrestus," lived in Rome. All other references are based on the Gospels.

GREEK TEXT

The text of the Greek Gospels should be the most trustworthy we possess for any ancient literature. While for some of the most important works of classical literature we have only a single mutilated manuscript copied late in the middle ages, and for none of them is the manuscript evidence overgenerous, manuscripts of the Greek Gospels and of their versions are counted by the thousands and many of them are of surprisingly early date.

TEXT IMPROVEMENTS

For well over a generation, the standard text has been that of Westcott and Hort. New discoveries of papyri, some as early as 200 A.D., have weakened seriously the prestige of the genealogical principle on which that text was constructed and with it the prestige of the Codex Vaticanus so generally made the basis of the text. A new text, which recognizes the fact that already in the second century variant *editions* were already in circulation, is demanded; meanwhile, each worker must form his own text, eclectic within rigidly fixed limits. The differences should not be exaggerated; in general they are minor and assume importance for the historian only when they relate to the presence or absence of passages in the text.

TRANSLATIONS

The best available translation is still that of the American Revised Version, of which another revision is now in preparation. Its text is normally that of Westcott and Hort; as a rule, the marginal translation is superior to that in the text. Of private translations, there is need to mention only those of James Moffatt, *The Holy Bible,* 1926, and of E. J. Goodspeed, *The New Testament, an American Translation,* 1923, whose chief virtue is its vivid colloquialism, which has tended however to blur the precision of technical terminology.

ARAMAIC ORIGINALS—OPPONENTS

These translations are all made from the Greek text, which alone is now extant. Jesus did not, however, preach in Greek but in Aramaic, and his sayings therefore must have been translated. The traditional view is that our present four Gospels and their written sources were all composed originally in Greek. This view is still defended by E. C. Colwell, *The Greek of the Fourth Gospel,* 1931; D. W. Riddle, "The Logic of the Theory of Translation Greek," *Journal of Biblical Literature,* LI, 1932, 13 ff.; "The Aramaic Gospels and the Synoptic Problem," *ibid.,* LIV, 1935, 127 ff.; E. J. Goodspeed, *New Chapters in New Testament Study,* 1937, 127 ff.

Aramaic Originals—Proponents

A detailed reply to Goodspeed is presented by A. T. Olm-stead, "Could an Aramaic Gospel be Written?" *Journal of Near Eastern Studies,* I, 1942, 41 ff. Other studies assuming an Aramaic original for longer or shorter sections of the Gospels are G. Dalman, *The Words of Jesus,* 1902; *Jesus-Jeshua,* 1929; Nathaniel Schmidt, *The Prophet of Nazareth,* 1905, 234 ff.; S. J. Case, "Kyrios as a Title for Christ," *Journal of Biblical Literature,* xxvi, 1907, 151 ff. C. F. Burney, *The Aramaic Origin of the Fourth Gospel,* 1922; *The Poetry of Our Lord,* 1925; J. A. Montgomery, *The Origin of the Gospel of St. John,* 1923; "Torrey's Aramaic Gospels," *Journal of Biblical Literature,* LIII, 1934, 79 ff.; Millar Burrows, "The Original Language of the Gospel of John," *ibid.,* XLIX, 1930, 95 ff.; "Principles for Testing the Translation Hypothesis in the Gospels," *ibid.,* LIII, 1934, 13 ff.; J. de Zwaan, "John wrote in Aramaic," *ibid.,* LVII, 1938, 155 ff.; W. R. Taylor, "Aramaic Gospel Sources and Form Criticism," *Expository Times,* LIX, 1937–38, 55 ff.; the chief protagonist of the Aramaic gospel, C. C. Torrey, has crowned a whole series of articles by *The Four Gospels: A New Translation,* 1933; cf. *Our Translated Gospels,* 1936; *Documents of the Primitive Church,* 1941. Torrey assumes that our four Gospels, virtually as they stand, are direct translations from the Aramaic; the present volume makes only the original Gospels written in that tongue.

Harmonies

There is no general agreement on the source criticism of these four Gospels. C. C. McCown, *The Search for the Real Jesus, a Century of Historical Study,* 1940, gives a penetrating if discouraging survey. Investigation of source problems begins with comparison of the four sources, best initiated by use of a "Harmony." Among them may be cited A. Huck, *Synopse der drei ersten Evangelien,* 3rd ed., 1906; E. D. Burton and E. J. Goodspeed, *A Harmony of the Synoptic Gospels in Greek,* 1920; W. A. Stevens and E. D. Burton, *A Harmony of the Gospels for Historical Study,* 1893.

SOURCE CRITICISM—AGNOSTIC

Typical recent books may be cited according to the schools they represent. The Christ myth hypothesis caused much excitement when popularized by W. B. Smith, *Der wachristliche Jesus,* 1906; *Ecce Deus,* 1913; and by Arthur Drews, *The Christ Myth,* 1910; but is now dead. A distinction without essential difference is found in the view that Jesus was indeed an historical personage but one of whom we know little or nothing. Illustrative is Charles Guignebert, *Jesus,* 1935. In America, the most outspoken advocates of this negative view have been C. T. Craig, "Current Trends in New Testament Study," *Journal of Biblical Literature,* LVII, 1938, 359 ff.; D. W. Riddle, "The Central Problem of the Gospels," *ibid.,* LX, 1941, 97 ff. The deliberate refusal of the *Cambridge Ancient History,* the last great synthesis of our knowledge of the ancient world, even to attempt a portrait of Jesus, is a glaring example of this agnosticism.

As a result, recent books on the Gospels have emphasized their significance for an understanding of the early church but have tacitly or explicitly ignored their value for a life of Jesus. Perhaps the most important is B. H. Streeter, *The Four Gospels,* 4 ed., 1930.

FORM CRITICISM

Form criticism, a technique borrowed from the folklorists who have long used it with conspicuous success, has been introduced recently into New Testament investigation. A long period of transmission by oral tradition must be assumed, an assumption also necessitated by the hypothesis that all Gospel sources were in Greek and late in date. Translations of the leading German exponents have been given by F. C. Grant, *Form Criticism, a New Method in New Testament Research,* 1934 (includes R. Bultmann, *The Study of the Synoptic Gospels;* K. Kundsin, *Primitive Christianity in the Light of Gospel Research); M. Dibelius, *The Message of Jesus Christ,* 1939; cf.

Gospel Criticism and Christology, 1935. Much the same view is held by D. W. Riddle, *The Gospels, Their Origin and Growth,* 1939. Form criticism tends to historical agnosticism; partial exceptions are C. H. Dodd, *History and the Gospel,* 1938; V. Taylor, *Formation of the Gospel Tradition,* 1933.

SYNOPTIC CRITICISM

Fortunately, form criticism has not entirely supplanted the older source criticism, which has followed in its virtues and its vices ordinary literary criticism. For the synoptic Gospels, its results may be accepted in so far as it proves a common source for the narratives of all three and another source for the sayings common to Matthew and Luke. Streeter, *Four Gospels,* has, however, proved that Luke's main source was independent.

MARK AS PRIMARY SOURCE

Most followers of the literary criticism assume also that Mark in its present form was actually the source of Matthew and Luke. This view was tested by the four competing narratives of the trial of Jesus at a meeting of the Society of Biblical Literature, December 31, 1940. Further evidence from the six competing stories of the Feeding of the Multitude has been given by the writer in the *Journal of Near Eastern Studies,* I, 1942, 70 ff. The present volume shows in detail that the unique source of Luke has high value, though members of this school have generally denied historical probability to everything not found in the narratives of Mark.

INTRODUCTIONS

So enormous is the literature presenting this until recently standard view that only a selection can be given. Among the introductions are A. Jülicher, *An Introduction to the New Testament,* 1904; James Moffatt, *An Introduction to the Literature of the New Testament,* 3 ed., 1918; E. F. Scott, *The Literature of the New Testament,* 1932; E. J. Goodspeed, *An Introduc-*

tion to the New Testament, 1937; Kirsopp Lake and Silva Lake, *An Introduction to the New Testament,* 1937; *cf.* M. J. Lagrange, *Introduction à l'Étude du Nouveau Testament,* 1933—— (Catholic).

GOSPELS

Among important works on the Gospels are V. H. Stanton, *The Gospels as Historical Documents,* 1903–20; F. C. Burkitt, *The Gospel History and Its Transmission,* 3 ed., 1911; *The Earliest Sources for the Life of Jesus,* 2 ed., 1922; B. S. Easton, *The Gospel before the Gospels,* 1928; *Christ in the Gospels,* 1930; E. D. Burton, *A Short Introduction to the Gospels,* revised by H. R. Willoughby, 1926; F. C. Grant, *The Growth of the Gospels,* 1933; *The Gospels of the Kingdom,* 1940; F. V. Filson, *Origins of the Gospels,* 1938.

SYNOPTIC PROBLEM

For the synoptic problem, we may consult E. D. Burton, *Some Principles of Literary Criticism and Their Application to the Synoptic Problem,* 1904; B. Weiss, *Die Quellen der synoptischen Überlieferung,* 1908; J. C. Hawkins, *Horae Synopticae,* 2 ed., 1909; W. Sanday, editor, *Oxford Studies in the Synoptic Problem,* 1911; J. Wellhausen, *Einleitung in die drei ersten Evangelien,* 2 ed., 1911; C. G. Montefiore, *The Synoptic Gospels,* 2 ed., 1927.

SAYINGS

Of special value for the so-called "Q" document is A. Harnack, *The Sayings of Jesus,* 1908; *cf.* E. F. Scott, *The Ethical Teaching of Jesus,* 1924; B. S. Easton, *What Jesus Taught,* 1938. For the Parables, see W. O. E. Oesterley, *The Gospel Parables in the Light of Their Jewish Background,* 1936; B. T. D. Smith, *The Parables of the Synoptic Gospels,* 1937.

COMMENTARIES: MATTHEW, MARK, LUKE

Earlier commentaries on the individual books should not be ignored; they give information on variants of the text, grammar and syntax, exegesis, and often translations which cannot be bettered. For Matthew, *cf.* W. C. Allen, *A Critical and Exegetical Commentary on the Gospel according to St. Matthew,* 1907; J. Wellhausen, *Das Evangelium Matthaei,* 2 ed., 1914; P. A. Micklem, *St. Matthew,* 1917; M. J. Lagrange, *Évangile selon Saint Matthieu,* 1923; E. Klostermann, *Das Mattäus Evangelium,* 2 ed., 1926; A. H. M'Neile, *The Gospel according to St. Matthew,* 1915. For Mark, A. Menzies, *The Earliest Gospel,* 1901; E. P. Gould, *A Critical and Exegetical Commentary on the Gospel according to St. Mark,* 1896; H. B. Swete, *The Gospel according to St. Mark,* 1898; J. Wellhausen, *Das Evangelium Marci,* 2 ed., 1909; B. W. Bacon, *The Gospel of Mark,* 1925; A. E. J. Rawlinson, *St. Mark,* 1925; E. Klostermann, *Das Markusevangelium,* 3 ed., 1936; M. J. Lagrange, *The Gospel according to St. Mark,* 1930. For Luke, A. Plummer, *A Critical and Exegetical Commentary on the Gospel according to St. Luke,* 1896; A. Wright, *The Gospel according to Luke,* 1900; J. Wellhausen, *Das Evangelium Lucae,* 1904; A. Harnack, *Luke the Physician,* 1907; W. M. Ramsay, *Luke the Physician,* 1908; H. J. Cadbury, *The Style and Literary Method of Luke,* 1919; *The Making of Luke-Acts,* 1927; M. J. Lagrange, *Évangile selon Saint Luc,* 1921; Lonsdale Ragg, *St. Luke,* 1922; A. F. Loisy, *L'Évangile selon Luc,* 1924; Vincent Taylor, *Behind the Third Gospel,* 1926; B. S. Easton, *The Gospel according to St. Luke,* 1926; E. Klostermann, *Das Lukasevangelium,* 2 ed., 1929; J. M. Creed, *The Gospel according to Luke,* 1930; W. Manson, *The Gospel of Luke,* 1930.

THE PROBLEM OF THE FOURTH GOSPEL

Discovery of a complete codex of all four Gospels dating little later than 200 A.D., F. G. Kenyon, *The Chester Beatty Biblical Papyri,* II, *The Gospels and Acts,* 1933–34, has compelled a drastic reduction downward of the late dates once assigned to the synoptic Gospels. Even more destructive of the late date of John is the finding of a scrap of that Gospel which cannot be placed later than 135 A.D., C. H. Roberts, *An Unpublished Fragment of the Fourth Gospel in the John Rylands Library,* 1935. The current view that John has little or no historical value is thereby challenged and the doubt of value is transferred to the books which hold this view.

John—Special Studies

Among more conservative studies are J. Drummond, *An Inquiry into the Character and Authorship of the Fourth Gospel,* 1904; W. Sanday, *The Criticism of the Fourth Gospel,* 1905; B. F. Westcott, *The Gospel according to St. John,* 1908; J. H. Bernard, *A Critical and Exegetical Commentary on the Gospel according to St. John,* 1929; M. J. Lagrange, *L'Évangile selon Saint Jean,* 2 ed., 1928 (Catholic) ; J. A. Robinson, *The Historical Character of St. John's Gospel,* 2 ed., 1929; H. S. Holland, *The Fourth Gospel,* 1923. Leaders of the radical attitude, H. H. Wendt, *The Gospel according to St. John,* 1902; B. W. Bacon, *The Fourth Gospel in Research and Debate,* 1910; *The Gospel of the Hellenists,* 1933; E. F. Scott, *The Fourth Gospel, Its Purpose and Theology,* 2 ed., 1908. Other works: F. W. Worsley, *The Fourth Gospel and the Synoptists,* 1909; H. L. Jackson, *The Problem of the Fourth Gospel,* 1918; A. Loisy, *Le Quatrième Évangile,* 2 ed., 1921; R. H. Strachan, *The Fourth Evangelist,* 2 ed., 1925; Percy Gardner, *The Ephesian Gospel,* 1915; L. Muirhead, *The Message of the Fourth Gospel,* 1925; A. E. Garvie, *The Beloved Disciple,* 1922; J. E. Carpenter, *The Johannine Writings,* 1927; G. H. C. Macgregor, *The Gospel of John,* 1928; V. Burch, *The Structure and Message of St. John's Gospel,* 1928; B. W. Robinson, *The Gospel of John,* 1928; H. Odeberg, *The Fourth Gospel,* 1929; E. S. Hoernle, *The Record of the Beloved Disciple,* 1931; G. W. Broomfield, *John, Peter, and the Fourth Gospel,* 1934; E. C. Colwell, *John Defends the Gospel,* 1936; P. Gardner Smith, *Saint John and the Synoptic Gospels,* 1938.

John—Sources

Earlier attempts to differentiate sources are listed by C. Clemen, *Die Entstehung des Johannesevangeliums*, 1912, 8 ff.; *cf.* W. F. Howard, *The Fourth Gospel in Recent Criticism and Discussion*, 1931. The author's discovery that the narratives proper are fully trustworthy while the interpolations agree with the long sermons in style and thought is the basis of this present life of Jesus.

Lives of Jesus

Preceding studies in source criticism have generally ignored the fact that all their conclusions are of tentative validity only until tested and proved through incorporation of the results in a full-length history. Earlier "conservative" Lives of Jesus are now considered out of date but a solid foundation with much valuable detailed illumination is due to such works as A. Edersheim, *The Life and Times of Jesus the Messiah*, 8th ed., 1896, and T. Keim, *The History of Jesus of Nazara*, 1873–83; to the Catholic studies of L. C. Fillion, *The Life of Christ*, 2 ed., 1928; M. J. Lagrange, *L'Évangile de Jésus Christ*, 1930; and F. Klein, *Jesus and His Apostles*, 1932; to T. R. Glover, *The Jesus of History*, 1917, non-critical but learned; and to A. C. Headlam, *The Life and Teaching of Jesus the Christ*, 1923, moderate. J. Klausner, *Jesus of Nazareth*, 1925, gives the Jewish point of view but follows current criticism. Representatives of the synoptic criticism are O. Holtzmann, *The Life of Jesus*, 1904; W. Bousset, *Jesus*, 1906; Nathaniel Schmidt, *The Prophet of Nazareth*, 1905; G. H. Gilbert, *Jesus*, 1912; F. C. Grant, *The Life and Times of Jesus*, 1921; G. A. Barton, *Jesus of Nazareth, a Biography*, 1922; A. H. McNeile, *Concerning Jesus*, 2 ed., 1924; S. J. Case, *Jesus, a New Biography*, 1927; J. Warshauer, *The Historical Life of Christ*, 1927; C. Gore, *Jesus of Nazareth*, 1929; F. Merrifield, *The Rediscovery of Jesus*, 1929; J. F. Bethune-Baker, *Early Traditions about Jesus*, 1930; J. MacKinnon, *The Historic Jesus*, 1931; F. C.

Burkitt, *Jesus Christ, an Historical Outline,* 1932; M. Goguel, *Life of Jesus,* 1933; P. Gardner-Smith, *The Christ of the Gospels,* 1938. In general, only the narrative of Mark is accepted, with "Q" for the teaching; in recent times, the amount of data accepted as historical grows steadily less. Not a few also attribute apocalyptic belief to Jesus himself.

GEOGRAPHY OF PALESTINE

Description of the events demands description of the stage. References to Palestine in this volume are based on personal knowledge, secured by continuous tramping over the country. Night after night in the villages introduced the author to native life. Much fuller descriptions are to be found in the writer's *History of Palestine and Syria,* 1931. The classic picture of Palestine is still that of George Adam Smith, *Historical Geography of the Holy Land,* 1894; *cf.* G. Dalman, *Sacred Sites and Ways,* 1935.

The map of Palestine (see page 134) in the time of Jesus has been checked with that of Roman Palestine, by M. Avi-Yonah, *Quarterly of the Department of Antiquities in Palestine,* V, 1936, 139 ff.

JERUSALEM

Jerusalem presents special problems. The plan used as end paper for this book has been constructed by the author and differs considerably from that familiar to the general reader. With the accompanying description of the Holy City it has been based, not merely on the ancient authorities mentioned in the notes, but particularly on minute and repeated examination of the ruins themselves during the years 1904–1905 and again in the spring of 1937. Results of personal examination have been checked by the archæological reports for which *cf.* L. A. Mayer and M. Avi-Yonah, "Concise Bibliography of Excavations in Palestine, Jerusalem," *Quarterly of the Department of Antiquities in Palestine,* I, 1932, 163 ff. The best English manual is still that of G. A. Smith, *Jerusalem,* 1908, though it often requires modification, especially on the course of the Second Wall. Important also is *Jérusalem, Recherches de Topographie, d'Archéologie, et d'Histoire,* I, *Jérusalem Antique,* by H. Vincent, 1912; II, *Jérusalem Nouvelle,* by H. Vincent and F. M. Abel, 1914–1926.

RECENT DISCOVERIES

Excellent accounts of the modern city and of its ancient ruins may be found in the guide books: Baedeker's *Palestine and Syria,* 3 ed., 1898, though badly antiquated, is valuable for the contributions of I. Benzinger; Cook's *Handbook to Palestine, Syria, and Iraq,* 6 ed., 1934, has an archæological appendix by John Garstang, former director of the Department of Antiquities for Palestine; Hachette's *Guide Bleu, Syrie, Palestine,* 1932, is particularly important for the plan of Herodian Jerusalem prepared by Père Hughes Vincent, the outstanding authority on Jerusalem topography, who has discussed the problem more fully in "Les Murs de Jérusalem d'après Néhémie," *Revue Biblique,* NS. I, 1904, 56 ff. More recent discoveries are listed in the *Bulletin of the American Schools of Oriental Research,* the *Palestine Exploration Quarterly,* the *Quarterly of the Department of Antiquities in Palestine,* and the *Revue Biblique.*

JOSEPHUS

For over two centuries, the background of Jesus' time has been well known through the translation of Josephus by William Whiston, often reprinted. Since 1926, a new translation and text, begun by H. St. J. Thackaray and continued by Ralph Marcus, has been in process of production in the *Loeb Classical Library.* Unfortunately the books of the *Antiquities* dealing with our period have not yet appeared; Whiston's translation is not safe and we must consult the original text as edited by B. Niese, *Flavii Josephi Opera,* 1885–95. Josephus was not a contemporary, he was born in 37 A.D. and wrote after 70 A.D., but his sources were excellent.

ROMAN EMPIRE

For the background history of the Roman empire, our best source is Tacitus, *Annals,* now edited and translated by C. H. Moore and J. Jackson in the *Loeb Classical Library,* 1931, 1937; Tacitus was not a contemporary, the *Annals* were still being written in 117 A.D., or more than a century after the accession of Tiberius. All authentic references to the Jews, including that to Jesus, were derived from Josephus. Supplementary information may be found in the *Lives of the Cæsars* by Suetonius, a later contemporary of Tacitus, edited and translated by J. C. Rolfe, 1914, in the *Loeb Classical Library.* This broader background is most recently sketched with full bibliography in the *Cambridge Ancient History, The Augustan Empire, 44 B.C.– A.D. 70,* edited by S. A. Cook, F. E. Adcock, and M. P. Charlesworth, X, 1934.

JEWISH HISTORY

All books dealing with the narrower background are based on E. Schürer, *Geschichte des jüdischen Volkes im Zeitalter Jesu Christi,* 4 ed., 1901–1909; unfortunately the English translation, *A History of the Jewish People in the Time of Jesus Christ,* 1890–1901, is based only on the second edition. Of later works, the best is Shailer Mathews, *New Testament Times in Palestine,* 1933; *cf.* also F. C. Grant, *The Economic Background of the Gospels,* 1926. F. B. Marsh, *The Reign of Tiberius,* 1931, should be read.

NEAR EAST

In these and similar works the "ancient history background" is treated as for all practical purposes identical with the general history of Greece and Rome, from whose standpoint events are viewed. The present volume has been written through the use of an almost complete history of the later ancient Near East extending from Cyrus to Muhammad, in which oriental sources are used side by side with the Greek and Latin, and in which the viewpoint is that of the Near East itself.

Pre-Christian Jewish Literature

This volume also emphasizes the fact that Jesus and his acquaintances were Jews, not Greeks, and that they were as yet little Romanized. We must therefore study their literature. Much of this, originally composed in Aramaic or Hebrew, is now available only in Greek translation or in secondary translations from the Greek. A generation of devoted investigation is now presented in translation, with full introductions and notes, under the editorship of R. H. Charles, *Apocrypha and Pseudepigrapha of the Old Testament*, 1913. More precise dating and interpretation are given by A. T. Olmstead, "Intertestamental Studies," *Journal of the American Oriental Society*, LVI, 1936, 242 ff. A huge new literature is at last made available for use by the recognition that the Aramaic Targums, greatly expanded translations of the Hebrew Bible, are, when freed from certain later additions or changes, pre-Christian in date and actually formed the Bible of Jesus; *see* Olmstead, "Could an Aramaic Gospel be Written?" *Journal of Near Eastern Studies*, I, 1942, 41 ff.

Post-Christian Literature

Later Talmudical literature has been well utilized. It is best approached through H. L. Strack, *Introduction to the Talmud and Midrash*, 1931. This whole literature has been pillaged by H. L. Strack and P. Billerbeck, *Kommentar zum Neuen Testament aus Talmud und Midrash*, 1923–28. *Cf.* C. G. Montefiore, *Rabbinic Literature and Gospel Teaching*, 1930. There is an excellent translation of the fundamental source by H. Danby, *The Mishnah*, 1923. I. Epstein, *The Babylonian Talmud*, 1935— is continuing the translation of that huge collection, but there is no adequate modern translation of the even more significant *Jerusalem Talmud*. The Midrashic material is collected and annotated by L. Ginzberg, *The Legends of the Jews*, 1913–38. Among the outstanding general works are G. F. Moore, *Judaism*, 1927–30; R. T. Herford, *Christianity in Talmud and Midrash*, 1903; L. Finkelstein, *The Pharisees*, 1938. Too much of this type of literature tacitly assumes that Talmud and Midrash represent the procedure and thought of the time of Jesus; actually much remains to be done in dating the portions which are pre-Christian. In this form of investigation, Finkelstein has shown himself a leader.

INDEX OF REFERENCES

INDEX OF NAMES AND SUBJECTS

INDEX OF REFERENCES

INDEX OF NAMES AND SUBJECTS

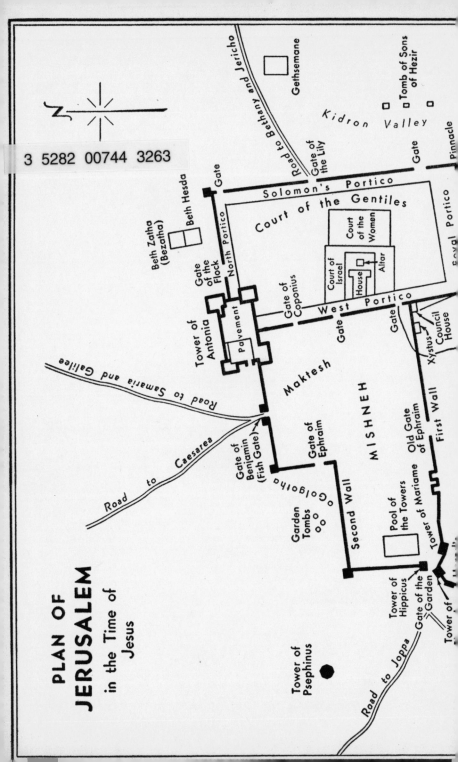

PLAN OF JERUSALEM
in the Time of Jesus

N

Tower of Psephinus

Road to Joppa

Gate of the Garden

Tower of Hippicus

Tower of Mariame

Pool of the Towers

Garden Tombs

Golgotha

Second Wall

Gate of Benjamin (Fish Gate)

Road to Caesarea

Road to Samaria and Galilee

Gate of Ephraim

MISHNEH

Old Gate of Ephraim

First Wall

Maketesh

Tower of Antonia

Pavement

Gate of the Flock

North Portico

Beth Zatha (Bezatha)

Beth Hesda

Gate

Gate of Coponius

West Portico

Gate

Gate

Xystus

Council House

Royal Portico

Court of the Gentiles

Solomon's Portico

Court of the Women

Court of Israel

House

Altar

Gate of the Lily

Road to Bethany and Jericho

Gethsemane

Tomb of Sons of Hezir

Kidron Valley

Gate

Pinnacle